From Stalingrad to Pillau

From Stalingrad to Pillau

A Red Army Artillery Officer Remembers
the Great Patriotic War

Isaak Kobylyanskiy

Edited by Stuart Britton

University Press of Kansas

Published by the University Press of Kansas (Lawrence, Kansas 66049), which
was organized by the Kansas Board of Regents and is operated and funded by
Emporia State University, Fort Hays State University, Kansas State University,
Pittsburg State University, the University of Kansas, and Wichita State University

ISBN 978-0-7006-1566-7

Contents

Contents

A photograph section appears following page 156.

Author's Note

I am a Soviet veteran of World War II or, more precisely, a veteran of the Great Patriotic War (GPW) of the Soviet people against fascist Germany.* I spent thirty-two months at the front and I'm sure that my generation, aged seventeen to twenty years in 1941, made a considerable contribution to our victory over the German forces. Most of these young fighters who came through the war were just soldiers, sergeants, and lieutenants, that is, people who really got to know the so-called truth of the foxholes. The main goal of this book is to share with my readers numerous pieces of the truth of the foxholes, which I acquired during the war from the age of nineteen.

While contemplating the structure of this book, I decided to start it with the story of my childhood and teens. I believe it would help my readers in the West to understand the conditions of those times and how they affected most personalities of the future young Soviet soldiers and officers.

The final pages of this book relate to the initial postwar year (1946). I describe there my personal experience of those days, but at the same time I tried to re-create a reliable picture of the unbelievably difficult life in my hometown, Kiev, Ukraine, in the initial postwar year.

Naturally, the main contents of the book are my reminiscences and reflections on wartime. Throughout the war I fought in a battery of regimental 76-mm field guns. According to regulations, they were always deployed close to the riflemen's trenches to provide our infantry units with direct support by fire and wheels maneuver.

I describe some battles that I participated in, but one can find many more reflections on human behavior and interrelations among our troops in the war. A series of pages depicts our wartime routine. I hope that all of this, which serves as a backdrop for what I narrate in this book, will be of no less interest to the readers than my personal war experience.

* In the Soviet Union, World War II is the war that began on 1 September 1939 and ended with the Japanese surrender in September 1945. The Great Patriotic War began on 22 June 1941 and concluded on 9 May 1945, and was fought exclusively on the Eastern Front.

I would like to emphasize that almost everything you will read in the book is based on the experience and impressions of a person who fought in a *particular* rifle regiment on *specific sections* of the tremendous Soviet-German front. It is quite likely that the conditions and circumstances that other soldiers and officers experienced in their units were notably different from mine. Moreover, I started fighting in October 1942; thus an extremely tragic period of the war was out of my sight. I'm also sure that other participants in the Great Patriotic War who were more experienced in life than I was could perceive the war differently than I did.

I do have one more reservation: it is possible that I failed to remember and mention some important events or facts, and that I was not quite accurate in some descriptions of events that happened long ago—no human's memory can be absolute. Nevertheless, I firmly promise that I have attempted to be truthful.

I emigrated from the former USSR to the United States in 1994, at the age of seventy-one. Since 1996 I have devoted myself to writing my personal memoirs, "The Story of My Life" (in Russian) for my descendants and closest friends. Naturally, my participation in the Great Patriotic War was represented in detail in these personal papers.

In 2004, the Russian publishers Yauza-Eksmo suggested that I write a Russian book of my war recollections for the sixtieth anniversary of the Soviet victory in the Great Patriotic War. I wrote the book on the basis of my "domestic" memoirs, and it was published in 2005 under the title *Direct Fire against the Enemy*. The edition sold out in a few months.

While working on *Direct Fire against the Enemy*, I began thinking a little about its future translation into English. I shared my intention with several American friends, and I narrated to them in English a couple of the episodes from my prospective Russian book. Many of their questions in response to my narration convinced me that any potential English-language book of my Great Patriotic War experience couldn't be just a translation of the Russian one, even a very liberal translation. Therefore, I decided to write the English rendition of my memoirs as a new book. Later, while writing it in 2005 and 2006, I followed this decision.

First of all, the text of the present book is full of explanations regarding specific Soviet terms, historical events, and phenomena

that have no analogues in the West. The book also contains end-
notes that are intended to assist further the reader's understanding
of some terms and specific events. While recounting some episodes
in English, I managed to find more expressive ways to describe the
events. I also got rid of several ambiguous expressions that I over-
looked in my Russian book. (Sorry, it was already too late to correct
them there!)

Another essential difference lies in the composition and contents
of the books: the English book contains more than 25 percent new
stories and additional material, while I have omitted many details
from the Russian book that were neither pertinent nor particularly
interesting to my Western audience. I also managed to provide this
new book with several additional photos, including two unique il-
lustrations from my private archives. They are published here for
the first time.

Acknowledgments

First of all I give my special acknowledgments to Mr. David M. Glantz, the editor of the *Journal of Slavic Military Studies* (formerly the *Journal of Soviet Military Studies*). In 2003 I sent him several fragments from my "domestic" memoirs, which I translated into English, having a very poor English vocabulary! Mr. Glantz edited and published them in the journal in 2003–2004. I have included some of these passages in the present book. I would like to express my sincere gratitude to Mr. Glantz not only for supporting my idea to create this book but also for his invaluable assistance in turning this idea into a reality.

I also acknowledge Mrs. Leah Watson and Mr. Todd Marvin, who freely helped me to "smooth" a considerable part of the rough texts that were written by a recent immigrant.

I address my special thanks to Mr. Stuart Britton, who not only thoroughly edited my manuscript but also motivated me to elucidate in this book several important events and phenomena in the former USSR.

Part I

A Teen on the Eve of War

Vinnitsa

My Parents

My father, Grigory Isaakovich Kobylyanskiy, was born in 1894 in the village of Lazarivka, Kiev oblast (province). There were six children in the Jewish family of scanty means. The main part of the family's living came from the prosperous, imperious, and strongly religious grandmother, who lived in a nearby big shtetl (Yiddish for a small town, village, or hamlet). She essentially raised my father from the age of six. For three years the local rabbi taught the boy reading, writing, and praying, all in Hebrew. In 1908 Grigory moved from the shtetl to the city of Kiev. Grigory's older sister was his guardian there. Her husband helped the teenager to get a job as an errand boy at a housing construction site. Soon, Grigory advanced to assistant foreman. He continued to gain experience in the field of building and to master Russian literacy through self-study, and quite soon he achieved the rank of technician. Between 1915 and 1918, my father worked for a railway construction company. At that time the company was laying a local branch line in the vicinity of Petrograd (now St. Petersburg), and Grigory was its official representative there. He stayed in Petrograd and while there witnessed the October Revolution of 1917.

Unfortunately, I never asked my father about his attitude toward the Revolution. Nevertheless, since he was a person who had been forced to earn his daily bread even in his childhood and who was cognizant of the humiliating "Jewish pale,"[1] I'm sure that he looked upon the Bolsheviks' victory favorably.

Not once during my childhood did I hear a word from him condemning the Soviet regime. Within my memory, my father always was a law-abiding citizen. When somebody would cite as an example an unlawfully prosperous acquaintance, he always replied: "I don't need that kind of wealth, I only want to sleep quietly at night."

My mother, Evgeniya Abramovna Kobylyanskaya, was born in 1896 in a shtetl of Yanushpol, Zhitomir oblast. She was the second

4   daughter (of six) in the family of a minor office worker at the local sugar refinery. In 1913 Evgeniya passed final exams at the Odessa female high school as a student who was allowed to take exams without regularly attending lectures. Then she entered the dental school in Kiev. In 1916 she worked as a civilian dentist in a military base hospital. In 1917 my future mother came back to Kiev. There she passed three uneasy years of the civil war and repeated changes of local power. In the terrible days of pogroms, her kindly Orthodox neighbors hid her.

My father and mother were married in 1920, and on 11 January 1923, their firstborn child arrived (that was me). In honor of my late grandfather I was named Isaak. The second child, my brother Tolya, was born in 1931.

By the time of my birth, both father and mother were unemployed and strapped for cash. They heated their small, single-room apartment with a *burzhuika* (a small, homemade metal oven), fueled by sawdust.

When I was just six months old, our family moved to the small and placid city of Vinnitsa, where my father started working in the bookkeeping office of the municipal bakery (the bread-baking plant). Thanks to his abilities and remarkable diligence he gradually moved up in his career. Father's strong sense of duty and good practical experience contributed to that, as well. The highlight was reached in 1937, when my father, a person without a complete education and, moreover, not a Party member, became a chief accountant at the Ukrainian State Association of Livestock Purchase, and our family (without me) moved from Vinnitsa to Kiev. (I followed them after completing my eighth grade in 1938.) During the war father worked in the rear supply services, which provided the army in the field with livestock and meat. In 1944 he returned to his prewar job in the liberated city.

My mother worked as a dentist in Vinnitsa, in Kiev, and during her time of evacuation in 1941–1944. After returning home, mother devoted herself to the household. I always remember my parents gratefully. They not only took care of my health and were concerned about my nutrition, clothes, and footwear, but also inculcated in me a constant thirst for knowledge.

Letter by Letter, Word by Word, Book by Book

When I was a four-year-old boy I already knew how to arrange my wooden alphabet blocks to create different words. From that point on, my parents fostered the development of my literacy in every possible way. Soon, a few thin children's books—from the innocent *Washtoholes* (about an animated washbasin eager to scrub children clean) to the politically aimed *Mister Twister*—replaced the ABC blocks. In 1928, a subscription to the monthly children's magazine *The Sparkle* was obtained. I was interested in reading all of this material.

Even at this early age, besides children's books, I liked to read headlines in newspapers. Once I paid particular attention to the heading "Final News." Knowing only one meaning of "final" (coming to the end), I was extremely surprised the next day, when I discovered the same headline in the newspaper. I felt I had been tricked.

Most of my early readings were from shabby, partly tattered preschool children's books published in the old alphabet as far back as before the October Revolution. Those were wonderful and absolutely apolitical books. Among a few books, which remained in my memory from then on, was the new Soviet poem, *Mister Twister*, about a fat and nasty American capitalist-racist.

From the age of eight, I became a permanent visitor to the local children's library that occupied just one room overflowing with books. At that time I could read pretty quickly, so sometimes I visited the library twice a day. It was so interesting to read about the famous seafarers James Cook, Ferdinand Magellan, Roald Amundsen, and, later, to "swallow" a lot of adventure stories!

One of the best children's books written by Soviet writers was the fascinating (but with clear class implications) tale *Three Fat Men* about a popular uprising in a fictitious city. The first book translated from English that I read was the touching antislavery novel *Uncle Tom's Cabin*. Later I read with great pleasure a few stories about American Indians, and I still remember my impression of the words *wigwam, grizzly, bison*. After a while I familiarized myself with Mark Twain's *Tom Sawyer* and *Huckleberry Finn*. I liked them very much.

The Soviet national press was still weak, and the inventory of our library was quite modest. Very quickly I exhausted all of its adventure books. So in the sixth and seventh grades, I satisfied my hunger for books by borrowing a lot of thick but shabby detective fiction from my friends. Those were handed over from one reader to another. Jules Verne, Alexandre Dumas, James F. Cooper, Arthur C. Doyle, and Victor Hugo were among my beloved authors.

That reading significantly enriched my vocabulary. I enjoyed new words such as *mustang, tomahawk, alligator, canyon, Pampas, musketeer, prefect, constable, mulatto, pirate, insurgent*. How exciting they sounded! (To this day, I can't understand the reason for my childhood reverence for everything from abroad. I don't remember being inspired with that idea by somebody. Was it indeed stuffed into my genes? If that's the case, why after I became an adult did my attitude toward everything foreign change to a carefully weighed one?)

Usually I got to keep the most interesting books just for a short while. I would have to read them at top speed. As a seventh grader I "devoured" a hundred pages an hour, skipping whole paragraphs not connected to the intrigue's main march of events. Under such conditions, how could I observe descriptions of landscapes or consider the sense of the author's digressions? Unfortunately, the bad habit of reading in haste sometimes affects me up to the present time. (In Russian it is called "reading diagonally"—reading a page along a diagonal from the beginning of the first line to the end of the last one. In America it is known as "skimming.")

In spite of my temporary passion for adventure, detective, and science fiction, I had time to read many other books. Particularly there were books written by Soviet authors for schoolchildren.

Besides my "independent" reading, I had two special subjects of literature at school: Russian and Ukrainian. However, the textbook materials about writers, poets, and their works were quite brief and too politicized. Nevertheless, by the end of our eighth grade we already knew some things of Pushkin, Lermontov, Nekrasov, Mayakovsky, Gogol, Leo Tolstoy, Chekhov, and Gorky, as well as of the Ukrainians Taras Shevchenko, Kotsyubinskiy, and Tychina. Unfortunately, most of what we were taught was so formal, "dryish," and even boring!

Along with fiction, I regularly read the children's newspaper the *Pioneers' Truth* and, in the last year of my life in Vinnitsa, the *Komsomol's Truth*. (Both newspapers were named after the children's and youth Communist organizations, respectively—see the next section of this chapter.)

In the first half of the 1930s my parents had subscribed to the ten-volume *Small Soviet Encyclopedia*. It became one of the most important sources of my knowledge in different spheres.

Simultaneously, we began receiving the multivolume collected works of Maksim Gorky. I tried to read the initial volumes, but I was still too young to make much sense of them. I became sufficiently mature to read and comprehend this author's works only a few years later, when I had already left Vinnitsa.

I was a ninth grader when I experienced genuine delight while reading non-detective fiction for the first time. That was *A Farewell to Arms*, written by Ernest Hemingway. Never before had I seen such a unity of substance (so congenial to my attitude!) and style, in the unusual, expressively dynamic manner of the author's writing.

When I glance back at the years of my youth, I realize that I gained most of my knowledge through reading, and much in my attitude and personality was formed under the influence of what I had read as a boy and teenager. At the age of about fifteen I was eager to inherit the best traits of my fictional heroes. I wanted to be courageous, steadfast and self-restrained, honest and unselfish, strong and nimble. I saw myself then as a future kind, faithful, and caring companion, friend, and husband. I mentally pictured how I would stand up for the weak and defeat enemies.

When I was twelve, someone presented me with a book containing four biographies. The subjects were the great inventors James Watt, George Stephenson, Robert Fulton, and Thomas Alva Edison. Under the influence of that book and of a lot of science fiction that I started to read somewhat later, I began to dream I would become a famous inventor. I dreamed of creating an unknown generator of odors or taste sensations. Maybe just this kind of reading impelled me several years later to choose the radio faculty of the Kiev Industrial Institute (KII). Moreover, at that time its name was "special faculty"—a very intriguing name!

There were also negative consequences of my passion for reading. I grew up in a country where the ruling clique of the Communist Party headed by Stalin had complete domination. The official name of that one-party system was "dictatorship of the proletariat."

The authority never tolerated otherwise-minded people, and it cruelly punished anyone who disagreed. Such people were named "enemies of the people," and many were executed. Being the masters of all mass media, publishing, and censorship, our rulers intended to bring up the Soviet people in the spirit of Communist ideology. A huge propaganda staff was established. It unceasingly unmasked the horrors and crying injustices of the "carrion" capitalist system, its merciless exploitation of the working masses, and its relationship with colonialism and imperialist wars. It also glorified our radiant future—communism. Political indoctrination began in elementary school. For example, the text from the ABC primer of those times taught the pupil: "We are not slaves. Slaves are dumb." In the reading part of the same textbook you could find a story about Lenin's childhood. A typical line from his favorite song went: "The rich man-kulak can't sleep at night. And the man who is poor as a church mouse dances and has fun."

Being absolutely honest, now I state openly: the pervasive propaganda produced its desired result, especially among the inexperienced youth and people of little education. For example, I had no doubt that everything written in our history and social science textbooks, and in the youth and "adult" newspapers, was true. I put absolute trust in the ideological tenets that society's and the state's interests are higher than a person's; that religion distracts employees from the fight for their rights; and that class solidarity is higher than patriotism. I'm sure I wasn't the only one who was convinced by those and similar dogmas. The worst of it was that during those years I accepted any published material as indisputable fact.

The absolute uniformity of the information furnished by mass media along with the absence of public disputes and polemic in the press (and all of that in conditions of mass fear of state repression) caused most of my generation to lose the ability to think critically. Probably, my parents' viewpoints, and those of other adults that I knew as well, were in conflict with the official line, but everyone kept such information concealed. There was never any private political talk in my presence. Maybe that was a way to protect children as well as themselves. As I understand now, just these circumstances were the origin of the conformism that was peculiar to me in my youth and began to vanish ultimately only after I had returned from the war.

While finishing this topic, where I have strayed far beyond my childhood, I'd like to emphasize again and again the important role of books in different periods of my life. I have to confess frankly that my attitude to the world, to people and society was coming not only from my education and life experience but also, to a certain extent, from some of the books I had read in my childhood and youth.

Schooldays: Elementary Classes

At the age of about eight I became a schoolboy. I think that I was fated to be the best student of my class from the very first day of school, and I would have to get used to that fact (nowadays, such a habit is called a "perfectionist's syndrome"). I gained the permanent position of class leader simply by chance. In 1930, the nearest school formed two first-grade classes: one for pupils who knew at least the ABCs; the other was for illiterate children. My parents brought me to the school on 31 August, by which point the "literate class" was already full. Because of that I was doomed to be the "best pupil" for several years in the "illiterate" class. My classmates were actually illiterate, so I was openly bored at school for quite a long time.

Being second-grade pupils, we became "Oktyabryata." It meant that we had mounted the first rung of the political ladder planned by the Communist Party for Soviet society: "Oktyabryata" (children of seven years or upward preparing for entry into the Young Pioneers); Young Pioneers (the pre-Komsomol organization for children aged ten or upward); Komsomol'tsy (members of the Komsomol, the Young Communist League); Communists. Three "Oktyabryata" sections were formed in our class, and as the best pupil I was appointed as a section leader. I became a Young Pioneer when I was a fourth grader (the equivalent of a fifth grader in America). As usual, my school results were absolutely perfect.

The Famine of 1933

The most terrible event in the years of my study in the elementary classes was the famine of 1933, which covered the Ukraine and several adjoining grain-producing Russian provinces. Actually, the main reason for this disaster derived from Marxist-Leninist theory about the petit bourgeois essence of the peasantry and Stalin's merciless way to get rid of it. He planned to annihilate the stratum of prosperous farmers and to force the rest of Soviet peasantry onto collective farms. The effects of this policy were tragic.

As you know, our family resided in a city, so I can share with you only what I saw there. Usually twice a week, on market days, a dozen or two female peasants would walk along our street in early mornings, bringing to market their vegetables, eggs, milk, home-made butter, cottage cheese, and so forth. That year they disappeared. As I recall, it was early spring when I, on my usual morning way to school, discovered strange human figures wearing shabby outer winter clothing, men and women with darkened, puffy faces and unbelievably swollen legs. They hardly shuffled their bare feet (no footwear size could hold such swollen feet) toward the main street. Initially I came across one or two such individuals, but in the next couple of days the number of these strangers increased visibly. Often, in exhaustion, these individuals would sit or lie down on the roadside to rest. Not all of them were then able to rise back to their feet.

At the time, I was sure that starvation made people thin, not stout. Therefore, once I realized the reason of their suffering, I became imbued with pity for these unhappy, dying people. Their appearances were so terrible that I, a ten-year-old boy, was afraid to look at them. (Earlier, whenever I came across a funeral procession, I had always been afraid to look at the deceased.) I didn't know who removed the corpses from the roadside, or when they did it, but by the time I would return home after school, there were no signs of the morning's terrible procession.

During the famine Vinnitsa residents were supplied with bread by ration cards, and I don't remember any evidence of starvation among neighboring families and my classmates. Nor did my childhood memory preserve any severe periods of malnutrition in our family, either.

I call to mind another incident of that awful time. I saw it at the small public market not far from my school. A barefoot, ragged, twenty-something-year-old man snatched away a crust of dark bread from a market woman's stall and then tried to run away. He was caught in a minute. I remember how he gobbled his spoil while being beaten unmercifully by several market men.

As another sign of the lean year I also remember pieces of hard sunflower-seed cake that some schoolchildren held in their pockets.

Former feed supplement for cattle had become a valuable foodstuff for people.

Not one of our newspapers of that time mentioned the famine. Instead, they published only triumphal reports of successful collectivization. Only during Gorbachev's glasnost (openness) campaign were the terrible facts of the famine revealed and published. People got to know that even cannibalism took place at that tragic time, and the number of Ukrainian victims of the famine that accompanied the "triumph of Stalin's collectivization" amounted to 7 million.

* * *

Let me now return to my schooling. Well, being convinced of my progress at school, my parents decided that apart from everything else I should also start to learn the German language. Soon, they found an inexpensive tutor, a forty-year-old German, Benke by last name, for me. The tutor and his family lived in a damp and dim small room. The family was of scanty means, and I still remember the unpleasant odor of burned cod-liver oil, which Mrs. Benke used to fry their meals.

I visited my tutor once a week. At first studying German seemed to be boring, but in less than about six months I already felt that it was bearing fruit, and thus it became interesting. Two years of studies with Mr. Benke laid a firm base of knowledge in the language. In subsequent years it helped me to read, write, and translate German text into Russian confidently. Many times in my life I remembered gratefully the wise decision of my parents and Mr. Benke's lessons. (My knowledge of the German language especially came in handy when I was at the front. Many of our regiment knew that I had a good command of German. Therefore, as soon as our scouts or riflemen captured a prisoner who would talk, they led him first to my fire platoon emplacements. There I would conduct an informal interrogation of the prisoner. I normally looked through the contents of the prisoner's wallet. Often, one could find there a few scabrous verses. While listening to my translation, our soldiers roared with laughter. Knowledge of the German language was of much benefit to me on the eve of the fall of Königsberg. You will read the story of that event in the second part of the book.)

Simultaneously Mr. Benke gave lessons to a pupil of the "literate class" in our school, Viktor Videnskiy by name. After several meetings there we became friends. Viktor was the best student in his class, and associating with him I understood that he was no less able and just as widely read as I was. The three of us, Viktor, his close friend Igor Voitsekhovskiy by name, and I, began to play chess regularly and with varying success. Igor was a thin, stooped, and very nearsighted boy of a purely noble nature. In appearance, he looked absolutely helpless. The friendship of the three of us went on until I left Vinnitsa for Kiev in June 1938. Moving ahead, I want to tell you how the fates of both my Vinnitsa schoolmates-friends turned out later on.

I'll start with the fate of Viktor Videnskiy.

In 1939, during a physical training lesson, Viktor accidentally fractured his forearm. Because the bones did not heal properly, he became unfit for military service. When the war began, Videnskiy was a Kiev University sophomore. In early July 1941, along with his mother, grandmother, and little brother, Viktor fled to Uzbekistan. (Years later I got to know that his father had been arrested in 1938 as an "enemy of the people," and then been executed.) The family starved there for a long time, and Viktor was treated for dysentery. After the treatment he continued his studies in Moscow State University, which at that time had been temporarily evacuated to the Central Asia region. Since the late 1950s Viktor Solomonovich Videnskiy has been a famous scientist in mathematics. He still continues to work as a part-time professor in St. Petersburg, and we remain in correspondence with each other.

The fate of Igor Voitsekhovskiy turned out absolutely different. I describe it in the following story.

My Schoolmates' Heroic Deeds and Tragic Fates in the War

German invaders occupied Vinnitsa in July 1941. Many years later I came to learn about the local youth underground resistance group. The youth underground resistance group was of valuable assistance to a large partisan formation that operated successfully against the invaders in the region of Vinnitsa and the surrounding provinces.

The most famous member of the group was familiar to me: Larisa Ratushnaya, a former student of the same High School Number 9 (renamed later to Number 6) that I had attended before leaving Vinnitsa. When the war began, Larisa (nickname Lyalya) had completed her third-year studies at Moscow State University, and she immediately volunteered to serve as a military nurse. After being captive for two weeks in August, she escaped from the prisoner-of-war camp and made her way back to Vinnitsa in October 1941. With Igor Voitsekhovskiy's recommendation she joined the youth resistance group and fulfilled numerous very important missions as a fearless partisan messenger.

Igor was an active member of the group. He succeeded in getting a job in the city clerk office. Igor was acceptable to the Germans for that job thanks to his personal attributes: he was of Ukrainian origin, not Jewish; he was not a member of Komsomol; and he appeared to be above suspicion. Making use of the opportunity to work there and scorning danger, Igor managed to alter a few of his former female classmates' papers, in effect turning those girls from Jews into Ukrainians. Moreover, he knew ahead of time the dates of forthcoming compulsory roundups of local youth for essentially slave labor in Germany. Through his friends, Igor passed information to many guys and girls, so they were able to "disappear" before the sweeps. His dangerous activities lasted a year until somebody informed on him to the police. Igor was caught and then hanged. After the end of the war the twenty-year-old hero was posthumously awarded with the medal "Partisan Glory."

Larisa's fate was no less dramatic. She survived until 18 March 1944, when a traitor killed her on a downtown street, just two days before the Red Army liberated Vinnitsa. On the twentieth anniversary of the Great Victory, 9 May 1965, Larisa Stepanovna Ratushnaya was awarded with the highest honorary title of "Hero of the Soviet Union" (posthumously). A monument to Lyalya was set up on the place where she was killed. The Vinnitsa Pioneers' and Schoolchildren's Palace was named after Larisa.

In the early 1970s, I unexpectedly received a letter from Vinnitsa. E. V. Gorb introduced herself as a local teacher and literary woman. I still don't know how she found my address. She asked me to share with her my recollections of Larisa Ratushnaya and Igor Voitsekhovskiy, since she was going to write a nonfictional narrative about both of them. I wrote a couple of pages about Igor and only a few lines about Lyalya, who was two years older than me. In a year or so I received from Mrs. Gorb a parcel with several consecutive issues of the Vinnitsa local newspaper in it. The issues contained the promised narrative under the title "Shine, Shine, My Star!" I was glad to find there some details that the author gleaned from my personal recollections.

Once, in the late 1980s, I had an opportunity to visit the city of my childhood for a couple of hours. Since 1938 Vinnitsa has increased in size many times over and was unrecognizable. I barely managed to find my old school, attended a meeting with young teachers, and visited the school museum of battle glory. I found there many familiar names; most of these schoolmates were killed in the war. Then, in memory of Igor and Larisa, I bowed before their bas-reliefs on the front wall of the building.

Just before leaving I entered the empty classroom where I studied fifty years ago. Sitting silently on the school bench I recollected my childhood, classmates, and teachers.

Schooldays: 1934–1938

In the fall of 1934 I became a fifth grader. Instead of only one teacher through all elementary classes, we now had several teachers, each for his or her particular discipline. My study in the middle and upper classes continued to bear excellent fruit, and I was able to find more time for activities beyond the classroom, such as sports, reading, public work, and . . . girls. (I describe my public work briefly at the end of this chapter.)

In 1936 our school moved into a newly built modern schoolhouse with a roomy gym. It was a pleasure for all of the students and teachers. A group of sports lovers built a volleyball court nearby.

In 1937 my parents moved to Kiev, but my new housemates were my father's former subordinates. They took care of me perfectly, and my mood was pretty good.

There was one national circumstance, however, that puzzled and confused me. It definitely darkened the situation in our country.

"The Fight against the Enemies of the People"

At this time, especially in 1937–1938, horrible events occurred in our country—they were part of the "fight against the enemies of the people and their accomplices." A surge of mass arrests and cruel punishments swept across the entire country. The media was full of official reports about the unveiling of anti-Soviet conspiracies that were headed by recent VIPs in the political, economic, and military

fields. The reports also alleged that these conspiracies were connected with foreign intelligence services.

Now all Soviet people were being taught that their main duty was
"to unmask the enemies of the people, spies and saboteurs." The
propaganda machine reeled off story after story about "how craftily
foreign intelligence services operated" and "remarkable examples of
Soviet citizens' vigilance."

For instance, I still remember a serialized espionage story that the
Pioneers' Truth published in several running issues, "Uncle Kolya—
the Fly Catcher." It was an intriguing narrative about a vigilant
Young Pioneer who detected a spy. The latter was concealed as an
entomologist with a small net in his hand, but his actual goal was to
photograph some Soviet military base. The brave Young Pioneer, at
risk to his own life, helped the Border Guards to catch the spy. (Not
only papers and magazines for young readers published such "educational" literary trash.)

Arrests and persecutions affected not only VIPs during this time
of terror. Many lower ranking bosses and local authorities were
also "taken" (everybody used this word at the time, instead of "arrested"). Moreover, many ordinary citizens became victims of the
mass terror, with no mention by the Soviet media. Even the author,
who was at that time "a quite Communistically thinking teen,"
couldn't understand how these important people and loyal citizens
could metamorphose overnight into enemies of the people, foreign
agents, and saboteurs of the economy. However, at that time I still
gave credence to our propaganda. I began to think more seriously
and to doubt whether the official words were true only some two
years later.

The steamroller of mass arrests and executions sped up, and the
fear of finding themselves caught under it compelled many families
to go through their family archives and albums. Anything that could
be interpreted as a compromising matter during a possible search
was wiped out.

At the time, my father was a bookkeeper in some office. There
were a couple of group photographs of the office staff in my father's
photo album. Naturally, their boss, a Communist Party member,
was in the center of each picture. In the spring of 1937, the boss was
"taken." The next day my father obliterated the boss's face in the
photographs with black ink.

Soon, similar circumstances prompted me to follow my father's example. I had a few certificates of merit for my "excellent study and active public work." One of them carried tiny oval portraits of our top two Ukrainian bosses, Kosior and Postyshev—the first and second secretaries of the Ukrainian Communist Party Central Committee, respectively.

Kosior was the first to be annihilated in the purges. (Nevertheless, fifty years later a monument to him was erected in Kiev.) As soon as it was declared that Kosior was "a mortal enemy of the people," I blotted out his picture thoroughly.

A year later the same fate befell Postyshev. This time I "acted" less resolutely—I just crossed out the former leader's image. There was a reason for my reluctance: since 1935 Postyshev had been known as an initiator and organizer of several good works on behalf of all Soviet children. The most memorable of them was to restore quasi legitimacy to the Christmas tree, which had been prohibited in the 1920s as "a means to attract children to a religious ceremony." Postyshev found a way to return a merry holiday to children. He just renamed the Christmas tree as the New Year's tree (the Orthodox Church Christmas Day is 7 January).

Fortunately, none of our numerous relatives and close acquaintances became a victim during these terrible years. Maybe that was one more reason why I didn't take the signs of this horrible period to my heart.

A Teenager's Attitude toward His Motherland. My Public Work

Despite this wave of mass arrests and terror, I remained a proud and loyal young Soviet patriot. How could a teenager at that time, who daily kept up with domestic and international events, not be proud of his country? How could he not love it? Absolutely all our media constantly reported with one accord about the unprecedented achievements of the Soviet national economy; the heroism of our polar explorers; our pilots' altitude and distance records in the sky; and the glorious victories of young Soviet musicians in a few international competitions! Let me mention a few important achievements and successful events that were in our media spotlight in the years 1934–1938; consequently, they were in the focus of my attention as well.

- The first five-year plan of industrialization for the country and collectivization of its agriculture was fulfilled or overfulfilled. Hundreds of factories and plants were built or reconstructed. More than 1,000 machine-tractor stations were established in the countryside.[2] The largest hydroelectric power plant in the USSR was built, which made the Dnieper River navigable to the Black Sea. The Turksib (Turkestan-Siberian railroad) was laid. It connected the remote Central Asian area to the national railroad system.
- Brave Soviet pilots rescued dozens of members of an arctic expeditionary team and the crew of the steamship *Chelyuskin,* which had been crushed by pack ice. To honor special feats of the Soviet people, the government instituted the highest national award—the status Hero of the Soviet Union. Along with the presentation of this title, they honored the recipient with the Order of Lenin and the Gold Star medal. Six polar airmen and the expedition director, Professor O. Yu. Shmidt, became the first Heroes of the Soviet Union.
- For the first time in world history, a Soviet team accomplished an aero-expedition to the North Pole. Here, on a mighty block of ice, the first in the world drifting meteorological station of long duration was founded. The station, with its four-man staff, functioned for about two years. There were four more Heroes of the Soviet Union when the station staff returned. The nation rejoiced over the feat of the brave team of four. Everywhere crowds of many thousands met them with lots of flowers.
- The first two nonstop flights from the USSR to America over the North Pole took place. The Soviet pilots flew a domestically designed aircraft, the ANT-25 (its principal designer was Andrey Nikolaevich Tupolev). The pilots Valeriy Chkalov and Mikhail Gromov became the next Heroes of the Soviet Union. (One previous attempt by the pilot Sigizmund Levanevskiy had ended in tragedy.) After the male pilots' distance flying accomplishments, a female crew consisting of Polina Osipenko, Valentina Grizodubova, and Marina Raskova set out on the record flight from

Moscow to the Far East. They became the first female Heroes of the Soviet Union. (A year or so later, Polina Osipenko and Valeriy Chkalov both perished in separate plane crashes.)

- Soviet aeronauts reached record altitudes. At first they surpassed the American record, 10,000 meters. The next crew exceeded 19,000 meters, but just after they started their descent, something went wrong and the balloon crashed. The three-man crew perished. The Soviet Union's numerous aviation records appeared to be quite natural against the backdrop of daily reporting about outstanding personal achievements in labor productivity. The coal miner Alexey Stakhanov surpassed by ten times the official rate of output in coal production. This achievement prompted what appeared to be a spontaneous labor movement to emulate Stakhanov's feat in different industries and in agriculture around the country. (Now, however, everyone knows that the movement was not spontaneous, but spread by directives "from above.")

- On 5 December 1936, at the Extraordinary All-Union Congress of Soviets, our leader Stalin made a speech about the project of the new Constitution of the USSR. That was the first time people all over the country could hear Stalin's voice by radio. Many, including me, were surprised at his strong Georgian accent. It was emphasized that the new Constitution would be the most democratic in the world. Delegates repeatedly interrupted Stalin's speech with loud cheers and tremendous ovations. Stormy applause and shouts of "Long live our leader comrade Stalin!" were heard over and over again. The new Constitution of the USSR, the so-called Stalin's Constitution, was approved unanimously. (I have already written about the peak of the stunning state propaganda at that time and how under the pretense of fighting against "enemies of the people" Stalin and his administration exterminated his real and potential political opponents or rivals for power.)

- In spite of all-round support by the USSR (including military supply and hundreds of hush-hush military volunteers), the Republicans lost the civil war in Spain. Following this defeat, our country implemented a remarkable humanitarian action: it sheltered several hundreds of Spanish children whose parents had been killed in the war, captured by General Franco's troops, or interned by the French government. All the Spanish children were accommodated in perfectly equipped special boarding schools with the best conditions for their studies, professional training, and leisure.

- I remember two jubilee celebrations that were important events in our national cultural life: the 100th anniversary of Pushkin's death and the 250th anniversary of the publication of the Georgian poet Shota Rustaveli's poem "The Warrior in the Tiger's Skin." The latter jubilee was celebrated with special solemnity, because our supreme leader, Stalin, was a Georgian. It was considered as the height of journalistic style to quote "The Warrior" on any occasion. For example, the following sarcastic lines from the poem could be used in numerous everyday situations: "Everybody imagines oneself to be a strategist while observing the battle from aside." When the matter concerned the heroic Republicans' fight in Spain, another quotation from Rustaveli was used: "Better death, but death with honor, than the shame of disgraceful days." It was constantly emphasized that the famous slogan of our time, proclaimed by the ardent Spanish Communist leader Dolores Ibarurri (the "Passionaria"), "Better to die standing than to live on bended knee," echoed the words about death and honor in Rustaveli's "The Warrior."
- Tremendous success accompanied young Soviet musicians who at last were able to participate in international music competitions. Most of the Soviet winners and laureates were students of Professor Petr Stolyarskiy from the Odessa School of Music. Their victories were celebrated in the Kremlin. Stalin personally presented the future outstanding performers David Oistrakh, Emil Gilels, Yakov Zak, Yakov Flier, and others who had glorified the country, with costly gifts.

Such a series of significant events, feats, outstanding successes, and records strengthened my deep conviction that the Soviet social order was the fairest and most progressive one on earth. I was sincerely pleased with each achievement of the Soviet people, either in the national economy or in sports, in the sky or at some musical competition. I was distressed when some efforts ended in failure and deeply mourned our every loss. But for all that, I wasn't a passive contemplator of what was going on. I always wanted and often tried to be involved in that impetuous life, to participate in creating our radiant future. Below, I present a couple of examples of what I did at that time as public work.

As a seventh grader I suggested my classmates gather used children's books and then donate the collection to some rural school library. Soon about fifty books were collected, and a few of us walked to a neighboring village. We easily found the squalid schoolhouse and gave our gift to the teacher who ran the school library. Everybody was pleased with the unexpected visitors; they kindly thanked us for the books. (But I still have the unpleasant memory of the tiny, unaired schoolhouse with its dense, heavy smell of sheepskin, tar, and unwashed bodies.)

The first election for members of the Supreme Soviet (main legislative body) of the USSR took place on 12 December 1937. I and a few other Young Pioneers were commissioned to help those who were unable to read the name of the candidate on the ballot (there was only one "candidate" per race in the Soviet Union at that time). The polling places were scheduled to open at 6:00 A.M. but there were already long lines of people waiting to vote by that time. It was still dark when I arrived at our schoolhouse, where a polling place was located. I was eager to be useful. Unfortunately, there was a long wait before anyone needed our help. Finally, around 3:00 P.M. an elderly woman appeared. She didn't refuse my help, and I was happy to accompany her into the polling booth. Soon my replacement arrived, and I went home with a proud feeling of my direct contribution to a historical event.

Perhaps it was my last public action in Vinnitsa. In a half year, I would be leaving the city of my childhood for Kiev.

Kiev

A Straight-A Student from the Provinces at a High School in the Capital

Soon after my arrival in Kiev, I went to the local District School Education Office for an assignment to a high school. They assigned me to High School Number 98 that was located in the central part of Kiev, not far from the building where our family resided.

At that time, many schools in Kiev had good accommodations. The best of them were several newly built, three-storied school buildings with spacious classrooms and well-equipped gymnasiums. By comparison to them, High School Number 98 looked miserable. It occupied the two upper floors of an old four-story building, and it was both cramped and uncomfortable.

During the first day of my studies at the new school I was able to form only a very general impression of my new classmates. They seemed noticeably more mature, more developed, and even bigger than the Vinnitsa teenagers. Most boys, and especially the girls, were better dressed than my former classmates.

At once I noticed two boys, who were wearing expensive suits (later I got to know that one of them was a professor's son, and the other's father managed a wine store). It was also striking that some girls wore high-heeled shoes. I also took note of a few extravagant (as I considered it) hairstyles. In Vinnitsa, these would have been considered excessively immodest for schoolgirls. However, I didn't want to jump to any final conclusions, as I understood that the time for my real familiarity with my new classmates was yet to come.

Unexpectedly in the very morning of the third day of studies, all male ninth graders, who were also members of Komsomol, were summoned to the teacher's room. We were informed that a supplemental recruiting for the ninth class of a nearby specialized artillery school (a so-called special school) had been announced. Those who wished to enroll in it would be released from lessons and had to appear at the special school within the hour. As a conscientious

member of Komsomol, who understood the country's need, I soon
appeared at the designated place along with a few other classmates.

About Special Schools

I have to digress here to describe briefly these special schools (well
known in Kiev as "*spets*-schools"), which had been organized not
long before in a few of the biggest cities of the USSR. The purpose
of these *spets*-schools was to produce within three or four years a
large number of highly trained junior officers for the Red Army
who had comprehensively mastered their particular military skill.
The length of studies at these *spets*-schools was three years, from
eighth to tenth grade. Only male teens were admitted. The entrants
were examined not only for their knowledge, particularly in math
and physics, but also for their health and, as one can guess, certain
biographical particulars. The government reckoned that after a perfect general education and preliminary military drill, all *spets*-school
graduates would continue their training as cadets at two-year military colleges.

The instruction in the *spets*-schools was good, but the students
there had a much greater workload than those in the regular high
schools. *Spets*-school students studied not only the full normal
course of general education but also received an expanded course of
physical education and military training. That lengthened the school
day. In addition, *spets*-school students spent one month each summer drilling at a military college annual camp.

To interest the best youths in these schools, *spets*-school students
received a wonderful privilege—a free military khaki uniform. That
kind of clothing instantly changed any lad into a slender and neat
young military man, the envy of all "civilian" schoolboys. The uniform was the object of every *spets*-schoolboy's permanent pride,
a symbol of special superiority over his regular school contempo-
raries. With particular pleasure and extra dash, every *spets*-school-
boy put his right hand to the peak of his service cap when saluting
every approaching serviceman. And how diligently, with a resolute,
ceremonial step, did he pass by a man of higher military rank!

There were more privileges for *spets*-schools—they received the
best schoolhouses in the city and highly skilled educational special-
ists. Moreover, additional instructors were hired to teach the future
officers some rules of etiquette and how to dance ballroom style

and other modern ("Western") dances. From time to time, *spets*-schools, where spacious halls were available, would host so-called evening friendship parties together with some regular high schools. The highlight of those parties was a dance in which the well-drilled *spets*-school students, with their excellent military bearing, always demonstrated their complete superiority over their "civilian" rivals to the girls who were present. That naturally made the male guests envious. They expressed their ill will toward *spets*-schoolboys with a particular nickname, "banana." And they boycotted those school-girls who preferred to be friends with "bananas," teased them, and sometimes made them cry.

A terrible ordeal awaited those *spets*-school graduates from the prewar enrollments. Almost all of them were involved in the terrible fighting from the very first months of the war. They fought for the motherland valiantly and skillfully, but not many of them returned from the war. The memory of this steadfast generation of Kiev artillery *spets*-school students and of their feats of arms was later immortalized in an impressive bas-relief established on the front of the building where they once had studied.

* * *

Let's return to 3 September 1938. Our small group of candidates arrived at the Artillery Special School, and the first point of business for each was a thorough medical examination. After my vision was checked, I was dismissed—the school wouldn't accept such nearsighted candidates. For other medical reasons they rejected two more of us. Eventually only two students from our group of five were accepted into the artillery *spets*-school (during the war one of them was killed in action, the second was seriously injured). So my efforts to take the road of a military career failed, and I returned to my school as an "ordinary" ninth grader.

With every passing day I became more familiar with the school, its teachers, and my classmates. It took me a while to begin to feel comfortable among my new classmates. I felt a kind of provincial inferiority complex throughout almost the entire first quarter of classes. Listening to my classmates' discussions during breaks, I discovered that I didn't understand some of the local slang; that I didn't know most details of school routine; and that I didn't react to some jokes that caused loud laughter among everyone else around me. I believed that I would become one of the gang soon, but meanwhile I felt some discomfort.

By contrast with those feelings, I didn't feel any inferiority in academic matters. Most teachers of this school were incomparably more professional than those in Vinnitsa. While listening to my new classmates' recitations, I realized that their average educational level and general knowledge were noticeably higher than that of my former classmates in Vinnitsa. Therefore I understood I had to work hard to be "best of the best" here, or at least "one of the best."

It was very difficult to study at home: our family of five (including my grandfather) lived together in a single tiny room. However, in spite of everything I achieved the desired goal: all my first quarter marks were "excellent."

Vera

In a month after I started attending the new school, I became good friends with two inseparable pals, both by the same first name—Boris (Boris Shpilskiy and Boris Golod). They once told me confidentially that the year before both had fallen in love with Vera Makovchik, "a daughter of an important railroad boss." They told me truthfully that neither of them had achieved any romantic success with Vera. After my friends' confession I started furtively to pay more and more attention to Vera, particularly to listen closely to her recitations at lessons. There were brighter and showier girls in that class, but this extremely unpretentious and at the same time self-confident brown-haired girl with her cordial-looking gray-green, slightly brown eyes (their shape was a little bit Asian) attracted me more and more.

At times after the main lesson, our school Komsomol held talks on different subjects in our classroom. The topics might be the arts, history, or science and technology. Students presented reports on the topics for group discussion.

The first report that I heard was dedicated to the composer Petr Ilich Tchaikovsky's life and creative work; Vera was the presenter. What I heard made a strong impression on me. Vera's report was obviously the result of meticulous research, which produced much information that was new to me. She organized the material carefully, and her clear speech and natural contact with the audience excited more interest in me toward Vera, and I wanted to get to know her better. Shortly before our fall vacation I gathered up my courage to ask Vera for a book about Tchaikovsky. Very likely, this was just a pretext for a chance to meet with Vera. One more month passed, and she occupied more and more place in my thoughts.

From time to time I met her among a group of classmates, along the way to or from school. Sometimes we strolled three or four together (Vera's constant companion was her closest friend, Lyusya Ezrova, who adored Vera). Not being sure about Vera's own feelings toward me, I carefully tried to find a way to befriend her.

I remember the memorable evening of 21 December 1938 to the smallest detail. After I finished doing my homework for the next day, I unexpectedly realized that I really wanted to see Vera right away. I thought up a reason and called her timidly from the telephone booth. (A home telephone was a rarity in Kiev at that time.) At first, pretending to be Vera, her thirteen-year-old sister, the prankster Nadya, had taken the receiver. However, after she heard that the matter concerned a draft of a truncated pyramid for geometry class, Nadya burst out laughing and called her sister. Vera told me I could borrow her draft temporarily. We agreed to meet in the lobby of the house where Vera lived (6 Theater Street).

Five minutes later, entering the lobby, I saw Vera wearing a friendly smile. She had her mother's fur coat casually thrown over her shoulders. There were no drafts in her hands. (The thought flitted through my head, "Maybe I'm supposed to be here for more than a short while!")

Vera invited me to follow her up to their apartment on the third floor. When we reached her door, from behind it I could hear the slightly distorted sound of a gramophone playing a beloved Russian folk song. It was "Metelitsa" ("Snowstorm"), being performed in the sentimental voice of Russia's favorite tenor, Lemeshev.

We entered the living room. I saw the slightly abashed Nadya sitting on the couch. She examined me with curiosity. Against the far wall stood the gramophone and a piano. Vera's nine-year-old sister, Lyuba, was rearranging music books there.

Vera imperceptibly helped me to shed the timidity that I experienced during the first minutes of being in an unfamiliar apartment. Soon I came to know that Vera had learned how to play the piano in her childhood. She even played some pieces from Tchaikovsky's "Seasons" for me, but confessed that she had not touched the instrument in a long time.

Soon Vera's mother, Agrippina Semenovna, entered the living room. Straight away she began talking about some novels and telling me the summary of a book she had recently read. Then she asked what I thought about some new movies. Everything was quite natural, and I had the sensation of being among old familiar friends.

After that visit I realized that, as regards to my relations with Vera, my stock obviously had gone up. From then on Vera and I started seeing each other quite frequently, and even Lyusya accompanied us less often. I learned a lot from Vera during our long evening walks. Unlike me, who grew up in mediocre Vinnitsa, Vera already had lived in three remarkable Soviet cities: Zaporozhe, where she was present at the launching of the world-renowned "Dnieproges" power plant; Leningrad, with its legendary Nevskiy Prospekt, the Petropavlovsk fortress, and its palaces and museums; and exotic Tashkent, the capital of Uzbekistan. Vera was a wonderful narrator, and all of Vera's stories were very interesting, so sometimes we suddenly discovered that it was already as late as past 11:00 P.M. To avoid our parents' anger and escape possible penalties, we would scurry home immediately.

Sometimes we dropped by Gastronom stores to buy candies made in Leningrad (instead of spending the daily thirty-five kopeks given to us by our parents to buy something for lunch, we put aside the money for candies). Being both a candy expert and a candy lover, Vera always made the best choice of the sweets.

At times we visited the Central Library, which was next to the Dynamo soccer stadium. In its reading hall we usually read some books not available for borrowing. I distinctly remember that we read Jaroslav Hasek's *Humoresques* and the romantic novelettes written by Stefan Zweig there. While reading Hasek, in spite of cautionary posters and the criticism of readers who sat nearby, we couldn't check our outbursts of loud laughter. Twice, we spent our time in that hall, gathering relevant quotations from some prerevolutionary volumes of articles written by half-forgotten literary critics.

In the spring of 1939, we agreed to exchange photographs. I gave Vera a tiny three-by-four-centimeter picture; in return, she gave me a professionally made, half-length portrait of herself. The picture showed the living image of the smiling Vera, with her ever-present short lock of hair curling down over the left corner of the forehead. She is looking at me kindly and cheerfully, with a scarcely revealed playful slyness. On the back—a dedicatory inscription "To Isaak as a sign of friendship. Vera. May 2, 1939. " (This priceless present was to pass through the whole war in a breast pocket of my combat blouse. Along with me it was soaked in the rain, submerged in rivers, and warmed by a campfire on a frosty day. As a result, the dear portrait became thoroughly damaged; however, I treasure it as much as ever, and I still keep it with care. Fortunately, there is another, perfect copy of that wonderful picture in our family archive.)

In spite of our frequent evening walks and other "extracurricular activities" that diverted us from our studies, both Vera and I finished the ninth school year as straight-A students.

The most memorable event of 1939 took place that November, when the second quarter of our last school year had just begun. It was an early evening when we met in the Pioneer Park. We walked along familiar paths and discussed a point of contention, which had recently arisen between us. As soon as Vera explained that she was not implicated in the situation, I instantly was relieved, and then I felt an overflowing happiness. In a few minutes I gathered myself up and told Vera that I loved her very much. And I heard Vera's voice under her breath, "Me too."

(During our entire lifetime together, Vera and I celebrated 11 November as the anniversary of our declaration of love—one of our main holidays. There were always flowers in our home on that day.)

In a week or so, late at night we visited the same park again. Sitting on the bench there, we launched into playful wrestling. When Vera's face appeared close by, I unexpectedly and almost unconsciously pulled my darling even closer to me and kissed her cheek. We both sat in frozen silence for a few seconds. I was afraid of Vera's possible protest or rebuke, but she continued to cling to me in silence. . . . There were many happy evenings afterward on the streets of Kiev, as well as on the benches in some unlit cozy nooks in the parks and public gardens where we favored each other with kisses. First they were timid and a little bit furtive, and then became more lingering and passionate. Sometimes we returned home well past midnight.

The tender affection that seized both of us didn't interrupt our contact with friends; we remained the straight-A students as before. We had time not only to go to the cinema regularly (and to some stage performances now and then) but also to take part in many school, after-school, and sporting events.

Very soon we graduated high school with certificates of merit. We both enrolled in the KII. Vera was admitted to the radio faculty, where we both wanted to go, but I wasn't as fortunate and wound up in the chemistry department.

A Freshman

The initial weeks of my institute studies were full of surprising discoveries. First, there were several different textbooks on the same subject. Second, our professors' lectures were absolutely different from the material in the textbooks. It was clear how important the student's written notes made during the lectures would become.

In general, my high school education was quite sufficient to master the new, more complicated subjects. Nevertheless, I had to exert myself quite considerably to do it. At that time our family was now living in a two-room (i.e., one-bedroom) apartment, so the conditions for at-home study were almost favorable.

Studies in the KII were much more difficult but also incomparably more interesting than in high school. Moreover, I was learning diligently not only because of my aforementioned "perfectionist's syndrome" but also because of my desire to receive a scholarship that was granted only to students who made progress. My results were outstanding: I achieved straight As in my four classes. That meant that I finished in the top 6 out of 600 KII freshmen. After that I became kind of a celebrity in the chemistry department. Soon I was co-opted into the faculty's Komsomol office. Vera's first semester results were not as impressive—mostly Bs.

After we successfully completed our first final exams, in the second semester of our freshman year, Vera and I grew bolder: we began skipping some lectures and did a tad bit more perfunctory work in our studies. Moreover, soon the spring of 1941 was in the air—it called us outdoors, out of the stuffy auditoriums. And we never denied ourselves the chance for a pleasant stroll along the familiar paths of parks that were beginning to green up in the spring sunshine. Starting in February we resumed going to plays, concerts, and the cinema. The previous fall, I had made Vera a fledgling soccer fan, and now she often accompanied me to the Dynamo stadium to watch matches.

I must add that at that time my interest in current domestic and international affairs increased rapidly: the world was changing before my eyes, and the Second World War had begun. Our newspapers and radio were my main sources of information.

Despite our rich cultural life, we still managed to come to the spring examination period not badly prepared. We successfully passed our initial final exams.

Meanwhile, we were waiting impatiently for Sunday, 22 June: that would be the opening day for the newly built, gigantic Central Stadium, which could hold up to 50,000 spectators. (The stadium had been under construction for several years, and its original name was Kosior Central Stadium, after the secretary-general of the Communist Party of Ukraine at the time. But after he became "an enemy of the people" and was executed, the stadium was renamed after the new secretary-general, Khrushchev. But Khrushchev Central Stadium was not its final name!)

I bought two tickets for the opening match for Vera and myself well in advance. In spite of the exam that was scheduled for the following Tuesday, all my thoughts were on the forthcoming match.

Saturday night my sleep was interrupted by some sounds that resembled distant peals of thunder. In my half-awake condition, I somehow associated the sounds with the routine practice antiaircraft fire that we had heard often that spring. I remember thinking to myself angrily, "What a nuisance are these training air-raid alarms; they just interrupt my sleep!" I rolled over and fell instantly back asleep.

I woke up in the morning later than usual. The weather was wonderful, and my mood was excellent because the anticipated soccer game was just a few hours away!

After taking my morning shower, I reentered our living room that also served as my bedroom. At that moment the black cardboard dish (our radio loudspeaker) announced in a rather unpleasant voice: "Attention! Stay tuned for an important government report at noon Moscow time." This strange sentence was repeated many times one after the other.

30   "Well," I thought, "the soccer match starts at 4:00 P.M. So, I have
      time to listen to that report. Then I'll get ready to go, and I'll fetch
      Vera on the way to the stadium."

      I waited until noon, listened to the report, and then found out—it
      was WAR!

Part II

The War

The War Begins

Kiev: The First Few Days of the War

In fact, at 12:00 P.M. sharp we heard the voice of the second in command in our government, People's Commissar of Foreign Affairs Vyacheslav M. Molotov. Slightly stammering, he announced: "Today, 22 June 1941, at 4:00 A.M. Germany treacherously, without declaration of war, attacked the USSR. German aircraft have bombed the cities of Kiev, Brest, Sevastopol, Odessa . . . " (I'm quoting from memory). Molotov's brief broadcast appeal to all citizens of the Soviet Union concluded with the words, "Our cause is just. The enemy will be defeated. Victory will be ours!" As soon as the broadcast ended, I heard my father give a loud sob.

Impressed by what I had just heard, I quickly dressed myself and ran to Vera. She already knew everything. However, neither of us recognized the seriousness of what had happened. For years we had been told over and over again that our Red Army was invincible. We believed that our "powerful and invincible" Red Army would deal with the impudent aggressors in just two or three days. And despite Molotov's somber statement, we innocently and cheerfully set out for the Khrushchev Central Stadium. It was still hours until the scheduled start of the match, but when we reached the stadium, an unbroken line of my fellow fans was already stretching into the city square adjoining the main entrance to the stadium. In the center of the square, we spotted several barrage balloons prepared for liftoff, attached to enormous spools of metal cable. Alas, we also noticed a handwritten notice: "Due to the war, the stadium opening has been postponed. The rescheduled date will be announced later, and all tickets will remain valid." Like it or not, we headed for home.

After dinner I forced myself to start preparing for my upcoming physics exam on Tuesday. I opened the textbook and tried to read it while listening to the reports coming through our radio in a constant stream. Every couple of minutes, I caught my attention drifting away from the textbook, and began listening more intently to the radio. Instead of the anticipated victory reports from the front, I heard only patriotic reports from meetings and assemblies, speeches by veterans of our Civil War, and the declarations of volunteers for the front. Broadcast messages on the course of the war were rare and largely unintelligible. Gradually, I forgot all about the exam and fell into deep thought.

At that time, I had a definite attitude toward Germany. I deeply appreciated the contribution of the German people to world culture. I knew about some outstanding German philosophers, writers, and composers from past centuries; I was particularly familiar with the numerous achievements of German scientists, especially in physics and chemistry. From childhood, my parents had taught me that the Germans were the tidiest, the most orderly, and most punctual people on the earth.

During the year and a half after the Molotov-Ribbentrop Non-Aggression Pact had been signed, our press wrote frequently and positively about Germany.[1] Our newspapers regularly published the daily reports of the German General Headquarters, which involuntarily prompted a reader's respect for the Wehrmacht. For example, I remember the brilliantly performed blitzkrieg operations and their rapid conquest of the Netherlands, Belgium, and Denmark as something special. The German slogans that I heard by radio, such as "End the domination of the Anglo-Saxon and Jewish plutocracy," were similar to the Communist Party's own current cliché, "Our main enemy is Western imperialism." Because the Soviet press never printed a word of condemnation about the German expansion in Europe, it logically followed—we were on their side.

Nevertheless, despite the now openly pro-German course of our propaganda, I (and most likely many others, who still recalled recent history) still harbored unfavorable feelings toward Hitler's Germany. After all, quite long before the beginning of "the Soviet-German friendship," the Soviet people had been made to understand that fascism was "the clearest and most naked form of imperialism" (in Stalin's unforgotten definition). The German aggression against Poland and other countries completely confirmed all of the ideas that I was still being taught about Germany a mere two years ago.

But that wasn't the only factor that shaped my worldview during the prewar times. I had come to hate Hitlerism after I learned about the tragic events associated with the Krystallnacht—Hitler's well-organized (in the best German style) mass pogroms of November 1938; about Hitler's and fascist Germans' fierce anti-Semitism; about their theory of Aryan supremacy; and about their scornful attitude toward Slavs and other people whom they considered inferior, fit only to serve as slaves. I had also managed to see a few Soviet antifascist movies that were popular in our country before the Soviet-German nonaggression pact was signed, and had read novels of the same nature by the German author Leo Feuchtwanger. All of this remained fresh in my memory, and the overnight change in our propaganda after the signing of the pact could not erase my convictions.

I have already written about my pride in the Soviet Union and its achievements when I was younger. What was it now, in my eighteenth year, at the outbreak of war?

I maintained my love for my motherland, as well as my pride in it. In recent years our Red Army had gained impressive victories over Japanese troops in the Far East (at Lake Khasan and at the Khalkin-Gol River in Mongolia). These victories had brought fame to a few new Heroes of the Soviet Union, including two prominent military leaders, Stern and Zhukov.

Furthermore, very important events took place during the 1939–1941 period. All our media regularly reported on them. The fact was that the USSR had bloodlessly increased its territory quite substantially. The new parts of our country were:

- Western Ukraine and western Belorussia from a partitioned Poland (the event was explained as "the reunification of Ukrainian and Belorussian lands and peoples").
- Bessarabia was ceded by Romania (the official explanation: "Romania has returned the former Russian land that was seized in 1917; by the way, northern Bukovina was also ceded—as compensation for the aforementioned seizure").
- Lithuania, Latvia, and Estonia (I don't remember exactly what we were taught at that time about the reasons for this annexation).

Each of the "acquisitions" was widely celebrated and documented by our media. The most impressive were the special issues of *kinokhronika* (newsreels) that reflected how cheerfully, with embraces, kisses, and flowers, crowds of local inhabitants greeted the advancing Red Army columns. I got pleasure from watching such scenes.

Each of the enumerated annexations was legalized very quickly: local representatives conventions were summoned and, on behalf of the local people, they appealed to the Supreme Soviet of the USSR to be admitted to the Soviet Union. Of course, there were no reasons for the Supreme Soviet to refuse such requests.

New local leaders appeared in each annexed land. I remember only two names: Villis Latsis, a Latvian writer, and some professor Kirkhensteins from Lithuania or Estonia.

At that time, I perceived the territorial expansion of the USSR as a positive achievement. We now know that it was a result of a secret protocol to the Molotov-Ribbentrop Non-Aggression Pact.

However, my belief in the wisdom of our actions was essentially undermined by an event that many had already forgotten. On the day in 1939 when the disgraceful war against Finland began, I heard a broadcast that, in a small town near Leningrad, "the representatives of the progressive forces of Finnish society have formed a People's-Democratic government headed by Otto Kuusinen, and have called upon the people to overthrow the imperialist regime of Mannerheim." But I knew perfectly well that Kuusinen was one of the leaders of the Communist International, the headquarters of which had always been located in Moscow. Further reports about this supposed "government" were never again heard.

Furthermore, my attitude toward our government's domestic policy was soon clouded by a new and more drastic law on labor discipline, which came into effect, I believe, in 1940: if you missed work without written permission for a day or more, or if you arrived twenty minutes or more late three times—you would be tried and sentenced to a year or two in prison. I believed in the need for strengthening labor discipline, but the cruelty of the new law's punishments seemed to far outweigh the crimes.

However, regardless of those and other similarly distressing facts, I remained a faithful patriot of my country. And now, on the evening of 22 June 1941, my thoughts whirled around a single question: "Where should my place be now?" According to peacetime law, I was still considered a preconscript, since a student was not subject to call-up before graduation. So what should I have done? Should I have simply sat, waiting for my call-up papers to arrive from the *voenkomat* (the military registration and enlistment office)? Or should I have awaited an order from my institute? Or should I have waited for special instructions from the local Komsomol committee? But the war was already here! My firm convictions didn't permit me to wait on the sidelines, and my character didn't permit me to idle about. Therefore, a decision had already ripened in my mind.

Late the next morning, without talking things over with anyone and without letting my parents and my sweetheart Vera know, I went to my local *voenkomat* to volunteer for the front. I wrote in my application that I was good in the German language, and I had already been awarded all of the four civil defense badges: "Voroshilov's Marksman," "Ready for Labor and Defense," "Ready for Medical Defense," and "Ready for Antiaircraft and Antichemical Defense."

When I approached the familiar building that housed the local *voenkomat,* I saw that the expansive courtyard in front of the building was crowded with hundreds of people, formed into several long lines. Passing by the line for those who had arrived in response to mobilization orders, I found the long line for volunteers and joined it. I recall a woman, a licensed medical specialist, and her seventeen-year-old daughter were standing in front of me in the line. They wanted to volunteer for work in a military hospital. After two hours of waiting, my turn came, and I entered a small room. A low-ranking officer greeted me with a handshake, read my application, expressed sincere gratitude, and . . . ordered me to wait for my call-up papers.

Meanwhile, the summer examination period at our institute continued, and the next day I had to sit for my physics exam. Instead of the designated auditorium for the exam, we students were sent to a room on the basement floor because air raids on the city were continuing. Having prepared inadequately for the oral exam, my answers were far from exemplary, which clearly surprised my examiner. He kindly offered me another chance to take the exam, so I could squeeze out the customary A. But I declined, telling him about my visit to the *voenkomat* the day before. As a result my grade was a B instead of my customary A.

From the very first hours of the war, the appearance of Kiev changed substantially. Following the strict directives of housing management, all tenants glued strips of paper in the form of two large Xs over each pane of glass. Sandbags appeared alongside many of the buildings. When it was dark, a strict blackout order was in force: everyone had to curtain off all windows so that no ray of light could make its way through. Streetlights were turned off. The headlights of streetcars, buses, and other vehicles were equipped with midnight blue lamps. All owners of any kind of radio equipment had to turn over their sets immediately to the authorities, and to save the receipt for them. Night duties were organized for the tenants of every apartment building, in case of fires caused by air raids. "Bomb shelter" signs with arrows pointing to the entrances appeared on the streets.

Under the influence of appeals by central and municipal authorities to expose and catch all spies, saboteurs, and the enemy's accomplices, many Kiev citizens were seized by a "spy mania." This was quite explainable: as you have read in chapter 1, for several years already, the powerful Soviet propaganda system had taught us to be vigilant to such threats. Mass-produced brochures, detective stories, plays, and films all featured skillful, dangerous undercover foreign spies and saboteurs.

There were many rumors during these days. Some saw a captured German saboteur wearing a Red Army colonel's uniform; others heard that a German paratrooper dressed as a Red Army soldier had unsuccessfully landed behind our lines and had been arrested on the spot. In any case, dozens of suspects were detained and handed over to municipal militia offices by our civilians.* A strange accent or a question such as, "What is the best way to get to [some street or special place]?" was enough reason for someone to be detained. After interrogation most of these detainees were released from custody.

After war was declared, most residents began hoarding supplies. Within a few days, the shelves of all the grocery stores were empty. Foodstuffs like flour, all kind of cereals, salt, sugar, fat and vegetable oil, canned goods and liquors, as well as soap, especially laundry soap, quickly disappeared. I remember when I entered a neighboring grocery on 5 July, the only items that were available for sale were numerous cans of "Chatka" (canned king crab from the Kamchatka Peninsula; in contrast to its postwar popularity, it was absolutely never in demand during prewar times).

On about 25 June, when the examination session was nearly finished, the Komsomol Office of our chemistry department commissioned me to be on duty at the institute's dormitory on Polevaya

---

* In the Soviet municipal government, "militia" is the equivalent of "local police" in our society and culture.

Street during the evenings. My shift was from 6:00 P.M. to midnight. For all five evenings of my duty, nothing dangerous happened either there or in the vicinity. Strictly observing my instructions, upon the sound of an air-raid warning, I immediately climbed to the roof of the building. But only a few times did I see in the distance searchlight beams, the flashes of antiaircraft fire, or the explosion of bombs dropped by the Germans. Usually, after about ten minutes an all-clear signal sounded. Apparently, the German bombers had orders to bomb other targets. As I recall, in Kiev their main objects of attack were the bridges across the Dnieper River.

On 27 June, just as I was about to report for duty, Vera unexpectedly came to see us at our home. It was a farewell visit: that evening, she together with her mother and three siblings would be leaving Kiev. Their initial destination was Moscow, but the final destination was still unknown. Vera promised to let me know as soon as they reached it.

I had expected to hear soon about the Red Army's successful actions, but the reports from our Supreme Command (the *Stavka*) remained vague. Within less than a week after the war began, some less seriously injured Red Army soldiers began appearing on the streets of Kiev, and many refugees from the western Ukraine (almost all of them were Jews from Poland) showed up at the railroad station. These events gave me good reason to take a more sober view of the frontline situation.

I remember that after a few more days, the reports from the *Stavka* grew far more alarming. It became known that most plants, factories, and institutions in the city were preparing for evacuation, and a veritable flood of Jews from the western part of the Ukraine poured into Kiev. These refugees, along with numerous local residents, crowded the railroad station, the freight yard station in Darnitsa, and the riverboat dock. All of them were desperate to leave Kiev as soon as possible at any price. They pressed together in dense masses as they boarded the freight cars and open flatcars on trains heading east, as well as the steamboats, launches, and barges heading downstream.

While nearly everybody was afraid to fall into the hands of the Germans, a few elderly Jews refused to be evacuated. They remembered 1918, during the time of the previous German occupation, and they convinced themselves that the Germans were civilized

40 people, and that no harm would come to them. (The future fate of these, as well as of tens of thousands of other local Jews, who were unable to evacuate, was indeed terrible—they ended up at Babi Yar, the site of one of the bloodiest massacres in world history.)[2]

On 29 June 1941, my institute's examination session came to an end, and Komsomol members were invited to take part in constructing defense lines along the Irpen River, 30 kilometers west of Kiev. I was glad finally to be of real use to the country. Late in the evening of the very same day, our group of about thirty students arrived at the outskirts of the village Belogorodka, which bordered on a pine forest. The Irpen River flowed nearby. We slept in a barn on a fragrant haystack. Just before dawn, we were awakened by the loud howl of passing airplanes, heading toward Kiev. Somewhere close by, a bomb exploded, evidently dropped prematurely by accident.

The morning of our first day of work was sunny. From a hillock on the edge of the forest, a panorama of the future lines of the antitank ditch opened before us. It stretched to the horizon and was crowded with hundreds of shirtless workers, equipped with shovels or carrying away the excavated earth on litters. A foreman approached us and pointed out the boundaries of the ditch segment that had been assigned to us. He explained to us that the near [friendly] wall of the ditch should be vertical, while the far [enemy] wall should be sloped. To a question on how steep the slope should be, the foreman confidently answered, "Fifty degrees—just as long as it is deep." He was surprised at the "stupidity" of the students, who stubbornly maintained that the angle of the slope should in that case be forty-five degrees.

On one side of us, a group of university students was working, but on the other side of us, professional excavators were laboring. We looked with envy from time to time at the gleaming, polished handles of their shovels, and at their agile and rhythmic movements. Despite all our efforts and our initial fervor, our productivity was significantly lower, and in the second half of the twelve-hour workday, it collapsed completely. Somehow, in the following days, we caught on to the work and managed to do quite a lot. While we worked on the ditch by the Irpen River, heavily loaded German Junkers flew over us three or four times a day in the direction of Kiev.

I don't remember how we spent the evenings, or where and how we were fed (I recall that they passed out bread for free and, not long before our departure, began selling strawberries for nine kopecks a kilogram). I remember that not far from our segment of the line, in a small field by the edge of the forest, there was a mysterious reinforced concrete construction, the foundations of which were sunk into the earth. Sometimes we could see a sentry patrolling back and forth near the bunker. This was one of the strongpoints of the former reserve line of defense for the old western borders of the country. By the war's outbreak, this line of defense had been imprudently disarmed.

By the middle of the sixth day of our excavation work, our segment of the ditch was ready for inspection. The nagging foreman found no flaws, and our group was permitted to return to Kiev. As soon as I reached the city, I began to worry about my parents and my little brother. As I made my way home, I looked all around, to see whether or not there were ruins of buildings, destroyed by enemy bombs. I was also impatient to find out what was happening at the front, as over the past six days, we had not been able to hear any radio or read any newspaper.

Once at home, I fell into the embrace of my mother, who was crying from joy when she saw that I was uninjured. Having learned that everyone in my family was safe, and all our things intact, I took a shower and ate a home-cooked meal. Only after this did my mother show me a notice from the *voenkomat:* on the morning of 6 July, I had to appear there with all my documents. Soon my highly concerned father showed up. He hugged me tightly and then began filling me in on the news. Reports from the front given by the Soviet Information Bureau (Sovinformburo) were vague as before but definitely grim, and local enterprises and institutions were preparing to evacuate the city.[3] Crowds of people were gathering at every point of departure. Despite threats from the authorities that they would arrest panicmongers, the atmosphere at the railroad stations and docks was extremely tense. Explaining that he could not leave his post at his establishment, my father looked at me hopefully and asked me to seek the help of Vera's father in getting my mother and little brother out of the city safely through all the crowds. Having finished this conversation with me, my father rushed off back to work and returned only after I was already asleep.

The next morning, I went to the *voenkomat,* where I received instructions to appear at the mustering point for preconscripts on

Shevchenko Boulevard by 4:00 P.M. on 9 July. I was to bring a change of underwear, some warm clothes, and enough food for one day. Everything was clear, and I had enough time before the muster, so I headed off to see if I could catch Vera's father, Vasiliy Aleksandrovich, at his office. When I reached his workplace, Vera's father soon courteously received me in his office. Before I even finished my explanation, he asked me for my home address, wrote it down, then ordered my mother and brother to be ready by 6:00 that evening, when his office car would pull up in front of our apartment.

Arriving back home, I began to help my mother pack all the needed clothes, shoes, and other items into knapsacks and a small suitcase. I remember how I stubbornly persuaded my mother several times not to take things that I considered excessive, and she had to repack her things over and over again. At last, not long before the designated time, everything was packed away, bound up, or buttoned up; Mama was resigning herself to the limited composition of the baggage, and I—to the weight of bags too heavy for my mother or little brother to lift. Precisely at 6:00, the car pulled up in front, we quickly loaded everything aboard, and drove by an unfamiliar route to a reserve rail line, a great distance away from the train station. A passenger train was standing there, under steam and ready to leave, guarded against unauthorized personnel by several militia officers. They were just finishing the loading of the families of staff and employees of the railroad administration into its cars. Mama and my brother, Tolya, were among the last passengers to board. I carried their bags aboard, and then we hastily said good-bye, since the train was already starting to move.

Happy that my mother and little brother had left in a passenger train that was inaccessible to the majority of people, I set off to my father's place of work, so I could inform him about their safe departure as soon as possible. It was still not dark, and the city was living in the anxious conditions of wartime. In the course of the day, I had noticed many more men in military uniform among the passersby. Trucks loaded with groups of armed Red Army soldiers traveled more often through the streets. On the Brest-Litovsk highway I saw several damaged tanks that were still capable of moving slowly under their own power. I came upon a considerable number of Red Army soldiers in dusty, sweat-soaked uniforms, slowly dragging themselves along with bandaged heads, arms, or legs. I saw even a small string of three wagons, loaded with domestic goods and wares, which had just completed a long journey from the west. Perched among their remaining household belongings were groups of exhausted refugees with faces blackened by dust. And now as I headed to my father, I unexpectedly became witness to a tragic event. A military truck sped past me and, without braking, turned sharply onto a bridge. The sudden turn threw a Red Army soldier head over heels off the back of the truck. He lay on the bridge motionlessly, with no sign of life, his head covered in blood. The truck stopped. His comrades leaped out, picked up the body, and laid it back on the truck. The truck then sped away again.

Having learned of my mother and Tolya's successful departure, my father was overjoyed. Now it remained for us to hope that the train would not come under air attack, and we had to patiently wait for word from Bashkiriya, where the train was headed.

In the remaining two days before my appearance at the military muster, I filled out my student's record book, received my summer stipend, and, being still a preconscript, I received a two-week supplement for students being mobilized for the war. I gathered up my things in preparation for departure and went in search of food to buy for my one-day ration. The latter task turned out to be not a simple matter. The neighboring produce store was empty of shoppers, and all that remained on the shelves were pyramids of the unpopular tins of crabmeat. I wandered around the city for a long time until I managed to buy something to eat. In some places, I detected the smell of smoke: certain offices were burning their files, to keep them out of enemy hands.

Once home again, I laid everything I had gathered into a small suitcase, except one item of particular pride to me—a new lined overcoat, carefully sewn in the latest style. This I decided to carry in my hands. There was still some time remaining, and I managed to find out from the railroad administration that the train, in which my mother and Tolya were traveling, had managed to cross the eastern border of Ukraine safely.

On the day I was due to report, my father came, checked the contents of my suitcase, then added a bar of soap he had managed to buy to the two loaves of bread and the stick of sausage I had purchased. He handed me a small amount of money, and then we set off to the assembly point. I went lightheartedly—after today I no longer had to make any personal decisions; instead, the government would decide everything for me, as well as for all my peers who were still not serving in the army. Soon we saw that the spacious courtyard, where we had been told to appear, was filled with young men, dressed every which way. The place was also packed with throngs of parents, girlfriends, and friends who had come to see us off. There were about 500 of us, all aged sixteen to eighteen (plus a few more older men, who had previously received deferments from military service). Many of the young men had managed to do without suitcases and instead carried comfortable backpacks over their shoulders. Instead of a coat, some of the guys had brought jackets or padded jackets, and this was also more sensible.

Soon some officers appeared, formed us into four ranks, and took a roll call. After the roll call, a military commissar declared, "According to the resolution of the GKO [the State Defense Committee], all of you are now part of the Red Army's strategic reserve, and, therefore, you are to march far to the east of Kiev." We were told that our destination was the city of Stalino (the present city of Donetsk), located about 600 kilometers east of Kiev, where a few other similar groups of young Kievans were already destined. There, under the direction of the local *voenkomat*, we were to work on state farms or in mines, until we were called into the army. Three officers, whom we were obliged to obey without question, would accompany our column.

After a few minutes, our column moved out onto Shevchenko Boulevard and slowly headed in the direction of Pechersk. Papa and other parents accompanied us until our first halt, which was announced near the Pechersk monasteries. Here we tightly embraced and kissed each other on the cheek, not knowing that our next meeting would not take place for another three years.

The command rang out to fall in, and the column resumed its march for the railroad bridge across the Dnieper River. The Germans had frequently tried to bomb the bridges across the river, but so far unsuccessfully. We were lucky, and we crossed the bridge in complete silence. On the opposite shore, I turned a lingering gaze back upon the familiar sight of the Pechersk monasteries' golden domes. "Goodbye, my Kiev! I am ready to overcome all difficulties and to surmount all obstacles, and I promise to do my best to return here as a victor!" was at that moment in my mind.

My Long Way to the Army

Leaving Kiev on 9 July 1941, I could not suppose that my path to the ranks of the Red Army would be so long in time (ten months) and in distance (on the order of 3,000 kilometers).

On the first evening we marched only a short distance, and soon after nightfall we bedded down in some empty storage facilities on a certain collective farm. I gradually became acquainted with my new surroundings. We had only a few students of higher education in our bunch. The majority in the group had less than high school education.

According to the calculations of the *voenkomat,* we should overcome the 600 kilometers to Stalino, our destination, in just a little more than two weeks. But the next day of our march, which resumed shortly after dawn, turned out to be very difficult. The merciless hot July sun; the deep ruts and bumps on the uneven dirt roads, which meandered through vast fields of ripened wheat; and the infrequent short breaks all combined to turn our well-formed column of happy fellows marching in uniform step from the day before into a despondent procession stretching hundreds of meters in length.

We suffered our first casualty when we stopped for dinner at some collective farm: one of the new reservists experienced heat exhaustion and lost consciousness. We left him at the collective farm's medical station. A full, hot meal and an hour's rest helped us, but by the end of the day we were deathly tired. Many of the men suffered blisters on their feet from their ill-fitting shoes. Despite my very uncomfortable load (a suitcase in one hand, my coat in the other), I didn't feel particularly weak or unhappy.

Our march took us through many rural villages, where our column would be greeted by women of various ages, sometimes approaching us alone, sometimes in small groups. Some would bring us earthenware pots filled with fresh milk; others carried cottage cheese, boiled eggs, or other kinds of food. They served each one of us who, leaving the column for a minute, stopped for a quick bite or drink. The most touching of all in these short encounters were the motherly parting words and the wishes for us to remain safe and unharmed, which rose from the hearts of these simple rural women, often as they wiped a tear with the corner of a white kerchief. In response to our words of gratitude, some said, "And perhaps, God willing, someone like me will one day treat my beloved son at the front in the same fashion."

The march continued, but day after day the discipline in our group deteriorated, the number of limping guys who could not keep up with the column grew, and the size of our unit dwindled. It is difficult to say what became of those we left behind. Our route of march was just a little south of the Kiev-Kharkov rail line; possibly, some of these fugitives reached the nearest station, where they took a seat on a train heading to the east, while others may have turned back to the west, toward their native home. In any case, by the end of the first week of our march, when the group was now melting away not by days, but by hours, the accompanying officers found a way that we could make the remaining distance in formation, and led us along the railroad bed. But at the very first station with a double track, a freight train was under steam, preparing to depart toward the east. While our officers discussed a plan of action, several of our guys climbed up on one of the train's flatcars and waved farewell. At that moment, I understood that there would be no further organized movement of the group.

We marched an additional 10 kilometers, and as evening fell, we reached another station on the railroad, where several trains were standing. Here the "unit" finally dissolved.

From that evening forward, I moved "by relay," each time transferring from a stopped train to one that was about to depart. In four days of such travel by transfer, I now found myself within the Donbas. Here everything looked as it did before the war, and local trains were running on schedule. Having reached Yasinovataya, a suburb of Stalino, on 20 July I found myself in the spacious apartment of the family of my mother's sister. In filthy clothes and tattered shoes, unwashed and unshaven, tired and hungry, I was too embarrassed to sit down at the table, before I had washed up and changed out of the sports shirt I had been wearing.

I appeared before the oblast *voenkomat* the next day. They checked my papers, registered me, and ordered me either to begin work immediately or to resume my studies at the local institute. The next day I began working in the metal shop of a coal mine. Every morning I handed out the tools and instruments to the shop workers and in the evening collected them back again. During the day, I marked the finished (military!) shop output—metal thermal containers used to deliver hot food to the soldiers at the front.

Approximately two weeks passed, when my aunt received a letter from my mother, who together with Tolya had been evacuated to the hinterlands of Bashkiriya. She was already working in a village named Inzer as a dentist at a local hospital. They gave her a room in a log house next to the hospital. We also received word from my father, whose office and staff of several workers were now situated in Kharkov. I was happy for this news from my parents, but I was still troubled—where, oh where, was my beloved Vera?

Trying to locate my beloved, I, counting only on a miracle, sent ten postcards to the cities where, as gossip had it, evacuees would most likely be staying. On each postcard I wrote the address, "[City], Main Post Office, General Delivery, Vera Vasilievna Makovchik." And the miracle happened! In the middle of August, I received a postcard, written in that familiar, precious handwriting, with the return address "Kuibyshev-5, General Delivery." Vera informed me that they were in Kuibyshev (present-day Samara), living not far from the train station in the same specially equipped coach-office car, Number YuZ-5, in which they had departed Kiev. Indescribably happy, I wrote Vera a detailed letter on the spot, and our correspondence was never again severed.

That same day that I received the postcard from Vera, I stopped working in the mine's machine shop and became an electrical mechanics student at the local industrial institute. Only two weeks of study passed, when I unexpectedly encountered a student with the last name Karlinskiy from Vera's department back at the KII. He told me an important bit of news: the KII had been evacuated to Tashkent, and I had to get there right away, as classes were about to resume. I offered to accompany him back to Tashkent. The next morning, I went to the oblast *voenkomat*. The officer on duty could not understand at all why I was showing him my Kiev student book, what Tashkent had to do with anything, and what sort of written permission I was seeking. He looked at me suspiciously, clearly doubting whether everything was right with my brain. He told me, "We're still not calling up second-year institute students, you can go to your institute and they'll register you there. We don't give out any references here. Happy travels!" Then he escorted me out of his office.

It didn't take long to gather my things, and if I am not mistaken, on 17 September Karlinskiy and I took our places on an open flatcar of a train ferrying glass to the east. So began the second leg of my long journey to the army.

This time we had to make our way to Tashkent—moreover, through Kuibyshev! Along the way, now having experience in such travel, we quickly figured out which of the multitude of freight trains, accumulating in the yards of rail junction stations, would leave first, where we would need to hop off in order to avoid getting sidetracked from our destination, and when we could dally long enough to get some food.

At this time the railroads of the country, especially in its European part, were overburdened. Hundreds of troop transports, hospital trains, and freight trains loaded with the machinery and equipment of evacuated factories were en route. Westward from the Volga River, passenger movement practically ceased. But at the same time, tens of thousands of evacuees were in motion to the east. The majority of these people, tortured by the long journey in freight cars or on open flatcars, were women, children, and the elderly. They looked terrible: in filthy clothes, unwashed, with darkened, haggard faces and uncombed hair. Many of them were sick and lice infested. But before them still lay such a long journey to the Urals, to Siberia, to Central Asia.

We looked at these most unfortunate families with great sympathy. They were often stuck waiting for long hours at the stations, not knowing when the train would depart or the name of the next station. The trains departed without announcements. Because of this, quite often immediately after a train stopped, dozens of people would pour out of the cars and on the spot, next to the train, in front of involuntary witnesses, hastily relieve themselves. Some people would rush to the station depot to try and find some food or get some water, but when they returned, they would find to their horror that the train had already left with the rest of their family.

According to GKO decree, food stations were established on the platforms of all railroad junctions in the European part of the USSR. Round-the-clock every evacuee could find some free food there: a few slices of bread, kasha (hot porridge), some sugar and salt, and boiled water. From time to time instead of the kasha, a borscht or vermicelli soup would appear, and you could even find pieces of meat in it, but such soup never lasted for very long.

In contrast to the majority of evacuees, Karlinskiy and I, being young, healthy fellows, unburdened with any household possessions or heavy luggage, often changed trains, found some kind of food, and relatively quickly traveled farther east. Once we reached Saratov, we bought tickets for a place on the deck of a river steamboat (we didn't have money for a cabin), which was heading up the Volga River to Kuibyshev. We moved slowly against the current, and I managed to get lost in admiration of the unique Volga landscapes, about which I had read so much. We suffered from hunger almost the entire long boat trip, as in our haste to get aboard the steamboat, we hadn't obtained any extra food. At last we reached our goal and arrived in Kuibyshev. At the sidetracks of the train station, I spent quite a long time searching for the passenger coach car YuZ-5.

It was in the afternoon when, with palpitating heart, I politely gave a knock on the locked door of Vera's car. There was no response. I knocked again, this time more vigorously and persistently. At last the door opened slightly, and I saw Vera's mother, Agrippina Semenovna, peering cautiously out. When she recognized the visitor, she joyfully invited me to enter and loudly called for Vera. Almost immediately, the happy, smiling Vera appeared before me at the entrance. Embarrassed to show our feelings in front of other people, we limited ourselves to a firm handshake, and the four of us, including Karlinskiy, stepped into the car.

In the coach car's salon, Vera's siblings, Nadya, Lyuba, and the three-year old Alik, affably greeted us. Within just a few minutes, a table was spread with food, and the famished guests ate to our hearts' content. Our joyful reunion was dampened by the news that, while we were traveling, Kiev had fallen to the enemy. Everyone was deeply worried about the lack of word about Vera's father, Vasiliy Aleksandrovich, who had remained in the city until the very final days.

After the abundant refreshments, Karlinskiy and I set off for the public bath. While we washed the road dirt off ourselves, our clothing underwent disinfection (a louse-killing heat treatment). Having returned to the coach car, we ate a bite of dinner with Vera and Agrippina Semenovna, and when it became dark, they laid out some comfortable bedding for us on the salon floor. That evening, Vera and I managed to sneak in a few hugs and kisses, but as soon as we heard the sound of someone's footsteps, we instantly moved away from each other.

The next morning arrived, and it was time to decide what to do next. Karlinskiy bought a train ticket to Tashkent, while I made an unsuccessful effort to enroll in the electrical department of the local industrial institute, where Vera was studying. Without a special residence permit for Kuibyshev, which had now become the second capital of the country, they wouldn't accept me into the institute. Obviously, I wanted to linger for as long as possible here with Vera, but I also wanted to make a short side trip to see my mother and brother in Baskiriya, before I went on to Tashkent.

The short days of my stay in Kuibyshev were filled with time together with Vera. We didn't part for a minute, and I would have felt totally happy, if I didn't have the sense of being a man with no status, no place of residence, and still no part in the war effort. I recall that when Vera and I encountered a column of young soldiers, I subconsciously experienced a certain sense of guilt before them.

On the eve of my departure for Bashkiriya, Vera and I went to the opera house, where masters of art from Moscow were putting on a benefit concert for the war fund. The majority of spectators were dressed in the latest fashion, and some looked like foreigners. Vera told me that the government of the country and foreign embassies had been relocated here from Moscow. She said you could occasionally see Foreign Minister Molotov, and that official "ZIS-110" cars and automobiles of foreign manufacture buzzed around the city.

I made my swift visit to Bashkiriya, to see my mother and little brother. Once that was done, I returned to Kuibyshev. The very next day, I left for Tashkent. Vera accompanied me, dragging along a bag heavy with food, which my beloved had lovingly prepared for my journey. Too soon came the parting kiss on the steps of the coach. The railway to Tashkent took ten days to travel.

In Tashkent

At last our train slowed to a stop, and through my car's window I could see the low building of the train station and its enormous inscription in the Russian and Uzbek languages: TASHKENT TOSHKENT.

It was the end of October, but I saw that everything around the station was still green and blooming.

One of the oldest cities in Central Asia, the capital of the Uzbek Soviet Socialist Republic of the USSR, Tashkent was an amazing blend of extreme antiquity and the present. Along with more or less contemporary, no higher than three-storied buildings in Tashkent's green central district, a large "old city" district existed, with thousands of small clay houses and a labyrinthine network of narrow roads and alleys.

According to GKO decree, many plants and factories from the western part of the USSR had been shifted to Tashkent after the war started. I remember that an evacuated aircraft-assembly plant was already operating here shortly before the 1942 New Year. Along with organized evacuees, many thousands of refugees poured into the city, and it had at least doubled in size from its prewar population.

I already knew that our evacuated KII had joined the Central Asia Industrial Institute (SAII). But it was just before evening when I reached the SAII and found the institute's offices were closed. A problem arose: where to find shelter for the night. I was lucky: one of the first people I met nearby was my good friend and former classmate Boris Shpilskiy. We were so delighted to see one another again that we exchanged kisses on the cheek, just like we were family. We celebrated our meeting at my initiative at the nearest café, and on my dime, since Boris had long been in dire financial straits. Over dinner, we exchanged news. After our meal, we went to the temporary dormitory, more precisely a shelter, where Boris was living at this time. The two genuine SAII dormitories were overcrowded.

The men's wing of this "dormitory" was only a large room, in which there were only three pieces of furniture: a small table in the center of the room, a barracks-style bed in the corner, and a badly worn armoire, which partially obscured the bed from passing eyes. On the floor along the walls were the modest belongings of the residents. Twenty plus students lived here, not only Kievans but also students who had arrived in Tashkent from other Ukrainian cities. In addition to them, there were usually also a few "illegals"—people who had still not informed authorities of their presence in the city, as was required by law. Sometimes the authorities carried out raids in search of such people.

Preparing for sleep, a resident would sweep the dust and trash out of his spot on the floor and spread out his "bedding": normally a few newspapers, sometimes an old mat or sack, while a briefcase or a stack of books, covered by a jacket, would serve as the pillow. Almost everyone slept in his clothes. Sometimes in the morning you could spot a new "illegal" under the table who had arrived during the night. A newlywed couple occupied the only bed in the corner of the room. The rest of the residents behaved tactfully, so as to give not even the hint of a double entendre about them.

The next morning, as soon as everyone had washed their face and gathered up their "bedding," we headed for the institute. Just a few meters from the "dormitory" began the rows of the Alaiskiy bazaar, which struck me with its rich bounty of fruits and vegetables, and the enormous size of the gifts of nature from Uzbekistan's mild, sunny climate.

The results of the first day's excursion to the institute were typical for those times. Institute officials informed me that they would re-enroll me, but only upon the condition that I find a place to live and obtain the necessary residence permit. I spent several days traveling through a bureaucratic maze, trying to obtain the requisite permit. But my initial appeals were fruitless, until I recollected the name of a distant relative who lived in Tashkent. I found this woman's address in an information office and immediately went to see her. Fortunately, she remembered my mother, although they had not seen each other in more than twenty years. The next day, I had in my hands a formal reference letter from this distant relative, testifying to her offer of living space to me, and supporting my application for a resident's permit.

In the beginning of December, I officially became a sophomore of the special faculty (my old-standing dream) of the SAII. However, I had little time for study: my primary concern was finding food, and I had to work full-time to earn my daily bread. I remember little of my studies here because I was hungry all the time. The city began bread rationing on 1 December, and the amount allotted to a student was only 400 grams a day (about 14 ounces)—plainly inadequate for a growing young man. So like the majority of other evacuated students, I concentrated on finding jobs to earn money for food.

I took on a variety of jobs. I first became a controller for Tashkent State Energy. It was my job to place limits on civilian energy

consumption by sealing electrical sockets in the apartments of civilian customers. This was necessary so that the factories that had
relocated to Tashkent would have enough energy to run their operations. I remember one well-to-do Uzbek family that tried to bribe
me with a place at their opulent dinner table. I was swallowing to
keep from drooling but declined the bribe and did my duty. I also
had many unpleasant moments with the wild dogs that often pa-
trolled the apartment courtyards.

I left this position soon enough and took on a variety of manual
labor jobs. Once, utterly famished, I even sold blood to a blood bank
and within the hour collapsed unconscious on the street.

With scientific study on the back burner because of my constant
hunger and search for food, in March I began work that continues
to stand out in my memory, for they were the first days in Tashkent
when I didn't feel hunger. I worked on a ten-student labor team in
a ropeyard that had been evacuated from Kharkov. The work with
the jute fiber was hot and dusty, and the dust filled our sweat pores
and breathing passages. We sneezed constantly. But I remember this
work fondly because after our three-hour shift, the factory foreman
would hand out food coupons to each of us. After we showered,
they would take us to the factory cafeteria in town, and a 200-gram
(about 7-ounce) chunk of bread accompanied each dinner. I would
save this bread and exchange it the next morning for eggs, cottage
cheese, or simple porridge and enjoy a full breakfast.

Often, the students were called upon to do unpaid, socially useful work; our earnings would go to the national defense fund. We
would have to tidy up some place, clean irrigation ditches, or stack
various materials. The hardest work was when we were taken to
help build the main irrigation canal several dozen kilometers from
Tashkent.

In such conditions, one couldn't even dream of full study. I
skipped the majority of lectures and went to the March–April 1942
exams unprepared, which strongly depressed me (surprisingly, the
grades I received were not bad at all). But my superficial education
in these circumstances bothered me far less than the fact that while
my motherland was caught up in a terrible struggle for her very
survival, I was sitting out the conflict far away.

Shortly after I completed the spring exams, several upperclass-
men from our faculty were accepted into military academies. I

hoped that after completing my second year of studies, I too would become a student at a military academy. Fate decreed otherwise. At the end of April, the *voenkomat* of the district where I was registered mistakenly ordered me: "Settle all accounts at your place of work in connection with your mobilization for the Red Army. Appear at the *voenkomat* on this date." Though, as a student, I was still not eligible for military service, I firmly resolved not to reveal my student status to the district *voenkomat*. The time had come for me to leave these hated conditions and my ineffective study at the institute. The *voenkomat* sent me to an artillery military college not far from the city of Alma-Ata. Finally, my long way to the army had come to an end.

On 14 May 1942, before leaving Tashkent I wrote my sweetheart, Vera, a farewell letter. Here are a few lines from it:

> I have pledged to myself to study military science without sparing strength or effort, so that I won't be left behind, but will be at the front. I'll be an honest and, I hope, a skilled Red [Army] officer. I want to take harsh vengeance on the enemy for all the evils they have done to millions of people like me. And if I must give my life, let it cost them as dearly as possible. Anyway, I promise: you'll never blush in shame or embarrassment for your chosen one. And I'll always carry your name in my heart, and I will return.

Three Months at a Military College and Seven Weeks in a Re-forming Division

A Cadet of the Artillery College

Well, on 15 May 1942, I found myself among a group of some fifteen recruits, who were heading by passenger train to the Ryazan Artillery College. In autumn 1941, the college had been evacuated from the city of Ryazan to the small town of Talgar in Kazakhstan. Talgar was located about 20 kilometers from the capital city of Alma-Ata (Kazakh for "Apples' Father"; today, the city of Astana is Kazakhstan's capital).

During most of our journey, a boundless steppe was visible out the windows: a vast green grassland decorated here and there with giant scarlet flower beds of blooming poppies—a uniquely wonderful scene.

Alma-Ata was very different from Tashkent and impressed me by its straight, broad streets bordered by flowering trees and beautiful buildings of recent construction. A gorgeous background completed the landscape, with the Alatau Mountains rising above the clouds; their distant peaks were barely discernible in the semitransparent haze.

That was the hardest and the hottest summer in the Great Patriotic War against Hitler's Germany. Because of the war, the usual two-year period of training for a lieutenant had been reduced by half. The obligatory quarantine period was shortened as well, and we very soon were taking the military oath and beginning our intensive studies.

The arriving group of recruits from Tashkent was assigned as a whole to the 3rd Training (sound-ranging) Battery of the First Training Battalion. The 1st Battery trained officers for weapon sections, the 2nd Battery trained fire control officers. Our specialty, in the 3rd Training Battery, was considered the most complicated, as it

56 required a good knowledge of trigonometry. Moreover, the majority of personnel of a sound-ranging battery are normally located quite far behind the front line of battle. (Incidentally, the famous author Aleksandr Solzhenitsyn served as an officer of such a battery during the war.) In the first months of training, all three batteries trained according to the same program.

We had at least ten lessons a day, except Sundays. So very soon we became exhausted. Everybody was impatiently waiting for the coming Sunday. On Sundays, we usually went to a neighboring collective farm to accomplish some agricultural operations there. Everyone liked these activities as a refreshing change of pace from our intensive training.

I described my daily routine in a letter to Vera, which I wrote on 16 June 1942: "How do we live? We get up at 5:00 A.M., exercise, and then wash in a nearby mountain stream. After breakfast there is training: seven hours before lunch, two hours after. We are supposed to have an hour of rest during the day, but this is rarely observed. On Sundays, they promise we will go to the theater or to concerts. Every officer I have met so far is a decent person and a good instructor. I can't say the same about our sergeant major."

In fact, the sergeant major combined some peculiar habits with a strict style of command. The most annoying thing was the evening roll call, when he would issue a seemingly interminable string of boring reprimands in the darkness of the summer night. We had to stand there in ranks, listening to his droning criticisms, while we frantically tried to keep our eyes open and remain awake. Once, I lost patience with his nightly sermon, and just after he finished, I loudly uttered, "Amen!" The cadets could hardly refrain from laughing, and the enraged sergeant major tried to find the one who had so deliberately violated military discipline. Fortunately, he failed to identify me: to my fellow cadets' credit, no one betrayed me.

I must confess that I didn't write Vera about certain difficulties that I encountered upon entering military life. These related specifically to aspects of my uniform.

The first problem of this kind arose just after I had received my boots. In contrast to most of the other new cadets, I hadn't worn this sort of footwear before. In the Red Army, we didn't wear socks. Rather, we wrapped *portyanki* (footcloths) around our feet and ankles before putting on our boots. I had only heard about these foot wraps before. I struggled to learn how to wrap my feet tightly and with no crimps, wrinkles, or loose corners. Then I began to imitate my well-experienced barrack mates' technique. It took me about a month before I learned the "art" of wrapping my feet properly. However, I performed the process very slowly, which was very bad for a cadet. You see, after you heard the early morning signal to arise, you had only a few seconds to wrap your feet, or else you would be late for the morning roll call. The inevitable consequence of tardiness was extra duty, and usually a most unpleasant one—to be on duty around the clock in the barrack (it meant also to scrub the floor of our twenty-five-stall latrine several times a day).

In order to evade the penalty for being late for roll call, all cadets made a special preparation before going to bed: everyone, after taking his boots off, carefully laid his wraps over the tops in a precise way. So, after you arose, it remained only to shove your feet along with the wraps into the boots. Later, when the sweetest commands "Stand at ease! Fall out!" finally rang out, you had an opportunity to wrap your feet again more properly and thoroughly.

Another problem regarding the uniform was a small component of it, the so-called *podvorotnichok* (a narrow ribbon of white cotton cloth sewn on the inside of a collar so, after the blouse is put on, only a tiny white strip peeps out over the collar). The cause of my troubles was my inability to do needlework. I had no sewing experience because this kind of chore was always my mom's exclusive business in our family.

I can't forget the sad episode that occurred on the day when I, together with a group of cadets, received my first pass and looked forward to escaping the college's grounds for a short while in the town (there was a rule in the college: the first pass was effective for only two hours, namely, from 2:00 P.M. until 4:00 P.M.).

A duty officer stood at the checkpoint. He examined the pass and then inspected everybody's appearance in a nagging fashion, trying to find the tiniest fault. Some cadets were ordered to adjust their military blouses and tighten their belts; others were forced to return to barracks in order to polish their boots better. And I was ordered to rip off my slightly crooked *podvorotnichok* and sew it back on "properly." I still remember with shame that I only managed to obtain a more or less acceptable result by 3:50 P.M., just minutes before the termination of pass, so that my long-awaited first pass never happened! (Nevertheless, quite soon I learned to wrap my feet skill-fully and to sew a *podvorotnichka* on a collar almost perfectly.)

* * *

The main subject at the college was, naturally, artillery science. This came to me quite easily, because, in contrast to the majority of my fellow cadets, I was strong in trigonometry and could quickly make mental calculations. Thus it was not hard for me to calculate instantly the proper angle of a gun's deflection on the artillery azimuth disc, given a certain range, and do the reverse calculation, while the other cadets in my training platoon lingered over mathematical compu-tations. I easily mastered the new terminology, such as "ellipse of dispersion," "registration mark," "drift," and others. Having work experience with instruments in my institute's laboratories, I learned more quickly than my fellow cadets how to use the "stereoscopes" and the "panorama" optical aiming devices, and how to lay the gun for direct fire. In general, within the first few weeks of study, I al-ready firmly grasped the fundamentals of artillery fire.

My eyeglasses, which I wore from first rise until the call for re-treat, served me well at the military college. First, they allowed me, a very nearsighted fellow, to spot any officer in time to prepare my-self to salute him, or to avoid the encounter. Second, thanks to my glasses I became a keen rifleman. And third, wearing them gave me a marked advantage over the other cadets in the classroom. Here, my glasses played an important role as a means of camouflage. Sup-porting my chin by one hand, I could doze quite calmly behind the cover of my thick spectacles. Teachers would instantly detect other drowsy cadets nearing sleep—and each one of us so badly wanted to sleep!

We studied and drilled almost without break for long hours ev-ery day. So every cadet was constantly sleepy, and almost every ca-det nodded off during lessons. I'll never forget an amusing episode that happened to cadet Gurgen Movsesyan. He was the cadet on duty that day. When the colonel who taught us artillery entered the classroom, Gurgen shouted, "Platoon, stand up! Attention!" and then reported our readiness for study. The lesson started, and within about ten minutes the colonel noticed that Gurgen had fallen asleep. Pointing at him with a finger, he quietly ordered Movsesyan's neigh-bor to wake him up. The latter poked Gurgen with his elbow. Being half asleep, Movsesyan jumped up and shouted, "Platoon, stand up! Attention! Break!" Everybody burst out laughing, including the colonel.

Only once did I have to serve guard duty, but I still remember how difficult these twenty-four hours were due to the disruptions in sleep. We had to serve four-hour shifts on duty, and had two hours of sleep off duty. I was keeping watch over the college's fuel depot in a shift that started after midnight. It was completely dark and silent around me. You couldn't squat or relax, nor exchange a word with anyone. After two hours of duty, your legs grew numb, but you didn't dare lean on your rifle, lest you would fall asleep instantly on your feet. This was dangerous, because at any moment the officer in charge or his assistant might appear. I could hardly wait for the shift change. It was not much easier to stand watch in the daytime under the baking sun, for even then you could hardly keep your eyes open, just like at night.

The most amazing thing for all of us was the amount of food suddenly available to us as cadets. Unlike our civilian life since the war had begun, when the search for food was a major preoccupation, here we received three nutritious meals a day.* After being half starved for a year or so, everybody quickly devoured his bulky meal. And the most desirable place to be on duty was the kitchen.

I clearly remember my own "kitchen duty." Four of us started our shift with cleaning the cauldrons after supper. We were in luck: the last course was boiled rice. It had been cooked with plenty of fat, raisins, and sugar. A delicious, golden brown crust covered the entire inner cooking surface of the large pot. After stuffing (more precisely, overstuffing) ourselves with this delicacy, we scraped off all the remaining crust and packed four buckets with it. Close to midnight, we secretly carried that precious load back to our platoon's tents. We quietly woke up our fellow cadets, and they emptied the buckets in no time. We didn't have to wait long for the consequences of our gluttony: many suffered from stomach problems for the next several days.

---

* Caloric content of wartime rations was tightly regulated in the USSR. Generally speaking, those in uniform ate better than those not in uniform, and uniformed personnel closest to the front lines ate best of all.

As we studied and trained, the news from the front lines in these months was quite alarming. The city of Rostov-on-Don, the historical gateway to the Caucasus, had fallen to the enemy, and the Germans had forced a crossing over the Don River. Now they were heading simultaneously in two directions, eastward toward Stalingrad and southward toward the Caucasus oil fields. They seemed very close to success. Meanwhile, we continued our measured pace of training and study. Here are the thoughts I shared with Vera in a letter dated 22 July 1942: " . . . I'm beginning to get a little fed up with the life of a scholar. I'm afraid I will spend the entire war studying, and thus not take part in the decisive operations of 1942. But I want my name written over the shattered fragments of the fascist regime as well, as one of the war's participants in 1941–1942."

Life at the military college continued to take its own course. In the middle of August, we were scheduled to have our first experience with firing cannons using live ammunition. Completely unexpectedly, an alarm sounded in the late afternoon of 14 August 1942, and all personnel fell into formation on the academy's parade ground, where the college's commander read orders for the entire academy. It was announced that, under Directive No. 227 of the Supreme High Command (this order later became famous as the "Not One Step Back" directive, written personally by Stalin), the following cadets were being dispatched as reinforcements for units of the operational army. My name was on the long list of cadets.

After farewell speeches by the battalion commanders, we set off to receive new uniforms, including greatcoats and boots made of ersatz leather, a minor cash stipend, and rucksacks tightly packed with dried rations. I remember only the smoked sausage, dried rye bread, and sugar.

Our column was scheduled to depart for the Alma-Ata train depot the following afternoon. This gave me a chance to write Vera a farewell letter before our departure from the college. I finished it with a line from a poem by the popular Soviet poet Konstantin Simonov: "Wait for me and I'll return!"

On the way to the train depot the next afternoon, I happened to notice our college's head clerk. He was holding a parcel in a large envelope. Without his notice, I managed to discern our destination on the envelope: Tuimazy, Tatar Autonomous Soviet Socialist Republic. Immediately, I had a slender hope to meet with Vera and my mother. I knew that Tuimazy was about a thousand miles from the battlefields, but that I would be there for just a short time, and then quickly wind up at the front.

At the railroad station, a typical Soviet troop train, which in Russian we call an "echelon," was already waiting for us. It was formed of numerous freight cars reequipped as railroad carriages for soldiers. Simple, plank bunk beds ran down the length of both sides of the car, enough to sleep about twenty-odd soldiers. We called such a troop car a *teplushka*.* We covered the simple planking with fresh hay from somewhere. In this *teplushka* we made the extremely long ride to the mysterious Tuimazy.

Before our echelon started off, I learned that our route would run through Kinel, a railroad junction close to the city of Kuibyshev, where Vera was still living at that time. I also asked some railroad authorities how long we'd be en route to Kinel. Once I had this information, without hesitation I sent a telegram to Vera, "Wait for me at the Kinel railroad terminal on 19 August."

There were numerous stops along our way, where we would hop out from the *teplushka* to buy the surprisingly inexpensive gifts of Central Asia—aromatic, honey-sweet melons. I purchased an enormous "best in show" melon for my meeting with Vera and announced this to all my neighbors in the *teplushka*.

Our echelon moved down the track with numerous long delays, so soon I had to write Vera a second telegram, postponing our meeting until 20 August.

Alas, our journey continued to stretch out in time, and I had to send three more such telegrams to Vera with new dates for our reunion. By this time, there was not a trace left of all my comrades' melons in our *teplushka*. Nevertheless, I stubbornly resisted the proposals from my comrades to "dispense" the single remaining melon in my lap. We were still far from Kinel.

At that time the small town of Kinel was a suburb of the city of Kuibyshev. Its local railroad terminal was one of busiest and most populated junctions in the USSR. It was the point where the endless human stream of refugees split into two parts: one, eastward, to the Ural region and Siberia; the second, southward, to the Central Asia

---

* The root of this word is *teplo*, or "heat." This conveyance was constructed in such a manner that it could retain heat, not an insignificant consideration in the USSR.

region. Hundreds of people gathered daily there in and around the small station building.

Well, 24 August came, and our train had finally reached within 30 kilometers of the Kinel station, but there it stopped on a nameless siding and didn't budge for three hours. I was sitting together with my acquaintance, Dima Repin from Leningrad, our feet dangling from the *teplushka*'s doorway, as we idly examined the freight cars and flatcars of the train that had long been sitting on the neighboring track. It was carrying machinery and evacuated families. At last the neighboring train rattled to a start, and its rail cars began slowly sliding past our *teplushka*. I dully noticed a passenger coach bringing up the tail of this train. I read its sign and couldn't believe my eyes: "YuZ-5." Vera's coach!

A railway worker with signal flags in her hands was standing on the rear platform of the coach. I instantly hopped off my train and ran along the railway embankment after the accelerating train, gesturing wildly to the woman to summon someone from inside the passenger coach. After a few seconds, when I had already started to fall behind, Vera's mother Agrippina Semenovna and sister Nadya appeared on the platform. Waving to each other, I managed to catch Nadya's cry: "Vera is waiting for you in Kinel!" And as their train pulled away, I saw that they could not restrain their emotional tears over this nearly miraculous chance encounter.

In little more than another hour, our train pulled into Kinel. The echelon's man in charge announced that our stop there would not be long, about half an hour. I leaped from my *teplushka* and ran into the overcrowded waiting hall. Dozens of evacuees were sleeping there on benches and on the floor. I ran around the small building, hastily looking at every sleeping or strolling woman that I passed, but none was my Vera. For a few minutes, I waited by the exit to the ladies' room and examined every woman who came out, but again, I had no success. Could Vera's appearance have changed beyond recognition after only nine months since our last parting? Of course not.

I asked the master of the terminal to use the loudspeaker to summon Vera to his office. That was done a few times too, and I stood waiting for Vera near the office entrance. Alas, nobody came.

Fortunately, we didn't depart on schedule. Somebody explained that our echelon had not yet received its full ration of bread from

Kuibyshev, and our departure had been delayed until the bread arrived.

Despairing to see Vera, I went into the small kiosk and bought an envelope and stamp. Then on a piece of paper I wrote sorrowful words of regret about our missed meeting, which quite possibly could have been our last. (Years later, it became widely known that of every hundred soldiers my age, only two returned from the war.) It was now almost dark, and I searched for a postbox to mail my letter. From the loudspeaker, I could hear "Metelitsa" playing, and I thought back to 21 December 1938, when I first met Vera in her home and "Metelitsa" had been playing on their gramophone.

Suddenly, I could hear the sound of a woman's steps behind me. I turned, and in the semidarkness, I could see a woman's figure approaching me. I peered more closely, straining to make out the face: it was Vera! Our joy was boundless!

I found my friend Repin, and together with Vera we located an empty freight truck, close to my train. Once inside, Vera told me about her adventures:

I have been waiting here for you since the day before yesterday. Actually, I haven't been in Kuibyshev for two weeks. I've been engaged in agricultural work with other students from the Kuibyshev Industrial Institute. I came home for the day on 21 August, and there I found your three telegrams. I instantly started getting ready for our meeting. I put together a large package of food and drink for us, including a stuffed pastry I made for you and a bottle of vodka, and then I put on some nice clothes and set off for Kinel. Here I waited, and I ran up to every military echelon that stopped—and we had no less than twenty such trains stopping here every twenty-four hours! I went up to each *teplushka* of the stopped train and inquired of the soldiers whether or not a "Kobylyanskiy" was inside. Of course, what young soldier couldn't take a sudden fancy for a sweet, nicely dressed young woman? So every *teplushka* produced its own smiling "Kobylyanskiy." Once I recognized their innocent fun, I would immediately run to the next car. The echelons ran day and night, leaving me hardly a minute for sleep. By the end of two days of waiting, exhausted, I sat down for a moment outside the train station, and instantly fell deeply asleep. For some reason, I suddenly awoke with a jolt, and in horror, realized I may have missed your train while sleeping. I ran back into the station.

Vera unpacked her bag, I opened the bottle of vodka, and we three started our unique supper. We drank to the meeting, enjoyed a hearty and tasty meal and finished with the wonderful melon.

Then Dima left us, and we spent the remainder of the night together. Vera and I had a good long talk, interrupted by the occasional hug or kiss. Both of us understood: our present meeting very likely could be our last one, but we believed in better fortune.

My echelon left at dawn. Three and a half long years lay ahead until I would see Vera again.

In Tuimazy

In three days we reached Tuimazy. Here representatives from main elements of the 300th Rifle Division selected from among the quite undereducated cadets whomever they happened to like at first glance. A sharp, fair-haired artillery lieutenant selected me as well as five other former cadets: my friend Dmitriy Repin, Alexander Ishchenko, Nikolay Kiselev, Vasiliy Panteleev, and Georgiy Senchenko. Thus we began our service together in the 1049th Rifle Regiment of the 300th Rifle Division. This division had started the war near Kremenchug in August 1941, had suffered heavy casualties over the next year, and now was undergoing re-formation. The lieutenant, who was representing a regimental battery of 76-mm field (or "infantry support") guns, led us into Tuimazy.

Our final destination was the outskirts of Tuimazy, where the regimental 76-mm field gun battery was located. Six dugouts provided shelter for the soldiers and sergeants of the battery, while our officers stayed in the little homes of several nearby Tuimazy residents. The six of us were introduced one by one to our battery commander, Senior Lieutenant Loshakov. I was appointed gunner.

All regimental detachments were undergoing intense training here as they prepared to go to the front. The artillerymen mastered the simple technique of fire over open sights (direct laying or direct fire), as well as the complicated method of fire using a reference point. To direct the latter, one must know how to use not only the panoramic sight but also the aiming circle, and he must be good in mental arithmetic as well. As you can imagine, thanks to my mathematical knowledge and recent artillery practice during the college drills, I was already prepared to control the fire of the entire battery.

During the field exercises, our deputy battery commander, Lieutenant Akimov, and the fire platoon commanders, Lieutenants
Moldakhmetov and Kamchatnyy, both still untested recent graduates
from a one-year artillery college, quite often made mistakes, so time
and again I helped them. Once it happened in Loshakov's presence.
The next day, I was appointed as gun crew commander of the first gun
of the battery and was promoted from sergeant to senior sergeant.

From Tuimazy to the Volga River

After seven weeks of replenishment and training, our infantry division boarded special freight trains equipped for military transportation and headed for the Stalingrad *Front*. On the third day we reached
the city of Kamyshin, which was an intermediate destination. Our
division hadn't been provided with horses yet, so trucks were to
meet us here to carry our regiment the rest of our 200-kilometer-
long way to Verkhne-Pogromnoye. Everybody was amazed by the
long column of brand-new trucks that arrived at the location where
we were waiting for them.

Wow! How many! What an unknown powerful model! It is so
different from Soviet trucks and much bigger than ours! Where are
they from? Who made them?

In a minute, a friendly driver answered all our questions. These
wonderful trucks, called Studebakers, had been shipped from the
United States as part of the American lend-lease program of assistance to the USSR. This column was part of a large transportation
unit, which was at the disposal of Stalingrad *Front* headquarters.

Soon we hooked the guns to the trucks and took our seats under
a tarpaulin cover. The battery started on the second part of its long
journey. There was an overcast sky all day long, and no German
planes were seen or heard. When we were within about 20 kilometers of our final destination, strange sounds resembling the remote
rumble of distant thunder were audible. Everybody understood: it
was the echo of the battle for Stalingrad. Most of us grew serious.
But at that time, Senior Sergeant Nikolay Kiselev, a former actor
from the city of Yaroslavl, a cheery and witty guy, joked: "It's like
Zeus the Thunderer is rolling huge logs along a cobblestone road in
the skies. Why is he too lazy to pave his road?" The joke cleared the
tense atmosphere that had just been hanging over us.

66   We reached Verkhne-Pogromnoye at the end of the day. I saw an
old traditional Russian village with a single street, which was lined
with log houses. All of the porches, doors, and windows on most
of the houses were skillfully decorated with carved wooden casings
and jambs. (Within some fifteen to twenty years after the war, the
area around Verkhne-Pogromnoye and neighboring villages along
the left [east] bank of the Volga developed rapidly and eventually
became the industrial city of Volzhskiy.)*

The direct distance between the village and our final destination—somewhere near the left bank of the Volga River—was about
2 kilometers. It was too far to roll our heavy guns there by hand.
Therefore four Studebakers along with our battery personnel were
to spend the night and the next day here. First of all, the trucks and
guns were hidden from aerial observation. For the same reason, we
were ordered to spend the daytime indoors only.

In the morning, Loshakov and Akimov participated in a regimental command's reconnaissance along the forested riverside. They
returned in the afternoon. They had spotted an important target
on the opposite bank and had selected good positions for both the
battery and its observation post (OP).

---

* Standing with one's back to the river's source (facing downstream), the "left" bank
is the land on the observer's left side, and the "right" bank is the land to the observer's right side. These forms are commonly used in Europe but are unfamiliar
to most Americans.

The Beginning on the Volga's Left Bank

First Time in Action

It was a gloomy late afternoon when our battery set off on the final leg of its route to battle. This time we drove very slowly along an extremely bumpy dirt road. It was growing more and more dark, but according to the order all lights were off. Finally, we reached the edge of a forest that stretched almost to the bank of the river. The Studebakers could go no farther. We stopped, unhooked the guns, and then unloaded the rest of our munitions and belongings. Everybody said good-bye to the drivers, and we started moving the guns by "human traction." It was so difficult in the darkness! Our problems were compounded when a heavy rain began falling. Only officers had waterproof capes, so in no time at all our military greatcoats were soaked through.

In about a half hour we reached a small clearing that had been chosen during the previous day's reconnaissance as the position for our battery's emplacements. Straightaway both fire platoons started digging four gun emplacements. The reconnaissance and fire control platoon, headed by Lieutenant Vinokurov, followed Loshakov to the opposite edge of the forest to the selected OP location. Two telephone operators began laying a 400-meter-long wire between our emplacement and the future OP.

Despite the darkness and ceaseless rain, we worked hand in hand to dig the gun emplacements and our foxholes. So quite soon that work was done, the parapets were covered with sod, and the guns were in position. Next, we camouflaged each gun's emplacement (so-called fire position) with a special net. Only then did we start to build two dugouts next to the clearing. Four men were assigned to hack and hew trees to cover the dugouts. All our tasks were completed about one hour before dawn. Taking turns, two sentries were posted, and everyone else (including me) dragged his exhausted body into a dugout and instantly went to sleep like a log. I did not suspect that a complete surprise was awaiting me.

It seemed to me that I had slept for just one minute when some-body shook me violently: "Double-quick to the telephone! Our battery commander is calling you!" I slipped my bare feet into my boots and ran to the emplacement, throwing the wet overcoat over my shoulders while fastening the belt at the same time. It was absolutely light outside. Akimov, Moldakhmetov, and Kamchatnyy were standing close to the telephone set. The operator stretched out the receiver to me. I took hold of it and introduced myself, and heard in response Loshakov's voice: "I order you to assume the position of the man in charge at the battery emplacements! Report to me ready for action in five minutes!"

"Yes, sir!" I replied immediately. But an order of this kind was so unexpected!

A question quickly flashed through my mind: Is that so? But look here, according to the service regulations, Deputy Battery Commander Akimov is the first in charge. And Moldakhmetov is after him, then—Kamchatnyy. But I had no time to complete my thoughts. I grew slightly nervous, and at the same time I felt a surge of pride: I was just given responsibility to fire the first shot of our battery in action! Now I had no right to blunder!

I knew inside and out how to control a battery's indirect fire from a covered position at the commands of the OP team. The battery fired about twenty rounds at three different targets without any errors. Then we received Loshakov's all-clear signal. In a couple of minutes Akimov was called to the telephone. After a quite long conversation, he ordered all of us to fall in and form up into two ranks. Akimov transmitted two messages from the OP, first, reporting that our battery had destroyed an enemy pillbox and neutralized two enemy mortar batteries; second, he passed along the battery commander's gratitude for the accurate fire of our fire platoons.

"We serve the Soviet Union!" we all responded together.

That is how my baptism of fire came about.

The Ensuing Events

We repeated our fire attacks for the next three days running, and the enemy's activity on this tiny sector of the front slackened. Then both fire platoons rolled their guns into direct fire positions on the very bank of the Volga. From here we could see the steep opposite bank of the Volga and several buildings of a small village called Latashanka. It lay just a few kilometers north of the outskirts of Stalingrad, where the bloody battle was raging at its height.

At the end of October, an order came down the chain of command to undertake an assault landing operation to seize Latashanka in order to draw away some of the enemy's forces from the fighting for Rynok, Spartakovka, and the factory districts in northern Stalingrad, and thereby relieve the pressure on the defenders. Two battalions of our rifle regiment were designated to form the landing force. By the dark of the night almost 700 troops embarked on four motorized barges that were moored near our bank. There was no strong resistance when they disembarked on the opposite shore at dawn, but the advance along the steep bank was slow. We heard the sounds of fighting from across the river. A report arrived that the landing force had managed to seize only a few peasants' houses by noon. Soon our headquarters lost radio contact with the landing force. Later, before sunset, heavier gunfire was heard, and in the evening a lone young soldier swam back across Volga with very bad news: several German self-propelled guns had arrived in the village and were pressing the landing party back. They needed immediate help.

Our command decided to reinforce the initial landing force. The supporting landing force was our 3rd Rifle Battalion, reinforced with a field gun platoon and an antitank gun platoon. All were to be ready to embark that evening. Battery commander Loshakov selected our first fire platoon to join the battalion. After sunset, we manhandled both guns of our fire platoon to the embarkation point that was not too far from our emplacements. Loshakov accompanied us to encourage us and wish good luck. Suddenly, our platoon commander, Lieutenant Moldakhmetov, fell ill with fever and left for the regimental medical company (I don't know what happened to him after that). On the spot, Loshakov summoned me and gave me command of the first fire platoon. (I would hold this post until November 1944. After Loshakov promoted me to platoon commander, my former gun layer Pavel Kalkatin was appointed gun crew commander, and Yusup Ismailov, an Uzbek, became the gunner. I was later awarded the rank of junior lieutenant in March 1943.)

Well, there were two motorized barges moored to the riverbank and waiting to carry us across. We embarked on our barge after the first one had already set off for the opposite bank, sailing slowly with muted engines. But this time the enemy reacted to our crossing. Just after it got dark, the Germans had begun to launch flares. So they discovered us and started shelling ceaselessly. Nevertheless, the first barge managed to reach the far bank, although there were many casualties among the troops it was carrying. But just after our barge left its mooring and its engine had started, a shell exploded beside us, causing a tremendous blast wave that deafened everybody and shook the barge like a small sliver of wood. The engine ceased operating, and the barge started drifting downstream. Several crewmen directed it back to the bank by pressing long poles against the riverbed. Fortunately, there were no casualties. That was the end of our battery's participation in the landing operation.

The fate of the troops at Latashanka was tragic. Most of at least 900 men were captured, killed, or injured. Only a few survived.

There was a lull in activity on our sector of the front following the fighting for Latashanka. One day in the middle of November 1942, an event of an absolutely different sort happened to me. Below I describe how I unexpectedly became a member of the Communist Party.

A Member of the Soviet Communist Party under Preferential Terms

That day our regiment's party organizer, Captain Prokhorov, along with Major Farber, an instructor of the division's political department, visited our battery emplacements. (All such instructors were assigned to visit all the infantry and artillery units in the division periodically, in order to inspire the soldiers with courage and, at the same time, to get wind of anything or rather anyone suspicious. Our battery was one of the detachments under Major Farber's observation.)

After giving a short lecture about the situation of the war, they approached me together with our deputy battery commander for political affairs, Senior Lieutenant Sysolyatin. They said to me, "We regard you as a warrior, who deserves the honor to become a communist." Farber advised me to submit an application for joining the VKP(b) as a candidate for a party membership (VKP[b] was the abbreviation for the prewar name of the Soviet Communist Party, namely, All-Union Communist Party [Bolshevik]).

Prokhorov declared that he had heard a lot about my conduct under fire, and therefore he was willing to give me a written recommendation for candidate membership as my sponsor.

Never before had I thought to join the Party so soon, as I considered myself too young and inexperienced for it. Nevertheless, I now felt flattered that such mature and responsible people were certain that I met the requirements for Party membership.

My readers may recall that around the age of fifteen, I began to be critical of a few of our government's decisions and actions. But I had never equated the Communist government's policies with the behavior and actions of individual ordinary VKP(b) members. I think that before the war, the total number of Communist Party members in the USSR numbered barely one-half of 1 percent of the country's adult population. I knew only four of them before the war. One was a printing house metalworker in his late forties, our next-door neighbor in Vinnitsa. Another was my thirty-five-year-old cousin, a military political worker, who had joined the Communist Party in 1930, while working at a coal mine. Two were forty-something-year-old high school principals, one living in Vinnitsa, the other in Kiev, and both were at the same time history teachers. Although each of these had different personalities and characteristics, all four were completely normal people and performed their duties quite well. I didn't see anything special in their manner of behaving or conduct. (At the same time, my teachers and the media taught me that pre-revolutionary Communists were the best fighters for the cause of the working masses against czarism. I believed it fully.)

As soon as the war started, all our media and every military unit newspaper began to publish such slogans as "Communists in the war—in the vanguard!" or "The only privilege given to a Party member is to take a lead in the struggle against the Nazi invaders."

Shortly after the war began, the requirements for admitting new VKP(b) members from among frontline soldiers and officers were simplified. The number of necessary sponsors decreased from three to one. The probation period for those who had excelled in battles was reduced from one year to three months.

While preparing my written application, I used a popular cliché of that time, "I want to go into battle as a communist." In a couple of days, I appeared before the head of the division's Party Commission,

Major Adamiya. It was a standard procedure. Because of his Georgian descent, he pronounced two questions in a thick Georgian accent. The first question was, "Do you love our homeland?" The second one was, "Do you love Stalin?" Twice I responded, "Yes," and I was admitted unanimously.

After the admission, I did not do anything special. I just continued to fight as well as I could.

The following February, Sysolyatin reminded me that it was already time to change my Party status from candidate member to full Party member. "No, I haven't excelled in battles as yet," was my response. That kind of dialogue took place a few times more until after an unforgettable battle at the "Ravine of Death," when I decided, "Now, I finally deserve to become a Party member under preferential terms."

That occurred in August 1943. I felt a little bit satisfied, but nothing changed in my soul and in my personality. I never took or even tried to take advantage of joining the VKP(b).

* * *

By the middle of November, our battery still lacked horses. This was tolerable as long as the front line in our sector remained static. However, a few days after the historic Stalingrad counteroffensive, Operation Uranus, began, our division received a lot of horses. This meant that we were now fully battle ready. It was the last week of November when we started our first long march.

However, our new horses were giving me unexpected problems. You see, I had never dealt with horses before.

Our new horses were numerous rust-colored, short-legged horses. They were a contribution from the Mongolia People's Republic, our satellite state. The horses were all of the same Mongolian breed, maybe the same kind that Genghis Khan's cavalry had used to conquer half the known world. They looked so similar to each other that, during our first march, I was unable to identify the eight horses that belonged to my platoon. Therefore, whenever there was a short halt in the march and our horsemen dismounted and moved away from their horses, I was afraid that I would not recognize my horses without their men.

My second problem became apparent the same day during the first long halt. Long before the war, I had read a lot about the traditions of certain Russian officers, who in past times had commanded in a careful and fatherly fashion. As the new fire platoon commander, I wanted to follow those examples, but sometimes I overdid it.

On this occasion, when we stopped to halt for an hour or two, my solicitous concern for my subordinates placed me in an embarrassing position. The horsemen freed the horses from their harnesses and were ready to lead them to a watering place. At that moment our field kitchen appeared with dinner for my platoon. I didn't want the horsemen's dinner to grow cold while they were watering the horses. So, with the best intentions, I ordered the horsemen to give fodder to their horses and eat their own meals, and take their horses for watering only after they had dined. That was a stupid, absurd idea born of complete ignorance, because *a horse never eats dry fodder before being watered*. But how could I know that? At the time I still was just a young city dweller, an ignorant know-nothing regarding how to care properly for horses. The "old" horsemen tried to hide their smiles at my foolishness.

We crossed the Volga River by a pontoon bridge downstream from Stalingrad, then advanced westward for several days. There were severe frosts in the Don River steppes that December. Two soldiers of an adjoining regiment, both Turkmen, froze to death. As we advanced, we had a few successful skirmishes with the Germans, when our 2nd Guards Army was promptly turned southward in order to block the path of German Field Marshal von Manstein's armored divisions. They were moving to break through to the trapped German Sixth Army in Stalingrad.[1] On 21 December, our division together with a cavalry division stopped Manstein's troops. (However, my battery didn't see much action in the ensuing struggle. Our regimental positions were on the outskirts of Pchelinskiy hamlet, at some distance from the main point of the German attack.)

A few days later, our division was transferred from the Stalingrad *Front* and was placed under command of the Southern *Front*. For its service in the Battle for Stalingrad, the 300th Rifle Division was honored with the title of "Guards" and renamed as the 87th Guards Rifle Division in April 1943.

We continued to pursue the withdrawing enemy, which occasionally led to clashes with its rearguard detachments. But we continued to press toward the Don River. We reached it around the time of the New Year and continued marching along its eastern bank in a southerly direction.

On 9 January 1943, while we were on the march, a low-flying German fighter caught our battery in broad daylight and made a strafing run. There was no place to take cover, and we suffered painful losses. Suleymanov, a middle-aged soldier, was killed, and eighteen-year-old Vanya Zhmak was wounded. We also lost nine horses in that attack.

We reached the Don River at a point across from a Cossack village called Razdorskaya on 13 January. The river was frozen solid, and two or three rifle battalions from our division crossed the river and attempted to seize Razdorskaya from the march. Although they reached the village, within two hours a German counterattack with tanks knocked our assault force back onto the ice and across the river. (I recall that on the frosty night before the assault, standing in my gun pit, I fell asleep, seemingly for a short while, and woke up from intolerable pain—the fingers on my hands were frostbitten.)

After the repulse at Razdorskaya, we continued our advance down the left bank of the frozen Don River. There were short skirmishes farther along our route. One bright frosty day during our march across the boundless white steppe, a sudden command rang out: "Regiment! To action! Get ready to repulse a tank attack from the south!"

In a minute all infantrymen scattered and lay down. At the same time we hurriedly prepared our battery's guns for firing with armor-piercing shells. Naturally, we had no time to dig four proper emplacements in the frozen ground. Three mounted scouts departed to check for the enemy tanks to the south. Long minutes of strained waiting crawled by as slowly as turtles, as we waited for their message. A half hour passed, and finally a new command arrived: "Regiment! As you were! Form march column!" Everybody breathed a sigh of relief.

Soon after that might-have-been battle, our regiment stayed for two days in a large hamlet called Karpovka, on the left bank of the Don River. The opposite bank was held by German troops, but there wasn't an intense exchange of fire. Nevertheless, an extraordinary incident took place there. I describe it below.

Zvonarev's Unfortunate Ice Fishing

A soldier of our control and reconnaissance platoon, Sergey Zvonarev, was the subject of the incident. Everybody in our battery knew him as a friendly and cheerful man. Unfortunately, at the same time, he was a true slob. Zvonarev learned that by night, when the Germans usually were quiet, some local villagers were successfully fishing through the ice on the river. Sergey decided to follow their example.

He didn't let anybody know when he set off for some ice fishing one moonless night. Sergey was wearing his winter camouflage coveralls. Zvonarev found several holes in the ice not far from the bank, but he saw human figures around them. So, Sergey, looking for a vacant hole, continued to walk farther from the bank. In some five minutes he came upon three men bent over more holes in the ice. They were wearing snow-white camouflage coveralls and seemed to be engrossed in fishing. At a distance of about 10 meters from the three, Zvonarev called out: "Hey, Slavs! Are the fish biting?" Unexpectedly all three drew themselves up to full height and instead of a response, Sergey heard: "Hände hoch!" (Hands up!)

We learned all the details of what had happened that night to Sergey ten days later from . . . Zvonarev himself. He reappeared in our march column during a stop in a right-bank Cossack village, the name of which now escapes me. The ill-starred fisherman told us that before dawn the Germans, who had captured him, left their position and in the ensuing week had retreated southward, taking the captive Sergey with them. They treated him kindly and fed him well (once he received even a chocolate candy as a treat). Nobody was appointed to look after him round the clock, and at a convenient moment Sergey hid in a villager's house. Then he found his way back to the regiment.

Not more than a half hour had passed since the "prodigal son's" return, when a NKVD officer of the regimental Special Department (*Osobyy Otdel*) appeared and ordered Zvonarev to follow him. We never heard another word about that reckless guy.[2]

There were only a few skirmishes in late January and early February 1943, while the German troops continued to retreat. We managed to cross the Don in early February over an ice-bound pontoon bridge near Bagaevskaya. The Germans frequently bombed this bridge, but on the day we crossed, a thick fog protected us. We continued our offensive toward the Donbas region—one of most industrialized areas in the European part of the USSR.

Our First Clash along the Mius River

It was mid-February when our division reached the left bank of a narrow river, only about 10 meters wide. It was the Mius River. On the opposite, somewhat elevated bank a few houses could be seen. Those were the outskirts of the German colony of Novaya Nadezhda (New Hope).[3]

Well-organized fire from Novaya Nadezhda was a sign that the enemy's troops intended to hold their positions there. Nevertheless, our infantrymen, who had not tasted defeat in the course of more than a month, didn't stop. At the end of the day they approached the frozen Mius River, paused to organize the attack under cover of the far bank, then rose to the attack. The assault enjoyed limited success, only managing to drive the Germans out of a few houses closest to the river. Further advance was impossible due to the increasing volume of German fire and the rising number of casualties on our side. (For some reason, our field guns remained behind during the attack.) Firing faded with the setting of the sun, and only the exchange of occasional machine gun bursts from the opposing sides broke the silence of the night. By this time each of our battery's platoons had received its specific order.

Being at the 1st Rifle Battalion commander's disposal, I received an order to cross the Mius and post both my guns among the infantry near the houses in our possession. Kamchatnyy's fire platoon had also taken position on the right bank of the river, but some 500 meters to the right of us. Their emplacements were just in front of an isolated brick building, seemingly a stable or a cowshed of a local collective farm. Since there had been no fighting there during the day, ammunition wagons of the supply platoon took their places just behind that building. The battery commander, the reconnaissance and fire control platoon, and the field kitchen remained on the left bank of the river, not far from the regimental command post.

At that time only two draft horses remained per gun in my platoon. It took the concerted effort of the gun crews and horses to get the guns across the icy surface of the river and up the steep far bank to the snow-covered, boggy meadow on the far side.

It was a starlit night, and I looked around. The nearest houses stood on a small hillock about 250 meters from the river. To the right of where we stood, I could make out two haystacks. Trying not to make any excessive noise, we advanced to the backyard of the nearest house. A rifle company commander, Senior Lieutenant Tarasov, was smoking there. After a handshake we considered where to place my guns. I placed Ismaylov's gun (Kalkatin had been injured recently) some 30 meters from the house, in a position where it could fire down the length of the street running through the village.

The second gun, Senchenko's, was currently inoperable, so we kept it in the yard to await the pending arrival of the regimental armorer. I ordered horsemen to shelter the limbers with the harnessed horses behind the haystacks. Then, after giving short instructions to both gun crew commanders, I entered the house.

It was a single-storied, brick building. From the lobby I went downstairs into a basement that was dimly illuminated by a *ploshka* (a saucer filled with oil that burned at a wick). Some ten officers and soldiers were there. Most smoked, and the men carried on low conversations. Tarasov lamented the losses he had suffered that day in his command. Only a handful of men remained in the ranks. The situation was similar in the other rifle companies, which were occupying neighboring buildings and yards. Tarasov advised me to lie down in the corner and get some sleep: "Don't worry, Germans never fight by night." However, I was still waiting for the arrival of the armorer. Moreover, the enemy was near.

Among others I met in the basement were two officers who were serving in mortar detachments. One, Lieutenant Vladimir Pedin, was the mustachioed, gloomy commander of the battalion's 82-mm mortar company. The other, Lieutenant Grigoriy Bamm, was a platoon commander in a 50-mm mortar company. In contrast to Pedin, he always wore a smile. (The frontline nickname for any mortar was "samovar"—a Russian tea urn, with an internal heating device—because a mortar resembled the tin pipe that connects to the samovar.) My conversation with the "samovarists" was brief: everybody had his own tasks.

I left the basement periodically to see that the sentries by the guns were still awake and to check on the horse handlers. Well past midnight the armorer Lieutenant Simunin arrived, carrying as always his heavy toolbox. He set to work on the broken gun, and after about an hour, both Simunin and Senchenko declared that the gun was now completely operable. Before the armorer left, he decided to warm up for a while and joined me in the basement.

The next time I climbed up the stairs and went outside, the moon was no longer visible, the night had become darker, and the desultory firing had stopped completely. The sentries were keeping vigil beside the guns, and I thought: "It seems that everything is calm. Now I can grab a bit of sleep."

I had just turned to return to the basement, when at that moment a sudden rattle of machine guns and the hiss and explosion of mortar shells shattered the silence. Tracer rounds flashed across the nighttime darkness in brilliant arcs. Flares rose one after the other in the depth of the village. A few mortar shells exploded just where our limbers were standing. One haystack burst into flame, then the other began to burn.

Our gun crews quickly prepared to fire down the street, but all we could see were gun flashes, and we were afraid of firing on our own troops. Suddenly the loud rattle of several German submachine guns firing simultaneously rang out, and just a moment later, a few of our infantrymen ran past us toward the river in a half crouch, followed by a few more. Then another group ran past our guns, with two or three machine gunners dragging their guns behind them. A real *drap-marsh* (in Russian colloquial frontline slang, a somewhat self-ironical expression that could be interpreted as a "skedaddle" or a "rout") had started. From the first moment that it started, nobody could stop this panicked flight.

I realized what was going on and ordered: "Bring up the limbers double quick! Prepare guns to march!" One limber appeared, but the second limber no longer had any horses. We hooked up Senchenko's gun, and I directed it to the river to join the retreating infantry. Simunin ran to help the second horseman drag away his limber. Ismaylov's crew with my assistance struggled to manhandle their horseless gun through the snow, but the river was still so far! Occasionally, several tardy infantry soldiers scurried past us for the river.

Finally, a group of mortar men with their dismantled "samovars" on their shoulders ran by and left us behind. We remained the lone group, struggling slowly across the snow-covered plain. We were exhausted, but we continued rolling the gun.

By this time Germans were beginning to emerge onto the outskirts of the colony and began directing aimed fire at us, though the low visibility slightly obscured us. When we were at a distance of some 70 meters from the river, an explosive bullet struck the gun shield. We dropped into the snow. I ordered Yusup Ismaylov, who was lying next to me, to remove the "panorama" (the optical sight) and the breech. Then we abandoned the gun and crawled to the river. The low visibility protected us, and we reached the river without any losses.

Under cover of the steep riverbank, we stopped and took stock. We found ourselves on the Mius River's mirrorlike, thick ice: two gun crews, one gun, one beautiful horse not in harness, and two limbers. We could see nearby the remains of the rifle battalion, about fifty infantrymen and a dozen mortar men.

It was now getting light, but fortunately the Germans remained inside Novaya Nadezhda. Otherwise, they could have arranged a real slaughter on the river ice. Gradually the number of infantrymen began to dwindle: Tarasov and the other company commanders were mustering their men and leading them downstream to a flat exit onto the eastern bank.

Ismaylov and I took turns clambering up the steep western bank of the river, where we could lie and observe what was going on. It was now completely quiet. Our abandoned gun was still where we had left it. Through the binoculars, I could see two Germans in white camouflage approaching each other from neighboring houses. I decided to wait until dark, then to try to sneak up to the abandoned gun and roll or drag it back to the river. I suggested the plan to Ismaylov and the crew, and they agreed.

At last two soldiers from our battery arrived, bringing orders from Senior Lieutenant Loshakov. The orders instructed me to return to the place of yesterday's jump-off point with my entire platoon. The orderlies also brought plenty of bread and about a dozen half-frozen pieces of boiled meat. While we were dealing with the food, they told us that Kamchatnyy's platoon had already withdrawn to the jump-off point and was digging gun emplacements and dugouts.

The orderlies informed me also of the loss in the supply platoon: Alexey Suchkov, the blacksmith, hadn't returned. The supply platoon had spent the night sheltered in the brick cowshed. When the fighting erupted in the colony, they all woke up. Then a mortar shell exploded right next to the cowshed and momentarily stunned them all. Lieutenant Brechko ordered everyone to fall back right away, but Suchkov, a tall, thin, fair-haired man in his forties, became mortally frightened. He climbed into a corncrib and grabbed its sides so tightly that no one could pry him loose. They had to leave him behind.

One more loss became apparent. The orderlies told me that Lieutenant Akimov was supposed to be with my platoon, and they had found that he wasn't here.

I executed Loshakov's order, but incompletely: I sent Senchenko's gun crew, their gun, and the sole remaining horse back to the battery. I asked the orderlies to deliver a request to Loshakov to send me a pair of horses and a horseman by early evening. I hoped that we would recover our gun when it got dark. Then we could haul it to the battery's emplacements.

Only six of us remained on the ice. The time hung heavily over the whole bright day as we waited for darkness. When it finally got dark, a full moon rose over the horizon, and that was in no way favorable to our risky plan. Flares that flew up from the outskirts of the colony every several minutes troubled us, too. Nevertheless, we kept careful watch over the situation in the meadow. As I watched, two German sentries, who appeared in the meadow about every fifteen minutes, were walking toward the gun, but they stopped some 50 meters short of it and turned back around. They quickly disappeared in the darkness.

At last the long-awaited horseman arrived with the requested horses. The German sentries were moving away from the gun, and I made the final decision—it was time! The three of us—Ismaylov, Maslov the gun loader, and I (only the three of us were wearing white camouflage coveralls)—left the riverbank and crept toward the gun. There was silence all around. When we reached the gun, we rose and began to roll the heavy gun across the snow. The task was so difficult, as the snow tended to pile up in front of the gun. After every few meters of progress, we lay down on the snow and rested for a minute. When we were about 10 meters from the river, something alerted the Germans, and they lobbed a few mortar salvos at the river. A few shells exploded not far from us. I shouted for the horsemen to pull the limber back a safe distance.

Once the mortar barrage ended, the entire remaining crew, waiting for us beneath the riverbank, climbed the steep slope and joined us in the meadow, to help us haul the gun to the edge of the bank. Once there, the gun rolled down the slope by itself.

While one of my soldiers went after the limber, Akimov

unexpectedly showed up. He answered our questions about where he had been evasively, and averted his eyes while he spoke. (The next day, a lieutenant from the regiment's Special Department persistently pressed me to recall any of Akimov's misdeeds or "anti-Soviet" statements, but I couldn't help him. It seemed some informer had already managed to report on Akimov.)

Around midnight we reached our battery position, together with our recovered gun. Loshakov and Sysolyatin greeted us as heroes and promised to recommend Ismaylov and me for decorations. Then Loshakov pointed out where he wanted me to position my guns and our dugout, and we went to work.

We came to a standstill on the Mius River line, and a rare period of positional warfare began. Neither side undertook offensive action, but we occasionally exchanged artillery fire. Soon an early thaw arrived.

The Mius Front and the Donbas

Our trench warfare on the Mius River left bank was not bloodless. Before the end of February, a single round of German artillery slammed into our battery area. Shrapnel killed our battery commander, Loshakov, and seriously wounded my friend from Leningrad, Senior Sergeant Dmitriy Repin. Lieutenant Lev Vinokurov became our new battery commander. During this lull in active operations, the front lines didn't shift, and we continued to face each other across the narrow Mius River. In March, our significantly battered division was withdrawn to a position behind the front lines for rest, reinforcement, and to prepare for the impending battles for the Donbas.

Two senior sergeants, gun crew commander Vladimir Tetyukov and gunner Yakov Zakernichnyy, reinforced my fire platoon in May after their release from a front hospital. Two young soldiers arrived from a training regiment. Among several others, a forty-five-year-old professional blacksmith, Andrey Shumchenko, and his seventeen-year-old son, Nikolay, arrived in the battery. They had been mobilized after the recent liberation of their village in the area of Rostov-on-Don. The senior Shumchenko replaced Suchkov, who had disappeared during our *drap-marsh* in mid-February. An eighteen-year-old graduate of an artillery college, Junior Lieutenant Grigoryan, an Armenian by origin, came to the battery shortly before mid-July.

Our division was in reserve from March to July. Several times during that period of inaction it was shifted from one settlement to another in two adjacent oblasts, Lugansk and Rostov-on-Don. We quickly tired of these movements. But our mood was excellent because, for the time being, we were safe from hostile fire.

In early May we settled in a small town of Vlasovka and stayed there for more than a week. This period deserves to be described separately.

Ten Blissful Days in Vlasovka

The peace and quiet and the gentle, warm weather all contributed to our common state of bliss. We placed equal value on the opportunity to heat plenty of water for bathing and washing. We received three regular hot meals a day. Moreover, regimental authorities rarely visited us, and our daily training wasn't burdensome. How could soldiers in war not be happy in these rare circumstances?

But I had an additional, personal reason to be in a good mood. The point is that since the previous fall I had been commanding a fire platoon without an officer's rank. Back in March 1943, I had been awarded the rank of junior lieutenant, but the corresponding written order arrived just when we moved to Vlasovka. That meant I now had the right to receive the "officer's ration" (including aromatic tobacco rather than the disgusting *makhorka*—crude shags—that the men received) equivalent to the rest of the battery's officers.

A big part of our battery was occupying a spacious yard, which belonged to the Korneev family. We placed two guns in a small orchard next to the house. Fifteen soldiers spent the nights in Korneev's barn, with hay as their bedding. Five officers stayed in the house. The supply platoon, our wagon train, the control and reconnaissance platoon, and others occupied two yards across the street. Our battery commander Vinokurov, who was by nature a recluse, preferred to stay alone in a small house beside them.

We five officers were quartered in the Korneev dining room. There were no beds there, so the mistress of the house gave us a few matted, Russian-style floor coverings and comforters. Three of our party were the political worker Stepan Sysolyatin, the deputy battery commander Alexey Akimov, and the supply platoon commander Grigoriy Brechko, all thirty-five years old. The other two were the fire platoon commanders, Ivan Kamchatnyy and I, both twenty years old. My friendship with Ivan started after Loshakov had ordered me to assume command of the first fire platoon. So my position became equal to that of Ivan, who commanded the second fire platoon. By the spring of 1943 we were already true friends.

Ivan Fedorovich Kamchatnyy (his nickname—Vanya) was born and grew up in a small Ukrainian village. In spite of the substantial differences in our prewar lives, we understood each other perfectly.

Vanya was much more experienced than I in how to get by under the conditions at the front, and he willingly shared his knowledge with me.

The first day of our stay in Vlasovka, we spent situating the personnel, as well as placing the guns, wagons, and horses. Shortly after dinner, a smiling Roman Makhlun, the battery sergeant major, entered our "officers' room" with a bag in his hand. He opened it and put the contents on the table. It was our combined officer's ration (my first ration was included in it!)—two herrings, a pack of tobacco, a 250-milliliter can of condensed milk, and five 200-gram packs of cookies. Unanimously we decided to dispose of the bulk of the ration immediately.

We had no problem dividing the tobacco into four parts (Sysolyatin was a nonsmoker), and in a minute all the smokers were in perfect bliss. Meanwhile, Sysolyatin prepared the herring and sliced the bread. Together, we pounced upon this choice food, and literally just a couple of minutes later the two youngest, Vanya and I, were clearing away the leftovers and doing the dishes. All that remained to be "mastered" was the can of condensed milk. Its contents were a mystery to everyone but me. So the other officers entrusted me with the task of opening the can and tasting the unfamiliar stuff inside. Having opened it, we discovered a viscous, dull-white substance inside. I poured out an equal portion into five saucers. Without waiting for anyone else, I tipped my saucer and sampled a tiny portion with the tip of my tongue. Sensing the sweetness, I immediately poured a large swallow into my mouth. The others followed my example, but the viscous, sweet liquid made Akimov sick. Rather than drink it all down straightaway, we prepared some tea and enjoyed it together with the sweet condensed milk. Alas, we never saw it again for the rest of the war.

We devoted most of the following days to combat training. After an early breakfast nearly all of our battery's personnel would set off for the so-called training ground—a vacant area about 4 kilometers from Vlasovka. A railroad branch line ran through this space, but the spots of rust on the rails gave evidence that no train had run through here for a long time. We set up our guns in the same position every day, so we didn't have to dig new emplacements each morning. Our drills were just practice, as we planned no real shooting. This didn't take much time, as most of our artillerymen were experienced veterans, and they quickly grew tired of such practice. Kamchatnyy and I sensed this and didn't want to overburden our men, so we announced plenty of breaks, both brief and long.

A viaduct ran near our "training ground" and offered a place of shade nearly all day long. This became our "classroom," where Sysolyatin would deliver his half-hour-long political lectures on both frontline and international news. This was our "dining hall," too, when the battery's field kitchen would roll up with our hot dinners around 2:00 P.M. The shade also offered the best place for numerous ten-minute smoking breaks during the day.

Yes, this was bliss for everybody!

(Unlike most of our men, I didn't idle away all my time in this soldier's paradise. I spent it on a more useful activity. Thanks to Vanya's friendly encouragement and his directions, I overcame my reluctance and mounted a horse for the first time in my life. At first, I held myself stiffly in the saddle while the horse walked or trotted. But Vanya continued to instruct me patiently. As a result, on the fifth day of our "combat training," I finally mastered the secret of relaxing and moving to the horse's own rhythm of motion. Only then did I begin to enjoy the sensation of riding in full measure.)

A notable event occurred on the seventh day of our idyllic stay in Vlasovka: a new chief of regimental artillery arrived. The previous chief, Captain Fedosov, had been killed in action near the Don River back in early January. The new chief, Captain Vasiliy Karpushinskiy, was introduced to us the next morning, as the battery was preparing to leave for our "training ground."

Vasiliy Nikitovich Karpushinskiy was an experienced frontline officer. He was in his late twenties, a handsome, dark-haired, slender man, neat and thoroughly clean-shaven. That morning Karpushinskiy followed the battery to the "training ground" and observed our drills. He promptly began to give us good practical advice. As every reader will understand, we quickly forgot all about our frequent smoke breaks.

We were lucky to be commanded by Karpushinskiy. He was not only a professional artilleryman but also a brave man with an even-tempered personality. We had to part with Karpushinskiy at midnight on 4 May 1944, when he was severely wounded close to the banks of the Belbek River near Sevastopol. He was taken to a hospital, and just a few hours later we began our final, triumphant storming of the city. (I didn't see Karpushinskiy again until 1969, an event that I describe in the appendix.)

As it always happens, we received the command to prepare for march unexpectedly. We had just finished our tenth supper in Vlasovka, and the sun was beginning to set. Most of our men were smoking idly. Suddenly Vinokurov appeared, called together all the men, and gave us the urgent order to prepare for march. This created an immediate uproar as everyone bustled about, but the fuss didn't last long; within the hour, our battery took its place in the regimental march column and moved out.

Before we left, the hostess of the house where we had been staying, Anna Vasilevna Korneeva, gave us each a motherly embrace and a kiss on the forehead. Five times, we heard her say, "May God protect you!"

* * *

Our next dwelling was the wooded Duvannaya ravine that stretched for several kilometers and was at least 100 meters wide. Once we arrived, the battery personnel took up their usual practice under the cover of the ravine's dense foliage that screened us from aerial observation: we began to dig shelters for personnel, horses and wagons, guns, ammunition, and the field kitchen. After our long period of rest and relaxation, everyone took to the work readily and, as it turned out, not in vain. We spent the next six weeks here, until mid-July.

In the hundreds of shelters and dugouts that lined the ravine, our whole division, now fully replenished with men, horses, arms, and equipment, was quartered here. Measured battle training began at sites located at a short distance from the ravine. Captain Karpushinskiy often observed and occasionally directed our battery's field exercises.

One day, out of pure curiosity, Kamchatnyy and I visited the neighboring mining town of Krasnodon. Some local inhabitants told us about the savage punishment of a group of teens, both male and female, all members of Komsomol, who tried to resist the German occupation. They had all been shot, and their bodies had been thrown down into a mine pit. While walking along a street in the town, we saw a short teenager, by sight no older than fifteen. A German submachine gun was hanging on his shoulder. We stopped him in order to take the weapon from him, but to our surprise the boy presented a certificate that confirmed his right to carry the gun. Some underground commander had signed the document. (Shortly thereafter the central Communist Party newspaper *Pravda* published a feature story, "The Young Guards," written by the famous Soviet writer Alexander Fadeev. The story told about the deeds and fate of the heroic Krasnodon youth underground group. Later Fadeev published a novel with the same title. Many years passed and . . . several members of the underground group fell under the shadow of suspicion about their real activities, and even the existence of this group began to be questioned. I have no right to judge whether someone was a hero or not, but everything I saw and heard on that day confirms that this group did exist and did operate.)

One day, shortly before the end of May, we were informed that the 2nd Guards Army commander would visit our division in order to award us with a Guards banner. According to the rules of ceremony, after the presentation of the banner, the entire division would have to march past the review stand, where the army, corps, and division commanders would stand and review the troops.

From that moment, everything changed in our daily routine. Instead of combat training (including even practice with live ammunition), endless marching drills occupied the bulk of our time. We underwent daily regimental inspections; the division inspections took place every other day. Faultfinding commanders always found at least one rough spot in our march. Marching songs had an important role in the drill, too, as each detachment in the division had its own marching song to master. Our battery's song was "The Artillery March." There was even a special division-wide competition in both ceremonial step and song performance.

In mid-June, on the eve of the long-awaited parade, we received fresh new uniforms. Everybody polished his boots and sewed on a fresh under-collar strip. Those were the last details of the preparation for the great event.

The day of the celebration was bright and hot. As usual, the master of ceremonies set a schedule for the division assembly that kept a considerable reserve. So did the commanders at each point in the line of command. As a result, our division stood in formation under the hot sun for more than two hours, waiting for the ceremony to begin.

Finally the ceremony started. In front of the division assembly, Lieutenant General Yakov Kreizer, commander of the 2nd Guards Army, handed the banner to Colonel Kirill Tymchik, commander of our 87th Guards Rifle Division. The red banner contained a golden embroidered inscription, "For Our Soviet Motherland!" Tymchik knelt on one knee and kissed the banner. Then the ceremonial march of the entire division took place beneath the stand. We marched in precise step, singing our brisk marching songs.

After the celebration, our combat training resumed for three more weeks. A difficult battle lay ahead of us.

Our Arduous Breakthrough Turned into the "Ravine of Death"

The general offensive of the 2nd Guards Army started in mid-July 1943. The goal of the offensive was to force a deep penetration into the German defenses with a subsequent advance into the central and western districts of the Donbas. According to the plan, our division initially was in the second echelon of the offensive. Thus, on the first day, only the guns of the division's artillery regiment fired, together with hundreds of other artillery pieces. The offensive developed very slowly. Only shortly before sunset did we manage to enter a small bridgehead, about 7 kilometers deep, which had been seized by the first echelon, near the village of Dmitrievka.[1] This was the extent of our advance on this long summer day. We were placed in an open field about a kilometer behind the front line. All detachments were ordered to dig in and camouflage everything. We finished these tasks long after midnight. Unfortunately, our sleep was very short.

Just as the day began to break, the hum of approaching German Stuka dive-bombers was audible. In a minute, a squadron of nine bombers formed "the snake" (a single line), then, while diving one after one, made a steep turn (the well-known German "carousel") and dropped their howling deadly bomb load on our position (because of their dive sirens we called these bombers "musicians"). The first element attacked, followed by the second and third elements, and then the first squadron of bombers flew away. But at the same time another squadron initiated the same maneuvers and conducted another triple bombardment. Without a pause, the third squadron came and the fourth. It seemed that there was no end to this hell. We had no antiaircraft guns, our fighters were nowhere to be seen, and the "musicians" had no reason to fear our rifle and sidearm fire. Unfortunately, the sky was absolutely cloudless, and the relentless bombardment continued with undiminished fury.

The bombers didn't strike our front line—it was too close to the German positions. Therefore, our division was exposed to the full brunt of their attacks. By noon the bright sky had darkened with dust and propellant gases, and it remained that way until dusk.

Deafened by the roar of aircraft engines, the howl of falling bombs, and the thunder of explosions, we lay in a state of constant tension. Only during the few short seconds of silence were we able to look round, to see if the German tanks and infantry were attacking. Fortunately, our frontline units avoided these raids and continued to press the enemy. They made some moderate advance during the day.

At long last, darkness arrived, and we were able to regain our senses and check our losses. By some miracle, our battery suffered no casualties. A close friend of mine, 120-mm mortar battery deputy commander Lieutenant Boris Glotov, was seriously wounded. (From this point on, I omit the "Guards" appellation from officers' ranks, in order to shorten the following text.)

At midnight we ate dinner and then moved forward to take position in the front line. Our regiment had the order to continue our offensive. By dawn, our battery was already situated along a belt of woods, less than a kilometer from the enemy's trenches. We prepared to commence direct fire.

Around us, we saw the evidence of yesterday's fierce fighting. There were many dead Soviet soldiers and several dead horses. The merciless July heat quickened the process of decomposition, and we could hardly endure the ever-present, putrid odor of decay—the eternal concomitant to death.

After a signal rocket we commenced rapid fire at the Germans' first-line trenches. After five minutes, when our infantry rose to the attack, we shifted our fire to the second line of the German defenses. Soon, German artillery and mortars spoke up in response to our fire. At first, their rounds fell harmlessly to the side of us, but then one shell finally struck the first gun of my platoon, seriously wounding the gun crew commander, Senior Sergeant Georgiy Senchenko, lightly wounding two of his crew, and damaging the gun. There were no other casualties in the battery.

That day our infantry did well and pushed the Germans back. After noon, we repositioned about 2 kilometers farther ahead. The 2nd Guards Army's offensive ground forward slowly; our regiment advanced, but suffered significant casualties. At the same time, in some ways it became easier for us to fight: the Germans didn't bomb the forward battle edge, our bridgehead was a bit larger, and we, after our long rest, were gradually getting reaccustomed to combat.

On the seventh day of the offensive, our advance stopped. The German defense became more organized and strong.

My platoon (with only one intact gun) was ordered to support our 1st Rifle Battalion. Its positions were on the top of a gently sloping elevation, amid a sunflower field, within some 100 meters of the German trenches. Once it became dark, both the gun commander Tetyukov and I went there to select an appropriate position for our gun.

Partway up the slope of the hill, about 500 meters from the battalion's positions, we unexpectedly came under "friendly" fire from a salvo of a Soviet multiple rocket launcher, the famous "Katyusha." It was a terrible minute: sixteen large-caliber rockets exploded around us one after another. It took us a minute or two to regain our senses and our breath. After this terrifying ordeal, I fully believed our newspaper reports that some German soldiers, caught in a barrage from "Stalin's Organs" (the German soldiers' nickname for the "Katyusha"), went crazy from the experience.

At last we reached the battalion command post atop the hill. The officers there were indignant at the stupid scoundrel whose error resulted in the "Katyusha" rockets landing a half kilometer short of the enemy trenches.

The battalion commander, Senior Lieutenant Nikolay Soin, approved our choice for the gun emplacement, which would be about 100 meters behind the riflemen's trenches. Then I sent Tetyukov back for the gun, gun crew, and shells. About an hour later they arrived at the chosen place, and we set to work doing our customary emplacement and foxhole digging. It was a moonlit night, and the soil was soft, so we completed all the digging, including a connecting trench to the infantry's trench line, well before dawn. Our signalman Nikolay Nazarenko connected my telephone set to the battalion wire. The driver Suyunov took the limber with the only pair of wheel horses and parked it behind a ruined one-story brick building at the foot of the hill.

The morning was quite calm, with only a desultory exchange of fire. To the left of our hill was a steep, wooded height. It was quiet there. To our right, behind a shallow hollow, stood a hill similar to our own. A chain of similar hills arced farther to the right, stretching back toward the river. Judging from the sound of fighting and the signal rockets, this chain of hills marked the boundary of the bridgehead captured by the 2nd Guards Army in the last week.

That morning, along with our cook and his assistant, the battery's newest member, Junior Lieutenant Grigoryan, came up. Vinokurov had sent him to us in order to "get the smell of gunpowder." He looked so young! I quickly filled him in on the present situation on our section of the front. Soon the 1st Rifle Battalion commander, Nikolay Soin, called me up by phone to tell me to come immediately to the battalion's observation post. Grigoryan followed me. Here, the battalion commander pointed out an enemy machine gun nest on a small knoll next to an isolated shrub. He asked me to neutralize the enemy machine gun (it was an informal sort of an order).

After returning to our position, I explained to Grigoryan how to estimate the distance from the gun emplacement to our target. After the crew prepared everything, Tetyukov gave the order to fire. After our first shot, the enemy machine gun fell silent, but we gave it several more rounds for good measure. We had been successful, and the battalion commander Soin telephoned us to express his gratitude. After this "baptism of fire," Grigoryan returned to the battery rear.

The next day it was again relatively calm on our sector, but the sounds of battle from the right grew noticeably stronger. When it became dark, the enemy's flares seemed to streak into the sky from visibly closer positions than from where they had appeared the night before. The next morning, it was clear that the Germans had pushed back our right-flank neighbor, and now the sounds of fighting carried to us almost from behind us. German bombers continued to work over our positions in the depth of the bridgehead. Among other messages that I heard by phone that day, I received word that our regiment commander had been seriously wounded.

By evening, the Germans had approached to within one kilometer of the regimental command post (CP). I realized with anxiety that our hill was now almost cut off. Nobody reached us with food and ammunition during the night, despite the fact that we were already out of antipersonnel shells. To keep informed about the current situation, I continuously monitored all the telephone exchanges between the battalion and the CP that night. Shortly before dawn, political deputy commander Major Tarasov's confident voice was heard, "No panic, comrades! The situation was completely restored during the night!" But from somewhere close beside our hill, German tanks rumbled and enemy illumination rockets flew skyward. Imperceptibly to myself, I fell asleep in my small entrenchment with the receiver at my ear.

I was awaked by a push on my shoulder and Nazarenko's angry cry, "Junior Lieutenant! Germans!" I leaped up. It was now completely light. Nazarenko silently pointed at the hollow to the right of us, where three Germans were walking calmly. The distance was about 150 meters. We quickly turned the gun and fired an armor-piercing shell, but the Germans quickly took cover behind a thick bush. We saw them, however, and our next shots were on target.

It was strangely quiet in front of us, and our telephone was deathly silent. I sent Nazarenko to find the break in the line and to ascertain what was going on in the battalion's trenches. He came back in a minute, "There's not a living soul there!" It meant that the battalion's riflemen had abandoned their positions during the night without saying a word. The situation was now extremely serious.

Tetyukov went for Suyunov but returned in some twenty minutes very worried: he had found no Suyunov, no limber, and no horses. Moreover, we could hear an exchange of gunfire from the CP's direction. I saw only one way out for us—to retreat, but what about the gun? We disabled it by removing the panorama sight. Then we took out the heavy breechblock, tossed it into a little ditch, and covered it over with dirt. Having done that, looking around, we descended into the valley in short bounds and headed for the isolated building that housed the regimental CP. Nobody from regimental command was visible. Rifle fire and submachine guns rattled quite nearby. A few soldiers, one by one, passed by us and disappeared into nearby vegetation. We followed them.

The scrub trees where we hid bordered a long and wide meadow. Some 30 meters away, a clump of dense shrubs stood like an island. One after another we made for this "island." There were some twenty soldiers and officers gathered there, Major Tarasov among them. Everyone was quite serious; they conversed in low voices. Making my way through the bushes to the opposite side of the "island," I peered out . . . and my heart sank: about 50 meters from us, two German tanks were standing about 70 meters apart, their turrets facing one another. From time to time, someone was shooting at our "island" from somewhere in short bursts of fire.

Then an unarmed Soviet soldier approached us from the direction of the tanks, bringing with him an ultimatum from the Germans. On behalf of the Germans he warned, "If you don't surrender within five minutes, the tanks will crush your lair with their tracks." Then the soldier went back.

What could we do? There was another "island" of dense shrubs some 70 meters ahead, but the tanks were between our current position and that sanctuary. Nevertheless, somebody rushed into the gap between the armored monsters. Another followed him, the third. Tarasov took off at a rush, and in a few seconds I started my own dash. I was running in a slight crouch; my heart pounding with nervousness and fear. Suddenly, when I had reached a point just between the tanks, a tremendous blow knocked me down.

I simultaneously felt intense pain in my right hip joint and caught the smell of burning cloth and flesh. Pressing the wound with my hand, I lay without stirring, being absolutely horror-struck—there was no way to avoid capture with such an injury. Tarasov lay 3 meters in front of me, groaning in a low voice, "Brothers, don't desert me!" Gradually I began to consider the situation: the tank shell obviously hadn't landed right next to me; otherwise I'd have been smashed completely. Maybe a clod of caked earth hit me? Very carefully I removed my hand from the hip and glanced at the palm: it was dry! I glanced forward—Tarasov, who had just been groaning, suddenly leaped to his feet and darted at full speed to a nearby shrub. I rushed after him, but my every step was very painful, and something else was making my running difficult. Somehow I reached the shrub. Lying there I discovered that the heel and the sole of my right boot were partly torn. I tore them off completely and shortly thereafter started my next rush to the next group of bushes standing by the far edge of the meadow. I found several soldiers already hiding there.

As far as 300 meters from this hiding place, we could see the mouth of a quite deep ravine, through which ran a rivulet, presumably a tributary to the Mius.[2] Hundreds of Soviet soldiers were gathered in the spacious meadow, mostly at the mouth of the ravine. Just yesterday they had been fighting on the hills.

I looked back at the enemy. To my surprise, both tanks rapidly backed up, while launching a series of colored flares. I couldn't understand what was going on and gave a glance upward—that was why the tanks were leaving! Nine "musicians" were starting their dive upon the meadow, packed with retreating Red Army troops. In seconds the whole area beside the ravine turned into absolute hell. Only the rare bomb failed to find victims. Scores of survivors were running to the ravine with the hope of hiding under its steep slopes. In fact, the 2nd Guards Army's retreat had turned into a tremendous *drap-marsh*.

Tetyukov appeared with the panorama sight in his hand. He and some others had stayed in the bushes close to the former CP until the tanks had departed and this bombardment had begun. We ran to the ravine together and down its steep slope, but I limped because of the pain. Dodging many corpses along the way, we dropped to the grass each time we heard the whistle of the next bomb. Soon we found ourselves at the five-meter-wide stream running through the ravine. The bodies of a few dead horses swollen to the size of hippopotamuses were floating on its surface. At that time the next nine "musicians" chose the entrance to the ravine as their target, just as we were reaching it. Bombs exploded very close to us, and an irresistible fear drove us down the steep bank of the stream and into its water, next to a dead horse. In a couple of minutes the bombardment came to an end. We shook off the water from our uniforms and footwear; then, along with other survivors, we moved slowly in the direction where our rear auxiliary detachments had been staying last week. Along the way, we helped several wounded soldiers and bumped into a few men from our regiment. Finally, we encountered organized groups of soldiers and officers; they were preparing defensive emplacements.

I remember also that two times some approaching lieutenants (their unusually clean uniforms were striking) explained to us where the temporary assembly point of our division was. It was clear that they weren't common infantry officers. Later we heard talks that our *drap-marsh* had been stopped by a blocking detachment. Nobody mentioned that it had shot down any retreating men.*

While we continued our way to the reassembly point, a powerful thunderstorm began—deliverance from any more Stuka attacks.

Soon we came upon Vinokurov and Kamchatnyy, and Vanya hugged me with affection. They explained that our horseman Suyunov had appeared there two hours before us, miraculously escaping the near encirclement with his limber and two fast horses. Suyunov had told them that we had been trapped in the pocket, and everyone had already considered us captured or killed.

Within a couple of hours after Tetyukov and I had returned, Ismaylov, Nazarenko, Khorkov, and Yusupov, one at a time, joined the battery. All of them were safe.

By the end of the day Vinokurov established contact with regimental headquarters. Before dawn, we received the order to withdraw our heavily battered division to the rear for urgent reinforcement and to prepare for new battles. We left the area, which from then on we called the "Ravine of Death."

In such a sad way our July battles at the Mius front came to an end. To crown it all, the beginning of August brought our battery a new misfortune. In a village some 30 kilometers behind the front lines, we came under a fierce aerial bombardment. Our battery commander Vinokurov was seriously injured. And the young Grigoryan, who had only one day of frontline experience, was killed.

Most of us were in a bad mood. After forcing the enemy back with unbelievable difficulties and a number of casualties, our offensive had come to grief.

The *Stavka* did not excuse the 2nd Guards Army's defeat. Lieutenant General Ya. G. Kreizer, the army commander, was immediately dismissed (Lieutenant General G. F. Zakharov was appointed in his stead). Moreover, all after-battle recommendations for decorating the bravest soldiers and officers were turned down.

(However this wasn't the end of the story. No more than ten days passed when the *Stavka* changed its mind: to repulse our offensive

* Blocking detachments were armed, organized units placed behind Soviet forces to prevent precipitous retreat. Authorized by the draconian Order Number 227 ("Not One Step Back"), they fired upon Soviet soldiers to halt movement and restore command and control.

and threatened breakthrough, the enemy had been forced to divert a significant part of his strength, especially the II S.S. Panzerkorps and bomber aircraft, from the Kursk-Orel battle. So our "failure" had been turned into success, and we were officially recognized for our effort. As the saying goes: "Better late than never.")

After describing our terrible experience during those two weeks, this seems like the appropriate time to shift gears. I'd like to pause and share with readers my personal reflections on fear in war.

Fear

I can hardly believe in the existence of people, with normal psyches, who never sense any fear. In any case, I can say that none of my numerous comrades in arms were those sorts of people. Yet it is one thing to feel fear, but quite another matter how one behaves in fearful situations. Most of my comrades did not lose their sense of reason, kept their composure, remembered the call of duty, and carried out their commander's orders. But there were rare others who lost their heads and could not act rationally because of fear. I call them "pathological cowards."

Remembering my behavior at the front, I think I belonged to the majority. Therefore I decided to talk here about fear and its gradations that I experienced during the war. (At the same time, I understand that perception of fear is absolutely unique to each individual. And I don't know whether or not I was a typical or an "average" representative of that majority. But assuming that I wasn't an exception, I decided to offer these reflections.)

Certainly, I feared being killed or seriously injured. I dreaded whatever might happen if the Germans took me prisoner. There were enough reasons for fear in war, especially for those, like me, who saw so many deaths around them. In contrast to my sense of duty and responsibility, which permanently existed from the day when I was ordered to be a gun crew commander, I experienced fear only in combat, moreover, not in every combat situation. As I accumulated battle experience, my ability to assess the situation grew. Often the information given by my commander helped; sometimes my own vision and appreciation of what was going on helped me determine the course of battle.

Summarizing my own feelings in the war, I can say that, in my opinion, there were three kinds of fear. I classify them below.

In case of lack of knowledge about what was going on, when you could only guess what would happen next or rely on your own forebodings, you would be seized by "subconscious" fear. This kind of fear, for example, most of us experienced when we first heard the remote echo of the battle for Stalingrad on our way to the Verkhne-Pogromnoye village (see chapter 4). I sensed a similar fear whenever we returned to the frontline trenches after a long period of rest and relaxation. Such a fear ruined my mood, made me unwilling to laugh or to joke, and caused me to smoke one hand-rolled cigarette after another.

The second sort of fear usually arose on the threshold of battle or during combat, when the situation was dangerous but more or less clear and it was possible somehow to foresee the future course of events. I call this kind of fear "conscious." It made you nervous, but at the same time it heightened your sense of perception and made you more self-disciplined.

The third type of fear, which I call "bodily" fear, is absolutely different. It is instinctive and arises instantly whenever you hear the growing hiss of murderous metal as it whizzes past you, the rising howl of an approaching shell, or whenever a bomb or shell explodes nearby. The explosion deafens you and tosses you like a piece of grain. This kind of fear deprives you of your will, and with inconceivable strength it presses you into the earth—the only thing that can protect you.

More than once I experienced this "bodily" fear, and I cannot forget the sensations. It is sufficient just to recall the last hours of our epic in the "Ravine of Death." After I narrowly avoided capture and escaped death or serious injury from a tank shell, I found myself in that open meadow under a long and terrible air bombardment. When a series of bombs exploded nearby, I instinctively dropped to the ground, hugged the earth as tightly as I could, and buried my face in it; I "protected" my head with both hands and squeezed my eyes shut. In spite of being a nonbeliever, I mentally addressed some unknown Almighty Highest Power, "Please let me survive! I'm so young; I don't have any child. If I should die, no trace of me will remain on Earth!" Those kinds of feelings and behaviors happened every time in such situations, when nothing depends on you, when you are defenseless, doomed to inaction, and must only submissively await your fate.

* * *

Many times in the war I experienced different kinds of fear, but I don't consider myself a particularly nervous person. Comparing my actions in dangerous situations with how the people around me behaved, I could say (without excessive modesty) that I was usually not worse than the majority. Moreover, often it turned out that I was more steadfast than many in our battery. (I am not speaking about those few pathological cowards that I met in the war. Those people were the clear exceptions, and the majority of the soldiers around me stood rather firm in combat.)

Our Model 1927/39 76-mm regimental infantry support guns were neither special antitank weapons nor long-range. Our usual mission was to support the infantry both on offense and on defense. Usually, the field guns of my fire platoon were located in direct fire positions—as a rule, about 100 meters behind our infantry's trenches. Sometimes it wasn't the best choice from the point of view of an artillery expert, but the infantrymen liked to see their supporting artillery as near as possible behind them. (Moreover, I remember two cases when my guns were in front of the riflemen whom we supported. Both of these unnatural situations happened when the infantry dug in on the edge of a forest. Each of the riflemen tried to dig his foxhole not on the very edge of the forest but a few meters back of it. Of course, this narrowed his field of fire, but his neighbors' fields of fire more than compensated for the shortage of his own field. And in this situation, where could we place our field guns in order to cover the whole zone of the rifle battalion or company with our fire? Naturally, only in front of the riflemen!)

* * *

Sometimes, battlefield experience indicated to you what you needed to fear most of all. Let us discuss one example of a threatening situation. It sometimes happened that our infantrymen, one after another and without organization, abandoned their trenches and ran away. Whenever this occurred, it would leave the supporting artillerymen in a clear dilemma. It was not only criminal but also disgraceful to abandon their undamaged gun. And to remove it to safety, without horses, only by effort of the gun crew, was not always possible (and, moreover, the pursuing Germans could easily catch up . . .). To try and defend the line with only a handful of soldiers instead of several dozens was also unrealistic.

Because of these reasons, after what happened on the outskirts of Novaya Nadezhda colony in February 1943 (see chapter 5), I was always on the alert for any sign of panic among our infantrymen, even the least sign. I already learned our first *drap-marsh*'s lesson well: panic is an avalanche-like process. It can be stopped only at the very beginning. If the number of people who are seized by panic exceeds a "critical amount," then only the fear of death can return them to rational behavior.

I still take pride in my determined action in a battle during the liberation of the Donbas. One evening the Germans stopped our 2nd Rifle Battalion's advance close to a railroad embankment. Fields of corn stretched out on both sides of it. Before dawn, both our infantry and my gun crews were fully entrenched and waiting for the command to begin our attack.

Unexpectedly, after a short mortar bombardment, the Germans beat us to the punch and launched a sudden attack of their own. We were ready to fire at them, when several of our infantrymen suddenly appeared running toward us. We couldn't fire at the Germans because this group of runaways was blocking our line of sight. There were not more than ten in the fleeing group, but I knew that if more soldiers followed their example and began to abandon the front trench, a real panic would ensue.

The fear of losing our guns enraged me to the highest degree; I snatched my pistol from its holster and dashed toward the panic-stricken runaways, firing into the air. Fortunately, my two gun crew commanders followed right behind me with their submachine guns tilted toward the retreating men. Shouting at the runaways in the foulest language I knew, I warned them that we would shoot them if they didn't return to the trench. The group stopped running, some glanced back, and . . . all of them turned back to their positions! We had interrupted the avalanche before it could really get started! Within a minute or two our guns began to speak. The German attack faltered.

* * *

Our bloody but unsuccessful combat in July was not the last fighting on the Mius front. In some two weeks, our forces were replenished and returned to the front line. We attacked again. This time our offensive took place farther south than our point of attack in July. We attacked the Germans in the village of Uspenka, near the town of Amvrosievka. The 2nd Guards Army's offensive was successful this time and finally cleared the way into the heart of the Donbas.

The Battle on the Outskirts of Vishnevy Hamlet: The Burning City of Stalino

It was the fourth night after our breakthrough of the German fortifications on the Mius front in August 1943, and we still were pursuing the retreating enemy. Usually we came to a halt at daybreak, and after thoroughly camouflaging our field guns and wagons, we had a good sleep in the daytime. But that moonless night was different. Our march along country roads was interrupted several times at some intersections because the regiment's advance guard hesitated over which road to take. (They didn't want to disturb the regiment's commanders, who were sleeping in their wagons.) As a result, it was already daylight when we approached the hamlet of Vishnevy, and an unexpected German reconnaissance plane performed a circle above our march column. Anyway, once the regiment reached the hamlet, we quietly started our breakfast.

Suddenly, there was an alarming announcement: a column of German tanks and trucks was moving toward Vishnevy! A lot of orders rang out, and all of our infantrymen ran down the gentle slope of a shallow, 1.5-kilometer-long ravine covered by blooming sunflowers. About 300 meters from the hamlet outskirts, they began furiously digging in. My platoon (with only one gun because the other two guns of our battery were under repair at that time) was ordered to engage the enemy over open sights. The second platoon (also with only one gun) was directed to a relatively safer covered position.

The gun crew commander, Vladimir Tetyukov, and I chose an apt place for laying direct fire right on the nearby edge of the slope. Then we gave the sign to our horseman, Suyunov, to bring up the gun and shells. Three more crewmen joined us: the gunner, Ismaylov; the charger, Khorkov; and the shell carrier, Yusupov. Suyunov brought up the gun and shells, and then he drove the limber to shelter behind a nearby house. In a few minutes the five of us hurriedly prepared the emplacement, set up the gun, and brought up and opened the shell boxes. We had just begun to dig foxholes for ourselves when a German tank with a dozen or more soldiers aboard appeared from behind a hillock on the opposite side of the ravine.

The tank was crawling slowly, and we were waiting for its maneuver. But in a minute two more tanks came into view, and then we saw a few more tanks and self-propelled guns. They were all moving slowly toward the ravine. If nothing was done about it, within five or six minutes the "Tigers" and "Ferdinands" [Editor's note: This should not be taken literally. In Red Army slang, all German tanks were "Tigers" and all German self-propelled guns were "Ferdinands"] would crush our still un-entrenched infantrymen. On the other hand, if we opened fire, we would be challenging a dozen armored monsters to an unequal duel. There was no time for reflection; the situation required immediate action.

In spite of the mortal risk, I gave the order, "To action!" The gun crew, directed by Tetyukov, prepared the shot, and I, while looking through my binoculars, estimated the distance to the leading "Tiger" and called out the number to set the sight. A few seconds passed, and the laying was completed. Tetyukov's order sounded, "Fire!" And in a split second a thundering roar pierced the seeming deathly quiet that had dominated the ravine quite recently.

Crouched on one knee to the right of the gun, where I had just recently stopped digging my foxhole, I looked through my field glasses for the point of explosion. What a horror! The shell exploded far to one side of the tank. I ran up to the panorama sight and took a short glance at the scale—there's the problem! Instead of the usual 30.00, it was set to 29.00. Evidently through his nervousness, Ismaylov had missed the proper setting by a whole point! Tetyukov adjusted the setting correctly, and the second shot rang out. This time the shell exploded exactly on the leading tank's track. And the soldiers who were sitting on it instantly disappeared as if being blown off by a strong gust of wind. The "Tiger" stopped moving, and we could hear the rattle of the German submachine guns (we called them *shmaissers*). Meanwhile, we redirected our aim to a neighboring self-propelled gun and hit it with our next shot. But at the same moment, a German shell flew over our heads with a threatening hiss—overshot by about 50 meters. We began to prepare to fire another round.

A sudden burst of tremendous force deafened me. Everything around was shrouded in suffocating propellant gases and rising dust. I lay on the ground, my head pounding. I raised it a little and took in a terrible view. Our gun was tilted unnaturally to one side. Ismaylov was lying beside it, writhing in pain while holding his head. Khorkov was slowly and carefully getting up off the ground. Yusupov was on his knees, and only Tetyukov was lying motionless. I walked up to the lifeless body of the gun commander—an enemy shell fragment had struck him in the temple. Ismaylov had a head wound, but it wasn't serious—a fragment just grazed his skin. Shell-shocked, Khorkov began to vomit. Somehow I bandaged Ismaylov's wound and sent Yusupov, who hadn't been touched, for Suyunov.

Then I looked over our gun. The shell had exploded beside the now-shattered left wheel. The gun shield was pierced in many places, and the aiming gear was damaged, too. When Yusupov and Suyunov returned, we took out the panorama sight, and the four of us (Khorkov couldn't help) carried Tetyukov's still-warm body to the hamlet outskirts in order to give him a proper burial in the nearby local cemetery and to pay our last respects to this tried and battle-tested warrior.

Thereafter, the five of us together, with a pair of horses harnessed to the limber, made our way to a nearby village, where the regimental medical company and artillery repair shop were situated.

While leaving the ravine, I looked back to find out what was going on there. The German tanks were still standing on the same line, and the enemy riflemen had not advanced either. To all appearances, our infantrymen were already entrenched well enough: one could hear the shots of our antitank rifles, the crackle of brisk submachine gun fire, and the quick "thump" of the company's 50-mm mortars. Then I heard a familiar sound—it was the first shot made by our second gun from its covered position.

While estimating the true value of what we had done, I asked myself: was it worth the irreplaceable loss of Tetyukov in the name of carrying out a combat order? My answer was yes, because otherwise the number of victims among our infantrymen would have been many times greater. Our two timely and well-aimed shots halted the enemy's advance for several minutes, giving our soldiers the time to finish digging in, and to open fire in time to repulse the attack.

* * *

After this memorable battle we continued liberating the Donbas, while constantly in pursuit of the retreating German forces. There were a few skirmishes and brief fights for some settlements. And on 6 September, shortly after sunset, without fighting we entered the heart of the Donbas—the city of Stalino.

Everything I experienced that evening remains unforgettable. Just before retreating from Stalino, German special incendiary commandos had set hundreds of houses on fire, most in the central part of the city. There was a terrible illumination when our troops passed through the streets. There were hundreds and hundreds of residents standing alongside the road and heartily greeting us. I'll never forget an elderly, gray-bearded man who continuously crossed himself and made low bows to us.

During one of our short halts, a group of women invited my friend Kamchatnyy and me to join them for a minute. In a nearby doorway they treated us to some homemade wine.

Later, at midnight I rode on horseback to the house where I had stayed for a month with my aunt in the summer of 1941 on my way from Kiev. The building was deserted, and two sections of it had been burned to the ground.

The next morning, as we were already leaving the city, a group of local inhabitants stood by the road and greeted us. Unexpectedly, an old and absolutely scraggy man left the group and approached the battery column. He hadn't shaved for a long time and was wearing some dirty, cast-off clothes. The man drew up to our wagons and said in a low, sad voice, "Lieutenant Brechko, I'm your blacksmith, Suchkov . . . " and began to cry. It was hard to recognize Alexey, who had refused to leave the Novaya Nadezhda cowshed during our first *drap-marsh*. Now he looked like the poorest beggar. Later Suchkov shared with us his terrible experience. The Germans had found him in the cowshed and had taken him prisoner. For almost five months he was kept in a prisoner-of-war camp. In mid-July the panic-stricken guards suddenly left the camp, and all the prisoners scattered (this was exactly when the Southern *Front* and the 2nd Guards Army had started its offensive on the Mius River). Since then Suchkov had been a fugitive. Without any identity papers, he had been experiencing another terrible time. Constantly afraid to bump into a policeman, he was suffering from fear and starvation.

Well, right away we fed Alexey and gave him a new uniform. Upon returning to the battery, Alexey became just a coachman, and Lieutenant Brechko retained Shumchenko as the blacksmith. In contrast to Zvonarev's fate, our regimental SMERSH group took no interest in Suchkov. So Alexey came off unhurt until the end of the war. Then a terrible tragedy claimed his life. It happened as follows.

In 1945, while we were still in East Prussia, Suchkov was demobilized because of his age. Rather than looking for a special train that would leave at some unknown time from some unknown place, Alexey preferred to wait and to return home with us, along with the rest of the division, because we were already about to depart for the USSR. It was impossible even to suppose that this decision would be a fatal one.

Our division (personnel, arms, ammunition, horses, etc.) left for the USSR aboard several specially equipped freight trains. All these trains stopped in Smolensk oblast, about 150 kilometers short of our destination. We had to make the rest of the way on our own. Suchkov and another demobilized coachman, Savoskin by name, took turns driving an ammunition wagon. During one halt in the march, both men were eating some cold food while sitting on the wagon. Meanwhile, the harnessed horses were grazing by the side of the road. As it reached for more grass, one of the horses triggered an antitank mine that had been buried there. There was a tremendous explosion! Suchkov and Savoskin both died in the blast.

Chapter 7

The Path to the Dnieper River's Mouth

After the enemy was driven out from the Donbas, our combat path ran westward, through Zaporozhe oblast toward the Dnieper River. Initially, it seemed that we were heading toward the city of Nikopol, but after a few days of marching, our division was redirected onto a much more southerly course than we had anticipated. Just at that time, after release from a front hospital, Vinokurov, our battery commander, returned to his post.

By the third week of September 1943, the Germans had stopped our 2nd Guards Army's advance near the Molochnaya River. Here they had established a well-fortified line of defenses (years later I read that its code name was "Wotan").[1] There were a few German colonies in addition to Ukrainian villages in this fertile area.

From mid-September, some names of towns and railroad stations that were familiar to me from my talks with Vera began to appear. This was the area where Vera had been born and had passed the years of her childhood. To my luck, on 20 September we entered the small town of Bolshoy Tokmak, where I knew that Vera's close relatives, the Nedoves family, had been living since the 1920s. Naturally, I was eager to see them.

Well-organized enemy fire stopped our regiment some 2 kilometers to the west of the town. An antitank ditch blocked our way to a small German colony (some Alt Muntal or other), which stood on a gentle elevation. We spent two relatively quiet weeks here as we prepared to resume our offensive, while the Germans launched rare bombing raids on the central part of Bolshoy Tokmak.

One night during this brief campaign lull, I made an attempt to find the Nedoves family. The town seemed to be absolutely deserted. During my hour-long walk in the dark, I knocked on dozens of doors, but no one ever answered. I was about to return to our position when for some reason a cellar near a small house drew my attention. I opened its door and caught a whiff of human scent. "Who is here?" I asked loudly. No one answered. I clicked the breech of my pistol: "Climb out immediately, otherwise I'll shoot you!" Right away a male voice responded, "Don't shoot! I'm a local resident, not a German." A man in his fifties appeared. He wasn't familiar with the Nedoves family but guided me to the local food store, the only brick building with a basement. There were at least twenty women, many with children, there. I asked about the Nedoveses, and two adolescent girls told me that Nadezhda Alexandrovna and Andrey Semenovich Nedoves were their teachers at the middle school. Both girls knew where the Nedoveses lived and guided me to a small house, about one kilometer from the store. Alas, the house was deserted, but now I knew where the family residence was located.

I returned to visit Vera's relatives two days later, this time in bright daylight. It was a success! I found all of them: Vera's own aunt, her husband, their fourteen-year-old son and two daughters, as well as the younger daughter's nineteen-year-old husband and their newly born son. We rapidly exchanged information. They were eager to know everything about the Makovchiks, Vera's parents' family. I answered many of their questions and gave them Vera's mailing address. In turn, I asked about their life there before we had liberated them. As they told me, in general, they had gone through two years of occupation quite safely. During the meeting, Vera's older cousin shared with me a quatrain that had been popular among the local youth involved in the underground resistance during the German occupation. It described the pending fate of the various nationalities under the "new order" established by the Germans. I have memorized it:

For the Germans—everything is good,
For the Jews—kaput,
For the Russians—the same,
For Ukrainians—the same, but later.

In my opinion, this was an exact and clear interpretation of Hitler's national policy on occupied territories of the USSR.

* * *

Our offensive resumed at the very end of September. We drove the enemy out of the Alt Muntal and the Prishib Hills area. Thereafter, heavy fighting lasted for about a week near the large German colony of Oktoberfeld. A terrible scene of an unsuccessful tank attack there still lingers in my mind. Without strong artillery support, a dozen of our T-34 tanks launched an attack on the German line in extended line formation. Very soon, enemy antitank fire from the right flank turned four of our tanks into burning torches. The rest stopped moving until dark.

A few days later the Germans finally retreated, and soon we crossed the border into Kherson oblast. We were on our way to the mouth of the Dnieper River.

On 3 November 1943, we entered the small town of Tsyurupinsk, which stood on the edge of the Dnieper River delta. Our front line lay along the Dnieper's left bank, across from the city of Kherson, about 3 kilometers from Tsyurupinsk. Almost impassable floodlands of the narrow twisting Konka River, a tributary to the Dnieper, separated Tsyurupinsk from the Dnieper. For the first few days, it was impossible to shift our heavy guns any closer to the Dnieper River because we couldn't find a longboat. So we set up temporary emplacements on the outskirts of Tsyurupinsk and began placing indirect fire on the Kherson freight train station. This was "blind fire" using coordinates that we obtained from topographic maps. Nobody was able to control and correct our fire, and we couldn't judge its effectiveness, but we liked the routine of these days. The battery fought, as we say today, "according to the clock." In the mornings, we would move into our firing positions, and once having completed our fire missions for the day, we would return at dusk to Tsyurupinsk, where we spent the nights in the homes of local residents. It was a blissful time, as the hospitable hosts were happy to share their homemade wine and tasty snacks with us, their liberators. On 6 November, wonderful news came: the Red Army had liberated Kiev, my home city. After drinking a considerable amount of celebratory wine, I saluted the event with six gunshots into the air.

As everybody knows, all good things must come to an end, and our "fighting by shifts" didn't last long. The next day, Lieutenant Brechko located two local fishermen who owned longboats that they had hidden from the Germans in a reedy arm of the Konka River. That same evening, the fishermen landed their longboats near the town. Once darkness fell, we loaded both Kamchatnyy's and my fire platoons aboard the longboats, and they floated us to a position in the floodlands. From then on, small boats became the only means of delivering food and shells to our positions.

The more or less dry glade, where we settled in, was overgrown with grass and willows. But the ground wasn't firm there, just a thin layer of soil covering bog. While digging into the ground with a spade, we found out that beneath the topsoil and bog, it was just swampy. Water kept seeping into our mucky trenches, and in order to make our shelters even a bit suitable for night sleep, we covered the bottom with layers of ammunition boxes.

While we were settling into the new location, two of our signalmen on board a small boat laid telephone wire from the OP to our position. The battery's OP was established on the very bank of the Dnieper's main channel, behind a half-submerged barge. The five men in the OP were Captain Karpushinskiy, Senior Lieutenant Vinokurov, and three soldiers from the fire control and reconnaissance platoon.

A high grain elevator stood on the opposite bank, and from time to time a locomotive with a couple of freight cars appeared on the railroad tracks that served the grain elevator. The Germans were using the calm on the east bank in order to haul away a huge stock of wheat from the grain elevator openly and regularly. Our appearance in the floodland put an end to this robbery. As soon as the telephone sets came to life, Vinokurov gave us the data for registering on the locomotive with only one gun. Two spotting rounds were enough to correct the data, and then we fired two salvos, one after another. Vinokurov telephoned: "Well done! Thank you and keep the aim!" There was not a sound heard from the grain elevator all day long the next day. But after midnight that night, a telephone call from the OP woke us up. They ordered us to repeat the salvo at the loading tracks. That put an end to German attempts to haul away the Ukrainian grain.

A couple of days later, the Germans seemed to be making an attempt to probe our positions on the eastern bank. We fired on a German launch, which was trying to make a landing on our bank.

In the end, just before our division was shifted out of the Dnieper's delta, the enemy detected our harassing battery and blanketed our gun positions with an accurate sheaf of fire. But luck was on our side—our savior turned out to be the swampy soil from which we had been constantly suffering. The enemy shells burrowed deeply into the soft ground before exploding, which muffled the explosion and greatly reduced the velocity of the shrapnel flying out of the muck. We had only one casualty from this barrage, a lightly wounded Vasiliy Panteleev, who soon returned to the battery.

A very special event happened during our fighting in the flood-lands. Before I describe it, I must provide a short introduction.

During our victorious campaign across Zaporozhe and Kherson oblasts we had liberated huge areas with tens of thousands of people from Nazi occupation. For a variety of reasons, there were many men of call-up age there. Very soon the local *voenkomats* conscripted them. Those who were found to have collaborated with the Germans were to be arrested and tried; all others were directed into the frontline forces. Regardless, according to the official attitude toward "the liberated," even these new soldiers were to remain under suspicion. In contrast to the official policy, they weren't prejudged in our battery. We always made the right appraisal as to "who's who" only after the battles were over. Let me narrate an appropriate short story about what happened in our battery at this time.

"Mysterious Are the Ways of the Lord"

A few of the newly "liberated" soldiers were assigned as replacements to our battery in October 1943. The youngest among them was Slava (the nickname of Vyacheslav) Tsybulskiy. He was just eighteen years old (some were in their midforties). His blond hair, blue eyes, athletic build, and neat appearance prompted positive feelings at first sight. I remember him as he just arrived at the battery wearing an old but clean military blouse, boots with black leg wrappings, and a field cap perched dashingly on his head. His answers to our usual questions (like "Where have you fought?" and "What are you skilled in?") were short and clear; his gestures—appropriate and fast. Everybody felt that the newcomer wanted to please his future commander.

I persistently asked the battery commander to place Tsybulskiy in my platoon, but Slava was made a telephone operator in the fire control and reconnaissance platoon. Over the next several days, we had a few short fights with the Germans who were retreating toward the lower Dnieper. As everybody supposed, Tsybulskiy proved himself to be a diligent, smart, and quite bold warrior. Soon we entered Tsyurupinsk, and for several days, Slava was at the OP on the bank of the Dnieper River.

One day, Tsybulskiy was sent back to Tsyurupinsk, where our battery rear services were located. Unexpectedly, Slava didn't return.

The next morning, we found out that the chief of the regimental SMERSH group, Major Vignanker, had arrested him.

It turned out that in fact Tsybulskiy was a native of Tsyurupinsk. Once the Germans came, he served as a local policeman under them and was remarkable for his special devotion to the new rulers. Tsybulskiy headed the search for local Jews who were hiding from the Germans and the police. He personally escorted seventy poor Jewish old men, women, and children to the place where they were to be shot, and actively took part in the executions. But by late September 1943, when the Soviet forces reached the Molochnaya River, Tsybulskiy realized that he had to disappear from Tsyurupinsk, where everybody knew of his monstrous crimes.

In due time he fled the town toward the northeast, as far as 250 kilometers away from Tsyurupinsk. Only there did Tsybulskiy present himself to the local *voenkomat*. He was assigned to our division at the time when we were advancing on a westerly path. If our division had not been redirected toward the mouth of the Dnieper, Tsybulskiy would hardly have been unmasked. But, as they say, "Mysterious are the ways of the Lord," and our combat path went through the hometown of the Germans' hireling and cruel butcher. As soon as he reappeared in the town, some neighbors recognized him. In a few days after the arrest an open trial took place in the town. Many bore witness against Tsybulskiy. The sentence was death by hanging. He was executed on a small square in the center of Tsyurupinsk. During those days I was still at the front line, and I was not present at the execution. Besides, I had no desire to look at the dead body of Tsybulskiy, whom I had so liked just five weeks before. I must add that the battery's other "liberated" recruits of that time, especially Khudoley and Derevenets, proved to be loyal and brave warriors.

* * *

In December 1943, our division was pulled out of its positions along the Dnieper River in order to replenish its rifle regiments, which had been substantially depleted by the constant skirmishes and the fighting along the Molochnaya River. We celebrated the New Year and Orthodox Church Christmas (7 January) in a big village named Chulakovka. The German occupiers, when they had hastily abandoned that part of Kherson oblast east of the Dnieper, had failed to haul away or destroy a huge amount of wheat in the local grain elevator. The residents of the village took this occasion to stock up on as much grain as they wanted. Thanks to these plentiful individual supplies, we drank here an ocean of *samogon* (moonshine).

This New Year's celebration remained in my memory above all others. On New Year's Eve the command of our 87th Guards Division organized a festive evening party on the occasion of the upcoming year, 1944. Only the senior officer staff took part in the party. About 100 people sat around a composite Π-shaped table in the auditorium of the local high school. My presence there was absolutely accidental. The division commander, Colonel Kirill Yakovlevich Tymchik, who sat at the center of the table, proposed an emotional toast to the New Year and to new victories. His short but heartfelt speech touched the audience, and I still remember, almost literally, Kirill Yakovlevich's words at the core of his speech. Here they are:

> I would like to begin my toast by reminding you, comrade officers, of some well-known facts. One can restore a half-ruined hut within a few weeks. And it is possible to build a new apartment building within a year. Moreover, it takes about three years to rebuild a big factory or plant. However, a new man, who would be a skilled builder or a good defender of the motherland, could appear no earlier than in some twenty years.
>
> Because of that I want you and I order you, comrade officers, to remember these facts and to always avoid the unnecessary expenditure of your soldiers' lives.

In a month we left Chulakovka for a *sovkhoz* (Soviet state farm) settlement, closer to the Crimea. A period of intense training for the planned storming of the Isthmus of Perekop began.

Fighting for the Crimea

Perekop

Our training continued for more than a month. In early March 1944, it seemed to everybody that we were already fully prepared to fight. But unexpectedly, during a regimental tactical exercise, a serious accident happened. The mortar men of a rifle company mistakenly "covered" our own detachment with their shells. There were several casualties, and some culprits were punished for this tragedy. But the training continued.

A belated spring and steady rains made all the local dirt roads impassable, so the ammunition for the coming offensive was delivered to the front line by thousands of soldiers. They formed a multikilometer human chain and passed the heavy shells from the hands of one man to the next. The bad weather caused repeated postponements of the date of the assault.

Finally, on 6 April 1944, our offensive on the Isthmus of Perekop began. By that time, our air force had already gained air superiority, but, unfortunately, the heavily overcast skies prevented our air force's planned preparatory bombardment of the enemy's trenches. Instead, our preparatory artillery bombardment was especially powerful. There was a hope that "the Fritzes" would retreat soon. Our division was in the second echelon and was due to follow up and to exploit any evidence of success by our first-echelon troops.

Our regiment was positioned about a half kilometer behind the frontline trenches. We all carefully monitored the initial progress of the battle in front of us. But the Germans were resisting desperately, and our first-echelon troops couldn't advance a step. Suddenly, we received an order—"Onward! Into battle!" And our deployed rifle units stepped forward to the firing line in full view of the enemy. We followed our infantry, dragging our guns along by hand. The growing weight of our additional fire forced the Germans to abandon their first line of trenches, but we were still far from real success.

Our regiment suffered the loss of many brave men in this action. The cheerful and courageous battalion commander, Captain Samson Minasyan, a favorite of most soldiers and officers, was killed. My friend Junior Lieutenant Vasiliy Bondarenko, who had been recently transferred into a rifle battalion, was also among the dead.

At night, the enemy pulled back to the next line of defense. Before midnight, for some strange reason, our regiment was withdrawn; we of course didn't know what was happening, but then we made a long flanking movement and stopped before a broad water obstacle, which turned out to be the Bay of Karkinit.

After a short halt an order came in, "Continue movement! Maintain silence!" It turned out that the bay was just knee deep here. In some twenty minutes our column reached the opposite shore. We continued marching as dawn broke and it gradually became light. Suddenly, a small hill appeared ahead of us, and we saw about twenty Germans at its base. They were quietly walking up the slope without any sign of worry. It was absolutely clear that they didn't expect us to come from this direction.

The regiment commander addressed himself to me: "Now, artilleryman, strike at the Fritzes!" I estimated the distance and ordered Panteleev (his gun was closest to me) to prepare to fire. Before all the soldiers' and officers' eyes, our crew deftly unlimbered the gun from the gun carriage, then turned it around and aimed it at the Germans. Thank God, the first shell landed squarely in the middle of the enemy group! Those who could still move began running for the top of the hill, but Panteleev fired again and again. Through my binoculars I saw that several Germans failed to reach the top. I think there were also some wounded men among those who escaped. Our soldiers and officers gathered around the artillerymen and congratulated us heartily.

Our flanking maneuver worked well. This was the first time in my war experience when we took the enemy by surprise. This time, after finding an entire rifle regiment on their left flank, the German forces fell back for several kilometers. Over the next two days we dislodged them from a few nearby settlements, which the Germans had converted into strongpoints. We had several further running fights as we advanced quickly down the western coast of the Crimea Peninsula.

Local residents, mostly women, welcomed us heartily both in the Russian and the Crimean Tatar villages. In a couple of days, we found out that in honor of our significant victory, Stalin had ordered the traditional twenty-four-salvo artillery salute in Moscow. Our Guards division was given the honorary title "Perekopskaya."

On 20 April, the division quartered in and around the recently liberated city of Evpatoriya. Our regiment was posted in a big village. Most of the local residents were Russian, but there were Crimean Tatar families there as well.

By that time, Red Army forces had liberated almost the entire Crimea. Therefore, we expected to rest for quite a long time.

Sevastopol

Alas, our hopes didn't come true. We moved out again, and within a week we had reached the close avenues of approach to Sevastopol from the Belbek River valley. By the end of April, we replaced an infantry division in the front lines there that had lost almost 90 percent of its personnel. To our right, the remnants of a penal battalion held their position.[1]

The German defense line had included all the dominating heights in our sector of operations. Therefore, many local attempts to break through their defenses had failed. German snipers struck anyone who carelessly showed even a bit of himself above the parapet. We were under constant shell fire. A few times, German night bombers heavily bombed the area where our regiment's rear detachments were situated. Every day, the number of our casualties in this static warfare grew. Our battery was no exception: within ten days we lost one officer and one soldier.

On 5 May, our resolute offensive started all around the line encircling Sevastopol. Our 2nd Guards Army was aimed at the Mekenzy Mountains; our neighbors to the left, at Sapun Mountain. The Germans resisted desperately but were forced to retreat. By late afternoon of 9 May, the Red Army seized the city and captured thousands of prisoners. The surviving enemy troops fell back to Cape Khersones. Victory was finally ours!

That evening, just as it fell dark, a fantastic salute in honor of the newly gained victory spontaneously began. At first, a few of our soldiers started shooting into the air. Following their example, hundreds, then thousands, of soldiers and officers began to shoot rifles, submachine guns, and pistols. Soon, artillerymen supported them: hundreds of guns of different caliber and dozens of "Katyushas" fired their shells and missiles at the enemies' last refuge on Cape Khersones. Signal rockets flared one after another. Scores of tracers pierced the dark Crimean sky, while flashes of gunfire periodically lit it up. It was a marvelous and unforgettable sight; it sounded like a real preparatory bombardment. That amazing salute lasted almost two hours until an order from above arrived: "Stop wasting ammunition!"

The next morning we left the city. The skeletal framework of the former dome, which had crowned the famous, now ruined "Panorama" building, remains in my memory as a symbol of the destroyed and deserted Sevastopol of that day.

We returned to the same village where the regiment had quartered before the march to Sevastopol. Our battery stayed in the very same households. Everything was calm all around us, and we were anticipating a long trek, because the distance between our current position outside Evpatoriya and the nearest front line was at least several hundred kilometers.

But here a very special and sobering event occurred right before our very eyes. I'd like to tell about it.

Eyewitness Testimony

On the fourth day of this relaxation we became unintentional eyewitnesses to an event that was (along with other undesirable facts) a state secret in the Soviet Union for quite a long time—the compulsory deportation of the Crimean Tatars. We had heard some things about these people the previous March from residents of the small Ukrainian town of Kalanchak. We had stayed there prior to our Perekop offensive.

Its residents told us that after the Germans had occupied the Crimea, the local Tatar elite sent a petition to Hitler. They asked him to grant the Crimea status as a German governor-general province. Moreover, it was said that the Tatars had asked the Führer for permission to drive out or annihilate all the non-Tatar population on the peninsula. (After the war I heard from Russian inhabitants of the Crimea at that time that during the German occupation most members of punitive expeditions against Soviet partisans were Crimean

Tatars.) On the other hand, the Tatar women, who met us on our way after the Perekop battle, seemed sincerely amiable. They told us about their husbands and brothers who were, reportedly, fighting at the front. After the war I read a lot about the outstanding fighter pilot, Twice Hero of Soviet Union, Akhmet-Khan-Sultan, who was a Crimean Tatar.

So, what then happened before my eyes on 15 May 1944? It was about 9:00 A.M. All five officers of our battery were, as usual, gathering for breakfast in the courtyard, where our supply platoon and its field kitchen were quartered. (The owner of the house was a Tatar in his late forties, Rakhim by name. There were also in the household his wife, Fatima, who looked older than he, and their thirteen-year-old daughter.)

The morning was calm. On a stool next to the house, a kerosene stove was softly hissing as its owner prepared some breakfast or lunch for the family.

As soon as our cook finished putting out the dishes, a Studebaker truck with a tarpaulin cover, which usually carried Red Army troops, stopped by the gate of the courtyard. A senior sergeant of the Ministry of Interior Troops, wearing a spiffy new uniform, leaped from the driver's compartment, holding a notebook in his hands. After entering the courtyard, the visitor politely saluted us and stepped toward the doorway. Rakhim emerged from the house to meet him. Looking into his notebook, the senior sergeant ascertained the identity of the man, then loudly declared: "According to government decree, you and your family are to be resettled. You have fifteen minutes to prepare."

Fatima stepped out of the house at that moment. Rakhim said a few words to her in their language, and she started wailing. But upon her husband's peremptory shout, Fatima instantly fell silent. In some ten minutes all three residents of the house, wearing their warm coats and each carrying a sack of household items, left the house and boarded the truck. The senior sergeant saluted us in parting, and the truck drove off. The kerosene stove continued to hiss.

The next afternoon we left the village and started our long march out of the Crimea. After walking a few kilometers along a narrow country road, we reached a wider road and continued marching. Soon, strange sounds like roaring caught our attention, wafting to us from the left. Several soldiers were sent to find out what was going on there. In a half hour they caught up with our column and told us what they had discovered. A kilometer from our route of march, they entered an absolutely deserted village. All signs indicated that it had been abandoned suddenly not later than the previous morning. None of the doors to the houses were locked. All utensils were in their places. In some houses, rising dough had overflowed onto the floor from its bowl. And the entire village resounded with wild howls from abandoned, suffering cows, which had not been milked for two days.

Years later I learned that not only the Crimean Tatars were expelled one and all. The same hard fate befell a few other "disloyal" peoples of the USSR.

* * *

Well, after a week of marching we reached a small railroad station named Snegirevka in the region of Nikolaev oblast. Several troop trains were waiting for our division there. For its successful battles for the Crimea, our division received a new honorific title, and its official designation now became the 87th Guards Perekopskaya Order of the Red Banner Rifle Division.

In the First Baltic *Front*

Transfer to Lithuania

As soon as all our horses, weapons, and ammunition were loaded onto their assigned flatcars, and all our troops into their assigned *teplushkas*, respectively, our train departed. Its destination was the Smolensk region, and the probable duration of the trip was a week or so. At first I had a glimmer of hope that Kiev would be on our route, but soon it became clear that we would bypass my home city.

Once, late at night we stopped at a railroad station called Romodan, about 150 kilometers to the west of Kiev. A friend of mine, Lieutenant Boris Voronin, and I were walking together alongside a neighboring train when a railroad man on duty announced through a megaphone: "Comrade officers! To everybody interested in reaching Kiev—the train with tanks on the second track departs in a few minutes." My heart instantly faltered. I said: "Boris, not a word of this!" We shook hands; I climbed onto the flatcar, settled down behind a tank, and waited impatiently for the train's departure. (What I did at that moment was an unauthorized leave of absence from my military unit in wartime. It was both crazy and highly risky. But the fact that Kiev was so close strongly tempted me. And I was so young!)

In spite of my fear of being caught in the city by a military patrol, I spent thirty-six hours there. First of all, I wanted to see my father. On my way to the office where he worked, I saw demolished and burned-down buildings here and there. At the office I was told that father was working together with a group of colleagues to help clear the heavily damaged Kreshchatik Street area. They were stacking a great deal of debris from the city's once most beautiful buildings.

Finally, the group returned, and I saw my dear father. We hadn't seen each other for almost three years. It was a touching reunion. Then we walked to his apartment. Along the way we passed the ruins of the building where our family had lived before the war. The rest of the day and a part of the night were spent in long, heart-to-heart conversation.

I had time to see not only my father but also Vera's parents and one female acquaintance of mine—a former classmate. Then I rushed in pursuit of our train; fortunately, I knew its number. I changed several trains before I found my regiment on the third day of the chase. The day before, the unit had been lodged in a miserable little village. There was a disturbing outcome to my absence: I was told that the regimental commander had promised to send me to a military tribunal for my unexcused absence. But he had no time to realize his threat, because the day after my return, the command "March!" sounded and our regiment left the village.

The country road was entirely sandy and stretched alongside a forest. It was very difficult to keep in formation after the long trip in *teplushkas* and freight cars. Every now and then our heavily laden wagons bogged down in deep sand. After just a few kilometers of marching, the column resembled a herd without a shepherd. This was when I received a most fortunate break. As we straggled along, the corps commander drove by in his staff car. The scene of our disorganization made his blood boil, and he instantly summoned our regimental commander and dismissed him. My "temporary desertion" was quickly forgotten.

The march seemed to go on forever but really lasted only two weeks. We passed through ruined Belorussian land in the wake of the successful Operation Bagration, which had demolished the German Army Group Center and had cleared Belorussia of the occupiers. We experienced almost no fighting along our route. In early July, we crossed the old (pre-1940) border of the USSR and entered the territory of Lithuania.

In Lithuania

Knowing with certainty that Lithuania had been a capitalist country for ages, I supposed that I would see there an absolutely different world. Therefore, after we crossed the border, I began to examine everything around me to compare it with signs and conditions of our Soviet way of life. Some were evident from the very first days in Lithuania.

The path of our regiment went exclusively through the countryside, and we saw mostly detached hamlets; villages were much more rare. Most hamlets didn't look prosperous; brick dwellings and buildings provided with electric power were exceptions.

At most rural road intersections, we saw something unusual for us—next to the road stood a three-meter-high wooden cross with a Christ figure. In some places you could also see at the intersection a man-made well with a balancing lifter made of a long wooden rod that was attached to the top of a short pole. Such a structure resembled the figure of some long-necked bird, so we called it "a crane" in my country.

* * *

For the first several days after we crossed into Lithuania, we didn't encounter any enemy troops. Our first skirmish, not quite a successful one, took place near the large village of Pogiry. We approached it rather carelessly in broad daylight. I was rambling through a field of tall, golden-yellow rye, searching for a good position for my two guns. Suddenly, I nearly bumped into a German soldier, who clearly hadn't expected to see me, either. Both of us fired a short burst at each other and then took to our heels. I don't know whether I wounded him or not, but I was injured in the thumb. It was very painful while they bandaged it at the regimental medical company. Nevertheless, the next morning I was back with my subordinates.

Throughout July, we advanced at a slow pace. Time and again, our battery stopped and deployed to support the rifle battalions by fire during brief skirmishes. Finally, in mid-August our division stopped on the bank of the Dubysa River. The Germans were well dug in behind it, and we required reinforcements. While we waited in front of this new obstacle, there were only periodic, short exchanges of fire with the enemy.

This more or less calm situation in the second half of August through the beginning of September 1944 gave me an opportunity to meet my friend Boris Glotov, the 120-mm mortar battery deputy commander, a few times. We had been missing each other since our last meeting, which took place in January when we were in Chulakovka before the Perekop offensive.

Boris was a remarkable person among our regimental officers, and I want to tell the readers more about him.

My Friend Boris Glotov

My readers may remember that Lieutenant Glotov had been seriously wounded on the first day of our offensive in July 1943 (see chapter 6). Actually, a splinter of a fragmentation bomb struck Glotov's chest and wounded his thorax. Usually injuries like Boris's were fatal, but fortunately, the splinter had penetrated the breast pocket of his field blouse, where he was carrying his Party membership card. The card had absorbed some of the energy of the splinter, and Boris recovered after one and a half months of treatment in a rear military hospital. In the interim, Lieutenant Fedor Bychkov took his place as the 120-mm mortar battery deputy commander. When Boris returned, the chief of regimental artillery, Captain Vasiliy Karpushinskiy, decided to hold Glotov in the regimental reserve. The regimental command approved Karpushinskiy's decision, and Boris often represented Karpushinskiy at headquarters or during visits to the batteries.

* * *

A good friend of mine, Boris Vladimirovich Glotov, was born in 1922. I don't remember his place of birth, but for some unclear reason the name of the city of Armavir, in the northern Caucasus, flashes through my mind. (It is also possible that the artillery college, where Boris received the lieutenant rank in 1942, was located in Armavir.)

His handsome, youthful appearance and excellent military bearing made Boris absolutely irresistible to teenage girls and young women. Most of the regimental officers liked him, too, regardless of the fact that he often behaved a little tactlessly, rather arrogantly, toward unfamiliar people.

I became acquainted with Boris in Vlasovka, when I was already a junior lieutenant. In the beginning it was just a nodding acquaintance, but gradually our relationship became closer. Believe it or not, but this change arose from . . . pieces of popular music that were our common favorites.

One evening, I accidentally overheard Glotov softly whistling a modern melody. It was one of the best pieces from the comic musical show *Much Ado about Silence*. (In January 1940, Utesov's famous jazz band had performed this show in Kiev. Vera and I were among the audience and remembered several pieces from the performance.) While listening to the first part of the familiar melody, I waited for Boris to complete it, and when he turned to the second part of the melody, I began whistling it loudly. Boris was surprised to find someone else here who knew his favorite variety musical piece, which he had heard on the radio. In a short while I was sharing my impressions of the whole Utesov show with Boris. Glotov, who had never attended such concerts in his modest city, showed keen interest in all the details of my story about the live performance. Then we changed the topic of conversation to other variety musical news, including the concert of the renowned Eddie Rozner's jazz band that had been performed in Kiev on the very eve of the German invasion. When time for good-bye came, both of us already realized that from then on we were now friends.

Boris was gifted with a good ear for music and had a firm musical memory. He was able to play the guitar and could instantly establish the chords for any known song. I wasn't as musically gifted as Boris was, but my musical memory was quite good, and I was able to hum a lot of contemporary songs. So, several times when we met in a convenient situation, we reminded each other of half-forgotten melodies from the repertoires of Soviet musical stars. However, most of our following contacts became more private and personal. Since Boris grew up in a city not as big as my Kiev was, he took an interest in the details of youthful life, activities, and even expressions of speech in a big city. And I tried to tell him everything about my local surroundings and personal experiences in Kiev, including prewar local slang, shibboleths, and jokes.

In turn, Boris shared with me the stories of his several love affairs (which he had never initiated). Being an occasional witness to the strong female attraction to my friend, I never doubted Boris's honesty as a narrator. I remember only one out of a half dozen of his stories of that sort. This one took place on a frosty day in a Don riverside Cossack village.

While walking along a sidewalk, Boris encountered a local eighteen-year-old girl. Just in order to start a chat, Glotov asked her: "Why is it so cold in your village?" In reply the girl invited Boris to warm himself for a while in her parents' house. The girl's mother immediately took an important role in the story. She gave Glotov a warm welcome, instantly stoked the oven, and in a couple

of minutes loudly said to her daughter: "Tamara, I'm leaving for
cousin Natasha's until late evening. Meanwhile, stay here and take
care of the comrade lieutenant, as it should be. Unmake the bed
and help him get warm." These last words were pronounced very
significantly. Tamara's response was much shorter, but clear: "Don't
worry, mom! I'll do my best! Bye-bye!"

The bedroom was small but cozy, with an icon in the corner.
The most impressive object in it, the bed, looked like a work of
nineteenth-century art. Its nickel-plated head and footboards were
striking. A flounce trimmed with lace was attached to the edge of a
snow-white slipcover. A tower of pillows covered with snow-white
lace pillow covers lay at the head of the bed. Nevertheless, Tamara
destroyed "the work of art" in a jiffy.

Boris's final love story developed in front of several regimental
officers' eyes. It started in November 1943, when our regimental
headquarters was located in the town of Tsyurupinsk, and our battery emplacements were on the Konka River floodlands, close to
the Dnieper River's left bank. Our supply platoon remained back in
Tsyurupinsk, and I had an opportunity to visit the town no more
than two or three times.

During that period, Boris was staying in a private house that
belonged to a family of three—a couple in their fifties, both local
teachers, and their twenty-year-old daughter, Galina. The family had
a guitar, and in the evenings Boris performed short concerts there.
Very soon a neighboring girl, Galina's friend Taya (nickname of
Taisiya), became a regular visitor to the house.

At her age of eighteen, Taya was a somewhat short, pretty girl
with blond hair and blue eyes. Her parents had left Tsyurupinsk for
Kherson two years ago, so the girl was the actual mistress of her
small house.

During the first meeting, Taya's gaze became fixed upon the
handsome guest. Very soon, everybody could notice that Taya had
fallen in love with Glotov. In fact, as soon as she turned her eyes
toward Boris, her look began to glow with love and warmth. More
than once, she invited Boris to visit her cozy home. At first Glotov
didn't return her feelings; for a week or so he remained quite cool.

But Taya couldn't bear her unrequited love, and one day while
alone with Boris, she burst into bitter sobbing. Boris's heart wasn't
made of stone; he tried to calm her and patted her head gently.

Instantly Taya clung to his chest and hugged him tightly. Gradually, her sobbing subsided, and Taya asked Boris to see her home. My friend returned from there late at night. The next day Boris moved into Taya's house and stayed there until the division's departure. Over these three weeks Taya conducted herself as Boris' lawful wife and looked as if she was in seventh heaven. Some officers told me later that Glotov looked a little ashamed by her efforts to display their intimacy openly to everyone, and he tried to keep a bit aloof from her in public.

It was a cold windy evening in mid-December 1943 when our regiment formed into a march column: we were leaving Tsyurupinsk for some unknown villages far from the Dnieper River. The only civilian who accompanied the column was Taya. She sat on a mortar battery's wagon until our first halt in a village, some 20 kilometers from Tsyurupinsk.

We thought that was the end of the story about Taya and Boris, until an unusual event happened in the second half of May 1944. After the liberation of Crimea, our division was on its way to an unknown railroad station in Nikolaev oblast. Our route was leading us to a temporary wooden bridge over the Dnieper River, 20 kilometers upstream from Kherson. We were very far behind the front lines, so the division openly marched in the daytime.

One morning we halted in a village about a day's march from the bridge. Quite unexpectedly, Taya suddenly appeared running alongside our column. Finally, she saw Boris, and hugged and kissed him passionately. The column started off, and Glotov sat Taya on a mortar battery's wagon, while he walked alongside. All day long they were together. But a guard at the bridge checkpoint stopped Taya. There were farewell kisses and Taya's tears on parting. And I'm still wondering about her mysterious feelings that led Taya to be in the right place at the right time. The next day we reached the station of Snegirevka, the starting point of our journey to Belorussia, Lithuania, and East Prussia.

Before I return to our division's movements and actions in this campaign, I'd like to finish the story about Boris Glotov. One day, now in Lithuania, we went together to the town of Shydlov (or maybe Shydluvai), where the regimental headquarters was located. Both of us had been summoned to receive decorations for the battles in the Crimea. While returning, we spotted a small signboard with a legend in unintelligible Lithuanian. But the letters FOTO made the inscription understandable. It was too late to drop in, so we decided to visit the studio the next day. The photographer snapped a picture of us, and I sent our photo to Vera. My beloved kept the picture.

My last meeting with Boris took place in the very beginning of September 1944. This time Boris suggested we get acquainted with two local girls that he had seen sitting on a bench behind a house on a previous day. I willingly supported the idea, and shortly before sunset we slowly strolled past the house. Soon two girls appeared on the bench. We entered the yard and, smiling, greeted them in German. The girls returned the "Guten Tag!" and began laughing, because in fact they didn't know the German language. Using gestures we asked them to let us join them on the bench, and they agreed. Then we introduced ourselves and asked them their names in German (naturally, I don't remember them now). It was getting dark, and gradually our hands began to wander. There wasn't a strong rebuff, but neither did either of the girls show any sign of pleasure. Soon we became tired of the course of events and with a quick "Auf Wiedersehen!" left them. We blamed our failure on two reasons: the language barrier and the frigidness of Baltic women.

On the way back Boris told me about a letter he had recently received from Tsyurupinsk. Taya had informed him that she was pregnant, but Boris considered this a maneuver to tie him to her.

When our division entered Lithuania, a new chief of regimental artillery, Senior Lieutenant Petrov, came into our regiment. In contrast to Karpushinskiy, who was a little fop, the round-shouldered Petrov always looked as if he was wearing somebody's old and wrinkled uniform. Small eyes, a pockmarked face, and rasping voice completed the picture of our new chief. It wasn't difficult to predict how the new, ugly chief would treat his handsome "reserve" subordinate.

Very soon the worst assumptions came true. Humiliating orders followed one after another, and the ambitious Boris could not restrain himself for very long. More than once he answered Petrov in an undisguisedly harsh manner. The tension of their relationship heightened day by day. Matters came to a head in late September. Glotov was transferred into the 262nd Guards Rifle Regiment of our division as a deputy 120-mm mortar battery commander. As for Petrov, he was seriously injured in mid-October. (Shortly after he was taken to the rear hospital, Vinokurov was assigned as the new chief of the regimental artillery. In November 1944 he recommended me for promotion to the position of battery commander, which I soon received. This was my last promotion in the army.)

After Boris Glotov's transfer out of the regiment, I didn't see him again. Our regiments fought not far one from another, but the paths of Boris's battery and my battery never crossed. Only in early March 1945 did I learn the dreadful news. A terrible misfortune had occurred in mid-February, when our division was retreating under strong German pressure on the Zemland (Samland) Peninsula (see the next chapter). Boris was the 120-mm mortar battery commander at that time.

After receiving an order to retreat, Glotov along with three of his subordinates left the battery OP. They walked in haste through a young coniferous forest. A small clearing was on their way, and all four of them carelessly entered it. In a moment a short burst of machine gun fire rang out, and Glotov fell on the spot. The mortar men crawled up to him: two bullets had struck Boris in his stomach, but he was still conscious. The soldiers dragged their commander back into the forest, and then one of them took his military overcoat off. They placed Glotov on it and carried him slowly. Boris moaned for a couple of minutes, then told the soldiers in a low voice: "Brothers, stop carrying me. Anyway I'll die soon, and you can escape. . . . " Glotov lapsed into silence and closed his eyes. His subordinates laid him on the ground, then silently stood in a crouch over him for a minute, as if bidding farewell to their dying commander. Then they stood up and quickly went on their way without looking back. The image of the young, vigorous, and smiling Boris Glotov is always on my mind.

* * *

For the months our division was in Lithuania, I had several meetings and interesting conversations with Russian-speaking Lithuanians and local Russians. I still remember one statement of a Lithuanian with a gray moustache: "Beyond dispute, you Russians as well as the Germans are great peoples. Nevertheless, the Lithuanian people, not a great one, have their own independent views on life and on spiritual values."

Once I met a Lithuanian-born Russian couple and answered their questions about the regulations and conditions on Soviet collective farms. I told them everything I knew from my former social studies and from the current newspapers. Both Russians nodded silently, then the woman said with emotion: "It's terrible to lose your main belongings, especially the land and livestock." They feared for their future, and my further explanations didn't lift their spirits. These and other similar contacts with Lithuanian countrymen sparked some new thinking in my mind.

Some Lithuanians told me how expensive hardware was in their country before the war. For example, you could receive only a small amount of nails in exchange for a pig.

After I met several Lithuanian families, a question emerged: why were most husbands so much older than their wives? An elderly and well-educated Lithuanian explained the essence of that phenomenon. Two reasons lay behind it. The first reason was a special law: by the right of succession, the land of an estate was indivisible; only one person could inherit it. As a rule, the eldest son inherited his parents' property, and the younger sons had to find their own way to make enough money to purchase their own estates. The second reason was the high unemployment in Lithuanian cities. Therefore, many male Lithuanians went to America in search of work. Those who were lucky earned enough in America in some fifteen years to return home to a good life in Lithuania. A man could then buy what he needed and choose a suitable young woman to marry. I found this explanation quite reasonable.

Two or three of my local interlocutors mentioned the name of the Lithuanian General Plekhavichus, who disappeared in the country during the Soviet rule in 1940–1941. I was told that after the Germans had occupied Lithuania, the patriotic general obtained Hitler's permission to form a Lithuanian division as a unit of the Wehrmacht. A universal call-up was declared, and many hundreds of young Lithuanians became soldiers of the division. The new recruits were armed and underwent several months of training. Then Plekhavichus received the order to merge his division with some German forces. Plekhavichus disobeyed the order: he and his men disappeared into the Lithuanian forests. After the Germans retreated from Lithuania, most of these temporary soldiers returned home wearing their civilian clothes. As I recall, none of my interlocutors mentioned what happened to their weapons.

Once in 1975, at a seaside resort in the Crimea, I sat close to a small group of resort visitors who were talking in some foreign language.

Unexpectedly, I recognized a couple of Lithuanian words and approached the group. First of all, I introduced myself and made sure that they were Lithuanians. Then I asked them if they were familiar with the name of General Plekhavichus. For some unknown reason their answers were evasive. One of them told that he had heard about Plekhavichus's postwar residence in the United States

In September our regiment made three ineffective efforts to break through the German positions on the Dubysa. We suffered losses without any compensating result. Only a full-scale offensive on the Shaulyay (Siauliai) sector of the front, which started on 5 October 1944, forced the enemy to retreat. For the next few days, the Germans were able to field only rearguard actions, and our division moved westward without substantial losses. We continued to press German troops back toward the "den of the enemy"—the land of East Prussia.

On 23 October we reached the left bank of the Neman (Nemunas, Niemen) River, just across from the historical city of Tilsit. The division's mission was to seize the city, and our regiment was designated to be the lead unit for the river crossing (a perilous task!). We spent a whole week building rafts for the crossing in a forest next to the river. Fortunately for us, the order to storm Tilsit was countermanded on the evening of 30 October, and the next day we received a new order. Our division was shifted to Latvia as a temporary reinforcement to our troops fighting on the Kurland [Courland] Peninsula. A powerful German grouping was trapped there but was stubbornly resisting all efforts to crush it.

To avoid being discovered by German aerial reconnaissance, we had to traverse the 200-kilometer distance to our new destination only by night. The cold, rainy weather and terrible dirt roads transformed our march into a nightmare. However, to be sure, there were five participants of that trip (I among them) who retained pleasant memories of the first leg of the march. Below is an amusing story about our experience.

Our Choral Singing Was of Great Use in a Remote Lithuanian Hamlet

The starting point of the designated march was about 10 kilometers behind the front lines. Leaden clouds stretched to the horizon.

Under this solid cloud cover, it was impossible to spot our column of march by aerial reconnaissance. Therefore, all regiments of our division were ordered to depart two hours before sunset.

As bad luck would have it, some ten minutes after our regiment began marching, the left wheel of my platoon's field gun suddenly emitted a crunching sound. The gun crew and I stepped out of the column immediately, and Zakernichnyy, the gun crew commander, ran for Simunin, the regimental armorer. Vinokurov, our battery commander, ordered me to stay there along with Zakernichnyy, Simunin, and both horsemen. The rest of the crew had to remain with the column. After the repair, the five of us would catch up with the column by following the division's road signs ("Tymchik's household").

Soon, Zakernichnyy and Simunin appeared. The latter opened his heavy metal box and took out a special wrench. After spending a minute on the wheel, the armorer told us that the bearing had crumbled. It would be possible to replace it within an hour and a half. At that moment it started raining in torrents, and our plan to repair the wheel on the spot instantly washed away.

According to my topographic map, there was an isolated hamlet not far from our present position, and we made our way along a narrow country track toward it. Soon we entered a small farm that was fenced with crooked poles. The farm seemed to be of modest means. Fortunately, the rain had stopped.

I explained to the master of the household, a sullen Lithuanian in his early fifties, that we would be staying with him until the next morning, when it would be possible for us to repair the wheel. Without saying a word, the owner opened the half-empty barn, and we rolled the gun and the limber into it. Gontarev and Maslov, the horsemen, watered the horses at the well and then led them into the barn. It was getting dark gradually, and the five of us, without waiting for an invitation, opened the front door and entered the house.

On the right of the entrance was the "hall" (the main room of the house), with a wooden table and three benches. The only window faced the barn. We went into the room and left the door to it wide open. In a minute all of us were sitting on two of the benches and idly exchanging some words with each other. We were hungry already. Unfortunately, at the time of breakdown, nobody imagined that the repair would be postponed until the next morning. Otherwise we would have brought along some food.

Across the entrance from the "hall" was another room, and its door too was wide open. We could see the figure of the home's mistress puttering about the stove there, but she never looked in our direction. Both owners emphatically ignored the uninvited guests.

It was absolutely obvious that nobody was about to invite us to have dinner. Therefore I left the "hall" and asked the relatively young mistress to boil a few cups of water for us. In broken Russian, I was told that both burners of the stove were occupied at that time; therefore, we would have to wait for the boiling water for at least one hour. Without even a slight prospect of some dinner, we were all depressed.

Probably under the influence of our situation, Gontarev, who has a tender tenor voice, started softly singing the sad song "I'm forgotten and forsaken. I became an orphan in my early youth. I have a bitter lot. . . . " At that moment Simunin took up the song. His rich baritone echoed Gontarev's melody. Then the rest of us joined in the song, and when we got to the second stanza, everyone was singing in a full voice. As the song came to its final words, we saw two very young curious listeners, who looked at us from the doorway. They were girls dressed in plain clothes, one a little older than twelve years of age, the other about nine.

When we finished the song, both of them remained standing in the doorway. It was obvious: they were waiting for another song. The presence of an audience encouraged us and we started singing the very popular song "Katyusha." Evidently the girls knew this song because shortly after they heard the few initial notes of its melody, pleased smiles appeared on their faces. When we went on to the next stanza, the master joined his daughters. This time the Lithuanian wasn't frowning; on the contrary, he looked at us quite kindly. In a minute he pushed the girls into the "hall" and called his wife. She stood beside him.

Seeing the audience had doubled, our "vocal quintet" became still more inspired. To impress our listeners, shortly after finishing "Katyusha," we chose the Russian folk song "Volga-Volga, Mother Volga" (and incorporated several fast "nursery rhymes" as playful tricks). The initial fluid stanza of the song went well. When it came to the end and, unexpectedly, the witty "nursery rhyme"—the playful "Liza-Liza-Lizaveta"—began to sound at an up-tempo, our listeners' faces broke into smiles. The family entered the "hall" and sat on the vacant bench.

The singers were getting more and more animated, so while singing the next "nursery rhyme," they drummed with their heels. Moreover, at that part of the song Gontarev, who always led off the songs, artistically whistled the melody. Our enthusiasm gripped the Lithuanian audience; all the listeners began to clap their hands, rhythmically keeping time with the song that ended triumphantly. The tired singers announced an intermission and went out for a smoke.

Because of a light rain shower, we opened the front door wide and smoked just inside the entrance. While smoking, we saw that the mistress along with her older daughter was peeling potatoes near a capacious cast-iron kettle. It seemed that things were moving nicely, and it meant a supper for us after all. Our mood lifted! After the kettle took its place on the stove, we introduced each other. Their family name was Paulauskas, her first name was Elenyte, his was Mykolas. The girls' names I don't remember. Then the second part of our concert started. At this time, we successfully performed four Russian and Ukrainian folk songs. As the final spice for our impromptu performance we performed the cheerful "You Kidded Me, You Put Me on the Spot." There was heel tapping and whistling to this song, too.

After the concert we smoked outdoors for a while. While returning into the "hall," we saw that a basin full of large pieces of boiled potato had appeared on the table. A plate with five bulbs of onion and a saucer full of salt were beside the basin. On top of it all, five large flat slices of gray bread lay on a soft canvas towel.

Five belly-pinched singers fell upon the food instantly, and we soon gobbled everything up. Instead of sweetened tea we drank just hot boiled water. Before saying "Good night!" we warmly thanked Elenyte for her generosity.

I appointed Gontarev and Maslov to be on duty and to spend the night in the barn. The rest of us slept on the floor in the "hall." I slept uneasily that night. At times it seemed that I heard a creak from the direction of the barn's gate. Fortunately, the night passed with no incidents and no more rain.

At dawn I woke up the team, and Simunin began fixing the wheel. The replacement of the bearing took less than one hour.

After watering the horses, our drivers, with Mykolas's permission, fed the horses with the master's hay.

At about nine in the morning Elenyte called us to breakfast. It was the same menu as at yesterday's supper. While eating, we discussed our further march. After we had emptied all the plates, we thanked both Lithuanians heartily.

It would have been proper to repay the hosts' kindness, but I had no cash. (As usual, after my monthly allotment to the defense fund, to the state loan, and the monthly remittance to my mother, the rest of my salary was automatically transferred directly into my personal account at the State Savings Bank. No personal checks were available, only the passbook.) There was no means to compensate our hosts' expenses, and I decided that if nothing else, maybe a written acknowledgment would be of use to them. (Recently every officer of our regiment had been given a sheet of thick paper with ten stamped coupons. Each coupon gave the right to make a purchase in any Voentorg, that is, a military trading network store. Of course, at the front we never even saw a Voentorg store.) Well, I cut out two adjacent coupons and wrote on the back a kind of "certificate of contribution." It was very short: "We received free of charge: food for five servicemen (twice); fodder for four horses (twice); a day and night shelter for our group of five." Then I wrote the date, my rank, and my full name and signed the certificate. Giving it to Mykolas, I was sure that nobody would compensate our hosts for their expenses, but I knew this piece of paper was a sign of their loyalty to the Red Army. Perhaps it would be prove useful someday.

Meanwhile, the crew wheeled the gun and the limber out of the barn, and then the gun was limbered. After the horsemen finished harnessing the horses, we all returned to the "hall" and, according to Russian tradition, sat down on the benches for a minute before starting on our journey. Then we said good-bye to the Paulauskases and set out along the track toward the main dirt road. The smiling Lithuanians waved their hands at us in farewell.

As we reached the main road, the three dismounted men sat on the trail of the gun carriage holding on to each other. The drivers prompted the horses, and our team rushed straight on. As we rode along, we kept close watch for road signs to "Tymchik's household." Periodically I checked our location on the topographic map.

From time to time the horsemen slowed the horses' pace for a few minutes to rest them. On these occasions we hopped off and walked behind the gun. Once we halted for a half hour in order to water the horses, but in general we were moving much faster than any infantry unit could. We overtook our regiment just as its elements were forming back into column to resume the march. Memories of our supper, breakfast, and entertainment in the Paulauskases' home were the sole pleasure during the rest of our difficult march to the Kurland Peninsula.

* * *

Our short-term collaboration with local Soviet troops didn't change the situation on the Kurland Peninsula. After a week of hard but unsuccessful fighting we started our trip back to rejoin our 2nd Guards Army.

While we had made our detour to Kurland, the forces of our Third Belorussian *Front* had crossed the East Prussia border to the south of our positions and had managed to take a few German frontier towns. But their success was only temporary: the Germans launched a counteroffensive and drove these units back across the border.

Our division continued to encounter some retreating enemy groups until mid-December, resulting in brief skirmishes. Then we stopped for several days in order to prepare for the decisive battles in East Prussia.

Initial Months on the Enemy's Land

East Prussia, which we entered in late December 1944, turned out to be totally different from our country as well as from neighboring Lithuania. Everywhere, in towns and in the countryside, you could see solid buildings with steep, red-tiled roofs. There were attributes of western European family life in the houses that amazed even those of us who had been city dwellers before the war. We also encountered many small hamlets and independent farms with roomy barns, cowsheds, and stables, all built of red brick. There was amazing order and cleanliness everywhere. The German roads that reminded us of a careful mother's well-groomed children especially impressed us all. Framed by straight rows of mature trees, the roads were all so clean, flat, and even! The crowns of mighty trees formed a continuous green archway over the road, and at that time I thought an entire armored division could successfully hide beneath them.

(Incidentally, in 1980, I had an occasion to visit this land again, now Kaliningrad oblast of the Russian Federation. I had a long conversation with the head of the motor transport company of the oblast. When the conversation turned to the local roads, the man passionately declared, "Swinish Germans! Why, while building and paving such wonderful and durable roads, didn't they make all pavement markings permanent? If they had done so, we'd have no such task every year, sometimes more than once.")

I remember in detail a few of the initial encounters on the land of the enemy. There was no significant fighting those days; the Germans continued to fall back. As far as I remember, in early January 1945 our division was placed under the command of the 43rd Army (in May we were passed back to the 2nd Guards Army).

One day in mid-January we met a group of several dozen unshaven men. They were all wearing the striped uniforms of prisoners of war. It looked like they had just left the camp where they had been held. The men stepped along to the east, walking freely and smiling merrily. They waved to us and extolled us loudly in French.

There were no more encounters for a few days; all of the farms and settlements in our path were deserted. Then we entered a large coniferous forest that was astonishingly clean. We met there a one-legged forester who was hauling away dried twigs and brush. The man, who was in his late fifties, told us that the forest was the personal property of Hitler's closest companion, Reichsmarshall Hermann Göring, chief of the German Luftwaffe (air force). The forest was his personal hunting preserve, and Göring had quite often visited there to hunt with his hounds.

While advancing through the deserted region, we occasionally received some information concerning German civilians in the form of various rumors and gossip that came from other detachments of our division. Of course, some news related to German women. Particularly, somebody once narrated that a group of six scouts from the adjacent rifle regiment had found three young women in a deserted manor. It was said that each of the three women made love with two Soviet scouts by turn all night long with no objections. (A very strict order about severe punishments for rapes and plunder was already in effect, but who knew what kind of relations took place at that time?)

Finally, on 30 January 1945, we ran into a few German civilians ourselves. It took place in the small town of Sidlung, near the city of Königsberg, East Prussia's capital. We entered the town at sunset after a short skirmish on its outskirts, whereupon the small German force had retreated hastily.

There were no signs of the war in the town. Through some windows one could see indoor lights. We checked out the nearby houses. Everything—power supply, water supply, even the toilets, was operating as usual. But—there were no inhabitants, although it was clear that they were somewhere nearby: radio sets were still playing in some of the homes.

I visited a few empty houses before I entered one where I found a group of elderly women sitting in the basement. Two of them were sitting in wheelchairs. During a short conversation with the group I understood: they were mortally frightened and were expecting some terrible Russian punishment.

In the house next door to this one, I found a couple in their late forties. They were amazed by my good knowledge of the German language. That pleased me, and I recited Heine's short poem

"Lorelei" for them; I had learned it by heart in secondary school. After perhaps deciding that this "Russian" would do no harm to them, they asked me if they should hide their fourteen-year-old daughter from the Soviet soldiers. Before answering them, I asked them to show me the girl. Then an awkward, long-legged girl crawled out from under the bed. She wasn't shaped like a real teenager yet, although she was quite tall. As for me, the girl had no sex appeal, but my advice was to hide her more carefully.

At that time our enemy was evidently weak. Therefore, I expected that we would enter Königsberg in short order. However, an order came to advance due westward, into the heart of the Zemland Peninsula. The enemy's resistance wasn't significant, so we advanced quite rapidly. We passed several small settlements and Hill 111.4, which dominated the peninsular landscape. Soon it became apparent that our topographic maps of the Zemland Peninsula were hopelessly obsolete. They showed neither the narrow-gauge railroad that ran along the strip of land, down which we marched, nor the squares of new forestland that held many spacious rectangular bunkers of reinforced concrete. It turned out that this part of the peninsula was the main German naval arsenal. Thousands and thousands of sea mines, shells, and bombs were stored in those bunkers. The Germans tried to defend every bunker, but we were stronger and in spite of combat casualties continued to press the enemy westward, toward the tip of the peninsula.

By early February we were quite close to the major German naval base of Pillau (it was renamed the city of Baltiysk after the war). But suddenly the enemy's forces launched strong counterattacks, as if they had been replaced or reinforced by fresh troops. The Germans counterattacked with the support of tanks and self-propelled guns. It had been several weeks since we had faced enemy armor, and now they were forcing us to retreat with heavy losses. Clearly, the two sides had switched roles. (Within a few days, we learned that two additional German divisions had recently transferred from Kurland to Pillau by sea and had entered the battle.)[1]

The enemy's pressure continued, and by that time we had to cling to every bunker. When the sky was clear, our low-flying ground attack aircraft, the Il-2, helped us to contain the enemy; occasionally the defensive fire of our long-range artillery put obstacles in the way of the German offensive. Nevertheless, the Germans pressed us back to the east.

There was one effort to stop this course of events. On 23 February (it was the anniversary of the Soviet army), another rifle regiment of our division, our neighbor on the right, was scheduled to counterattack the enemy. To strengthen the thrust, our battery was attached to that regiment, and we took our position in its formation. The start of the attack was set for 6:00 A.M., but a half hour before, the Germans rained down upon us such a storm of artillery that it completely ruined our attack preparations. Moreover, when at dawn four enemy tanks and a line of soldiers with assault rifles started approaching our trenches, many of us were affected with panic. As a result, the planned attack turned into a *drap-marsh*. Fortunately, our limbers came up just in time, and my battery saved its guns and had no personnel losses.

The Unforgettable Battle for the Hill 111.4

On 28 February, the line of our severely battered rifle companies lay at the base of Hill 111.4, which we had passed three weeks before. The regimental command post was placed on top of the hill. If we lost this strategically important point, our troops would have to withdraw eastward for at least another 20 kilometers. It would substantively weaken the present threat to Königsberg. Because of that, we received a stringent order that prevented any further retreat; besides, after three straight weeks of misfortune, we hated to continue retreating as well. Certainly, at the same time the Germans were strongly drawn to the predominant hill, looming just before them.

Before the war, a wonderful winter mountain ski resort with a famous ski jump had been located there. The flat top of the hill, somewhat smaller than a soccer ground, was crowned with a tall structure built in the style of a medieval fortress tower. (After the war I learned that the name of the tower was Bismarckturm, in honor of the former chancellor of Germany, Bismark.) In case we were forced to retreat, our combat engineers had mined the tower with a substantial amount of explosives and established round-the-clock duty beside it. About 30 meters below the top of the hill, in a two-meter-deep ditch, many shelters and dugouts housed the command post with a squad of guards and two regimental battery commanders with their orderlies. There were about thirty of us there.

During the daytime, our companies supported by my battery's guns managed to repel two or three German infantry attempts to approach the hill. As it grew dark, the shooting faded away. All of us relaxed, and after a late supper with "100 grams" of vodka we fell into deep sleep.

But the night turned out to be full of unexpected events. In the middle of the night a low sound of a flare, fired from the top of the hill, woke us up. We heard distinctly strange voices from upslope: they were Germans, who had reached the top of the hill by some miracle. One more flare soared into the sky. Naturally, it was a signal to their command that the infiltrators had seized the hill. All our telephones were silent; evidently the uninvited "guests" had cut our telephone wires on their silent climb to the top. None of us knew the size of the party of infiltrators. The fate of the two combat engineers, who were on duty near the tower, was unknown as well.

An anxious, oppressive atmosphere crept over our group in the darkness of the night. It was unclear what to do. All of us in the ditch spoke to each other in a whisper. I was very nervous.

Later, at dawn, I discovered that during the night our regiment commander, Lieutenant Colonel Rubtsov, had changed out of his military greatcoat into a soldier's padded jacket without shoulder straps. It was a clear sign that he thought capture was likely, and I became actually scared. At that time I wore a German officer's raincoat with a Soviet lieutenant's badge of ranks (not a bigwig!), so I didn't change out of it. I only tore to shreds a few letters from my sweetheart, which I had been keeping in the pockets of the raincoat.

Finally a tremendous explosion sounded from the top of the hill, and the entire hill shook violently. There was the long rumble of falling debris, and we could hear the groaning of casualties. We were sure that after the explosion of the mined Bismarckturm, we would easily be able to defeat the shaken remnants of the enemy group. With our usual "Hurrah!" we tried to climb the slope to the top. But the rapid fire of rifles and submachine guns, and numerous bursts of hand grenade explosions, greeted us. We were forced to drop to the ground and scuttled back to our ditch. Rubtsov sent an orderly to the rifle battalions for reinforcements. Within some thirty minutes a group of fifteen men reached our ditch in support. Together with them we tried to assault the hilltop from two opposite directions, but this effort was unsuccessful, too.

Looking for a way out, I remembered my portable FM radio A7 and reported to Rubtsov that it might be possible for us to make radio contact with my battery's supply platoon commander. The platoon was located not far from the divisional headquarters. Without confidence of success, I put Rubtsov's message on the air in veiled language to deliver an artillery strike on the top of the hill. In response, I learned that only "Katyushas" would be able to respond to my request for artillery support. Given the inaccuracy of the rockets, it was risky to accept such support, but we had no alternative.

In twenty minutes or so we heard the familiar howling sounds of two "Katyushas," and right after that, the threatening rustle of wind over our heads before some three dozen shells exploded on the hilltop. When the thundering roar stopped, we went into the attack for the third time.

This time the Germans couldn't withstand our "Hurrah!" and fled downhill at the sound of our cheers. We gave chase, and almost all the runaways were caught. I had to take off after one of the Germans who was particularly elusive. While chasing him, I became more and more angry. I think, in those minutes, I looked like a predatory animal while hunting prey. When I finally caught up with the soldier, my left hand gripped his collar, and my right hand with a pistol in it struck him on the chin as hard as I could. The German staggered, dropped his submachine gun, and then obediently followed my orders. When we returned to our ditch, the last captive (there were about forty of them) descended the hilltop. The young man was the commander of the group, a senior lieutenant. Supporting his bleeding right forearm with his left arm, he loudly addressed everyone in German, "Ich will leben! Neunzehn Jahren alt! (I want to live! I'm nineteen years old!)"

So, on the night of 1 March 1945, we had regained control of this hill, which remained in my memory for life. There were no further retreats. Moreover, the enemy attack had spent its force. The front line stopped advancing, and our division was transferred to the close rear area for a whole month of replenishment and combat training before the storming of Königsberg.

Let me suggest to you, my reader, to take a temporary relief from the sounds of the war, too. You'll find some peaceful stories in the next chapter.

Chapter 11

Some Fortunate Finds in East Prussia

In the course of the successful offensives of late fall 1944 and early 1945, our detachments discovered several warehouses that had been abandoned by the retreating German troops. Besides weapons and ammunition, we found other sorts of property in these warehouses. There were spare parts, lubricants, and methylated spirits, but also different kinds of food. We less frequently came upon warehouses full of wine, brandy, and schnapps too.

Naturally, soldiers in the advanced detachments were the "pioneers" who discovered the spoils. Initially they grabbed and consumed everything that seemed edible and drinkable without discrimination. Soon we began hearing sad rumors of incidents where drinking the methylated spirits that they had found had poisoned groups of these "pioneers." In most cases the outcome was fatal; sometimes the victims were blinded. Then numerous articles appeared in our newspapers on this topic. Some sources, including official military orders, stated that retreating Germans had poisoned the foodstuff and liquors before leaving it for us to find. In awe of the terrible potential outcomes, everybody (me, too) became extremely cautious regarding all captured food supplies, liquors, and so on.

Some of our battery's members had their own experience as "food and liquor finders." Here are two true stories on this subject.

How Our Wise Sergeant Major Handled the Priceless Spoils

A piece of rare luck fell to our regimental artillerymen's lot in late January, when the regiment was in pursuit of the retreating enemy. That day the 120-mm mortar battery's food and clothing team along with our team bumped into an abandoned storage facility while inspecting a remote German hamlet. They found four metal casks there: two of 200-liter capacity and two of 100-liter capacity. Each cask had a numerical marking.

The "pioneer" of that discovery was Sergeant Major Petrenko from the mortar battery. Without delay he opened the first big cask by releasing its cap. Right away everybody smelled the familiar attractive scent of alcohol. The "pioneer" shook the cask slightly and then put his forefinger into the opening for a moment. He withdrew his moistened finger, sniffed it carefully, and then finally licked it clean. Like a professional alcohol taster, Petrenko paused for a second before cheerfully proclaiming: "That's it! Undiluted alcohol! As pure as God's tear!"

Petrenko divided the rich "spoils" fraternally, and our battery's Sergeant Major Shkalenkov became the manager of 300 liters of the precious liquid. Vasiliy Ivanovich Shkalenkov, a forty-five-year-old Belorussian, had been serving in our battery since the early fall of 1943. He was an experienced man of extraordinary fate that had more than once turned against him in life.

As I heard from Vasiliy Ivanovich himself, in the mid-1930s he had been a prosperous chairman of a collective farm in Belorussia. However, in 1938 he was arrested and sentenced for some shady dealings and served the punishment somewhere in the Far East. Shortly after the war began, he started pressing to be released and sent to the front line. In the spring of 1943, Shkalenkov got everything that he wanted.

Vasiliy Ivanovich was an excellent manager and supervised the battery's food and clothing team perfectly well. He made friends with both chiefs of regimental services: PFS (food and forage supply) and OVS (clothing and wagon train supply), Senior Lieutenants Udovichenko and Onufreychuk, respectively. They were deferential to Shkalenkov, who used this friendship to keep our battery better supplied than all the others.

Knowing Vasiliy Ivanovich's thrift, I was fully confident that the priceless liquid "trophy" had fallen into reliable hands. Actually, both casks were immediately locked up in the sergeant major's pantry. After the day of the find everybody in our battery received fifty grams of pure alcohol daily.

On the next day Shkalenkov decided out of curiosity to check the contents of the 100-liter cask. He put a thin rubber tube into the cask's opening and set the tube's end into a glass. To his great surprise, the running liquid wasn't clear: its color resembled that of weak tea. Moreover, he smelled a delicious aroma from the liquid. Without hesitation Vasiliy Ivanovich took a good sip of the drink. For a half minute he didn't breathe, utterly delighted with the savor of the drink.

Coincidentally, I was visiting our rear service team at that time, and the slyly smiling Shkalenkov invited me to drop by his pantry for a short while. Here he asked me to try the drink from the glass. I took a thimbleful and felt as if I was in seventh heaven. Never before had I tasted a strong drink with such a wonderful flavor as this one. My first reaction was the phrase "Nectar and ambrosia!" Trying to guess what I had drunk, I turned over in my mind all the names of drinks or spirits I had ever tasted or at least had heard or read about. Vodka? Whiskey? Brandy? Irish cream? Cognac? No, no, no. Finally, one more name came up—Jamaican rum; it seemed to me that I had read about it somewhere. Oh, of course, it was Robert L. Stevenson's *Treasure Island;* I even knew by heart the famous song, with the lines "Fifteen men on a dead man's chest / Yo-ho-ho, and a bottle of rum!"

So, I named the wonderful drink, and the sergeant major liked the name. Then we considered Shkalenkov's plan on how to handle the invaluable find.

First of all, we should be fair with respect to our fellow mortar men whose casks held only pure alcohol. Thus, we had to offer them fifty liters of rum in exchange for an equal quantity of pure alcohol.

Second, the number of the rum consumers had to be restricted to seven: the battery commander, the four platoon commanders, the sergeant major, and his aide, Alexey Nemukhin. The daily ration of rum must be fixed—no more than two half-liter flasks every other day (by turns with pure alcohol) for each of us in the circle. (I performed a quick mental arithmetic: the disposable quantity of rum would be enough for at least three months because one of the platoon commanders, Ivan Kamchatnyy, was going to go on leave.)

The last item of the plan stated that it would be acceptable to expend frugal doses of rum as well as moderate portions of pure alcohol to treat some "very useful persons" at the sergeant major's discretion. Vasiliy Ivanovich was also permitted to exchange the recently obtained drinks for food or some especially necessary goods.

(Here, I must make note of the great importance of liquor at the front. During the Great Patriotic War, vodka became a virtual unit of currency. Moreover, the rum was a special rarity at that time, so its value was many times higher.

Much later, when Stalin was already dead, and the universal fear of being arrested gradually diminished, handing over a bottle of alcohol became a usual and very effective form of bribery. It was considered quasi-legal and helped to solve many different problems.)

I admired Vasiliy Ivanovich's wisdom and approved his plan unconditionally.

You've read in the previous chapter about the numerous hard, sometimes dramatic battles that we fought across the Zemland Peninsula in February 1945 (with my battery usually attached to a rifle battalion). Very seldom did the battery field kitchen reach the battery emplacements or my OP by day. Nevertheless, whether by daylight or in the darkness of night, Aleksandr Bezuglov, the cook, always managed to hand me a flask of rum when the kitchen arrived. As a rule, I shared the delivered rum with two of my subordinates, the reconnaissance platoon commander and his fire platoon colleague, and with the rifle battalion commander.

Once, shortly before the end of February, the sergeant major's assistant unexpectedly arrived along with Bezuglov. Nemukhin's look was very anxious. I asked him why he had come here without my request. And Alexey gave me a detailed explanation, starting from the end.

The previous night Vasiliy Ivanovich Shkalenkov, our sergeant major, had left for his native Belorussia. He possessed a paper—an extract from the People's Commissariat of Defense's order regarding Shkalenkov's extraordinary demobilization for reasons of his age and state of health. Nemukhin told me that the chief of the personnel department and the regimental medical company commander had quickly moved all the paperwork through the requisite channels for the discharge. Both were given in advance two small ten-liter jerricans, one filled with pure alcohol, the other with rum, as a most effective incentive for their work and for their superiors at division headquarters. Shkalenkov's discharge was ready within three weeks.

Alexey took a deep breath and continued to relay the unbelievable news: "This morning by the regiment commander's order I was appointed our battery sergeant major. And I ought to report to you on the real situation concerning the liquors. Actually it is bad. We have only about ten liters of rum now; and the amount remaining of pure alcohol is just a bit more. What are your instructions?"

More than sixty years have passed since that moment, but I still remember my feelings after Nemukhin's stunning report. It was so unexpected! It was like lightning coming out of the blue. My first reaction was indignation: "How could it occur without at least letting me know? After all, I was Shkalenkov's direct commander, and there was no legal way to manage the deal without my personal written approval!" (What a naive person was I as a twenty-two-year-old Guards lieutenant at that time!)

Shortly after, while calming down, I began to think more clearly. Some reasonable considerations entered my train of thought: "What are you so excited about? The man had a real wealth at his unrestricted disposal and he handled it wisely. He had a rare opportunity and he seized it. He did his best for himself. And you are unable to change the existing 'rules of society games.'"

Finally I became quite calm and gave Nemukhin detailed instructions concerning our own liquor (the "People's Commissar's vodka" must be distributed as usual).

First of all, the remaining alcohol must be conserved and consumed sparingly.

Second, our rum must be delivered only to those officers who were at the front line. The consumption of rum must be reduced to a drink every other day, alternating with the pure alcohol. And the supply platoon commander, Lieutenant Brechko, along with the new sergeant major and his still unappointed aide should be satisfied with a half flask of pure alcohol a day for the three of them.

I knew Alexey Nemukhin as an honest, conscientious, and dutiful person. Therefore, I was fully confident that he would exactly obey all the instructions I had just given him. Later events confirmed the accuracy of my expectations.

* * *

A week after Nemukhin's visit, our division was withdrawn from the front line in order to take on substantial personnel replacements and undergo extensive training for the coming assault on Königsberg. Since we all were in the rear area now, I decided to equalize the pure alcohol's ration for every officer, preserving the scanty amount of remaining rum for the more difficult days ahead.

Such days came on 6 April 1945, when the storming of Königsberg began. Nemukhin resumed the delivery of rum to the front line in full. And we emptied the last flask of rum before dawn on 10 April, when Senior Lieutenant Nikolai Soin and I enjoyed a "liquid celebration" in honor of our victory in that night's memorable combat. You'll read about this event at the end of the next chapter.

Now let me proceed to the second story.

Volynkin's Mysterious Find

Stepan Volynkin was our wagon driver in his late forties. Everybody in the battery knew him as a person whose thirst to scavenge and scrounge anything useful from our surrounding neighborhood was unquenchable.

In early March 1945 our regiment was encamped in a forest, and we were all living in dugouts. Once Volynkin entreated Alexey Nemukhin to let him go for a short drive. Stepan promised not to return empty-handed. Actually, he returned with a mysterious find: a 100-liter metal cask lay in Volynkin's wagon.

The cask was filled with a mysterious light yellow, odorless, fatty substance that resembled congealed melted butter. After exploring the find, Nemukhin asked me to take a look at the unknown substance. By sight it reminded me of a type of Soviet technical grease. Being overcautious, I hesitated to reach a firm decision even about using it as a lubricant for our weapon: what if the substance had an acid admixture? So Alexey received no advice from me.

However, in some two hours a smiling Nemukhin reentered the small dugout where Lieutenant Mitrofan Dmitriev and I were staying. Alexey placed a tin can, which was half filled with the "substance," on a ledge that we used as a table. Then he took a two-inch-long piece of packthread from his pocket, dipped it into the "matter," and, using a rifle cartridge with a hole in it, made a wick. After he brought a burning match to the wick, our dugout became illuminated with a steady bright light. It was much better than the traditional Russian *ploshka* because there was no smell of burning and no trace of soot. From then on we called these lamps "Nemukhin *ploshkas*," and all our battery's dugouts were illuminated day and night (we were able to burn them for a year or longer).

Three days passed, and Volynkin unexpectedly entered my dugout. He held a mess kit covered by a clean piece of a white fabric.

While smiling slyly, Stepan uncovered the kit and said, "I brought you a couple of warm '*oladyas*' [soft, thick pancakes fried in fat] to taste."

The pancakes turned out to be fat and extremely delicious, and I looked at Volynkin approvingly and at the same time questioningly. With this unspoken prompt, Stepan continued:

> From now on my find will be of real benefit to us all. To tell you the truth, I was dissatisfied with Nemukhin's decision on how to use this "substance." From the day when we first opened the cask, I felt that the stuff had to be edible. However, having heard plenty of rumors about poisoned food, I had patiently restrained my desire to try it for two days. Then, remembering that a man can die but once, I yielded to temptation. To avoid doing much harm to anyone else, I decided first to test the substance by myself. I did it yesterday evening. After I awoke this morning alive and feeling fine, I shared everything regarding my find with Bezuglov, the cook. Then we fried a lot of pancakes and stuffed ourselves up to the neck.

When Volynkin finished his monologue, I went to Nemukhin to try the substance out for myself. I scooped a little of the substance up with a spoon and, without hesitation, directed it into my mouth for the final tasting. I wasn't in a hurry to determine what the stuff really was. After a few seconds, I decided, but without real confidence, that the substance was probably *margarine*. I wasn't quite certain because I knew about it just by hearsay during the prewar years.

At that time most Kievans had already heard about a new sort of fat, in addition to the popular forms, such as butter, vegetable oil, and so on. The new fat was inexpensive and was already appearing on the shelves of city grocery stores. I heard from my parents that this margarine was only popular among poor city dwellers. I was certain that the majority of our prewar rural population had never even heard the word "margarine." (There was no reaction among our soldiers, when I loudly explained that the mysterious substance was actually German margarine, and that it was quite safe to consume.)

From that day forward, the nourishment of the men in our battery became much richer in calories. Margarine consumption was placed under Nemukhin's observation. Unfortunately, we only had about 100 liters of margarine available. We used it all up within the next two months.

The Fall of Königsberg

Königsberg was well prepared to offer long-term resistance to attacking troops. During numerous tactical exercises in March 1945, our commanders informed us that three defensive rings encircled Königsberg. The first of them consisted of fifteen old forts with massive stonewalls. A deep, water-filled ditch surrounded every fort. At least one fort covered every sector around the city with its fire. After the war, official data were published: before our assault, the Königsberg garrison numbered 130,000 officers and men, with over 200 tanks and up to 4,000 guns and mortars.

According to the general plan of our attack, special groups were formed to penetrate the fortification system. The name of such a group was *shturmovoy otryad* (assault detachment). One such group was created in our regiment. The 1st Rifle Battalion commander, Senior Lieutenant Nikolay Soin, was appointed as the storm troop commander. The troop consisted of Soin's battalion, my battery, and two SU-76s (self-propelled 76-mm guns). Our general mission was to lead the attack in the direction of the fort Number 5-A Lendorf.

I am not going to describe below the entire battle of Königsberg, nor special details of the operation, such as the powerful preparatory artillery bombardment, the sieges of some forts, or the difficult street fighting. I only want to talk about several particularly memorable events from the three initial days of our offensive and to describe in detail what happened on the unforgettable night before the garrison's capitulation.

Our attack began late in the morning of 6 April 1945. According to the general plan, our assault detachment advanced in the designated direction, and at noon we reached the fort Number 5-A Lendorf. But it was not our job to capture the fort. We bypassed it to the west and continued moving forward, while it was the 2nd Rifle Battalion's mission to encircle the fort and force its garrison to surrender.

Overcoming German resistance, we continued our advance. Before sunset we approached the narrow Landgraben Canal that flowed along the outskirts of the city. Soin's troop was halted close to a bridge across the canal by heavy-caliber machine gun fire. My battery fired a few shells at the enemy in return, but the machine gun seemingly had changed its position and continued to fire.

At dawn the next day, both SU-76s crossed the canal, the rest of the troop following closely behind them. Hard street fighting went on all day long. By the morning of 8 April, we found ourselves in the aristocratic quarters of the city. It wasn't easy to get our bearings in the central part of Königsberg. Besides, other assault detachments were operating on adjacent streets, and we stopped at almost every intersection to get more specific information on our current position, the enemy's position, and the overall situation.

During one of these halts, the signboard of a small hotel attracted my attention. Out of curiosity, I opened the entrance door and entered a spacious lobby. It was crowded with elderly women. There were at least five infirm persons sitting in wheelchairs among them. Two of them also suffered from hand tremors. Everybody looked terrified.

At the far end of the hall, there was some loud commotion. An elderly German was standing in the center of a group of four or five Soviet soldiers, who did not seem to be from our unit. The short and gray-haired German was wearing a dark blue uniform with gilt buttons, lace, and shoulder straps. The soldiers, evidently taking the German for an important military officer, were trying to drag him toward the exit. The old man resisted with all his might, shouting over and over again "Ich bin der portier!" "Ich bin der portier!" ("I'm the doorman!"). I couldn't remain indifferent to this situation, while understanding what the man was shouting. I intervened, explaining what the man was saying and why he was wearing this uniform (at the time, most of my compatriots were from rural areas and had never seen a doorman before). Then I advised the German to change out of his uniform immediately.

My translator's mission didn't stop yet, though. Just after the incident with the doorman was over, I heard from the corner of the lobby a loud female voice pronouncing in German, "Leave me alone, please. I'm fifty and I'm old enough to be your mother. . . ." Then I saw an unfamiliar Soviet soldier, who was embracing the resisting woman. I asked the solder if he understood what she had just said and, without waiting for his answer, I translated her words. This soldier, who was in his midtwenties, momentarily grew angry, stepped away from the woman, cursed in Russian at the top of his voice, and headed for the exit.

We continued to advance, and at noon our assault detachment approached the bridge across the Pregel River in the central part of the city. From this vantage point, we could see the outlines of two large buildings. Later I learned that these were the Royal Castle and the Königsberg Cathedral. They were prominent works of old architecture, but both now showed heavy damage caused by Royal Air Force (RAF) bombing raids in late August 1944 and Soviet bombardments prior to our final assault.

Soon we encountered guardsmen of Colonel Tolstikov's 1st Guards Rifle Division, part of the 11th Guards Army that was advancing from the opposite side of the river.[1] That meeting was one of the crucial events foreseen in the general plan for the battle. We had thus split the defending German force in two, which strengthened our confidence in achieving final victory. Soon after this linkup, our assault detachment redeployed to the northern outskirts of the city. Before dusk we took up position on the grounds of a German military hospital that was still intact and operational. There was a terrible spectacle by the blank wall, which fenced the grounds near the south side of the main building. We saw there a stack of several dozen scorched corpses—horrific evidence of the recent Anglo-American bombing raid.

The regimental headquarters settled down in a private house, about half a kilometer to the south of us, nearer to the center of the city. Our signalmen connected us with the headquarters by wire.

Nikolay Soin, four other officers, and I occupied a small corner room in the left wing of the main hospital building. Two guns of my battery were placed on the right side of the building, their muzzles facing an empty lot to the northeast. (The rest of my guns as well as the supply platoon hadn't yet found the right way to the hospital.) Two of Soin's soldiers—our sentries—dug themselves a small foxhole in the street, just outside the wall of the hospital wing. We could see them through the window. The situation had been quiet for the last several hours, but we hadn't managed to eat. However, the reigning calm and the moonless night put our exhausted soldiers into a deep sleep, in spite of their hunger. Some officers were dozing while sitting in chairs.

It was already far into the night when we were awakened by a strange noise. Simultaneously both sentries ran into our room shouting "Germans! Tanks!" Next we heard a gunshot not far from us, and shortly thereafter—a close burst of submachine gun fire. The telephone buzzed. Rubtsov, the regimental commander, was trying to figure out the strange situation: the headquarters personnel were fending off a German attack, while we were still in our position forward of them. All of us went outside, listening to the footsteps of running people and a desultory shooting in the street. We tried to discern what was going on in the street in the pitch darkness through a wire-mesh fence.

At that moment two armed German soldiers tumbled over the fence, practically falling on our heads. We quickly seized them and grabbed their carbines. Both Germans were unshaven and looked jaded, their age was around forty. One of them had been injured recently: his head was swathed in bandages. We took them back into our room and questioned them meticulously about the size of their group and how they had happened to appear in the midst of the Soviet positions. I served as the interpreter.

Here is what they told us, plus what we saw and learned for ourselves after dawn broke:

At the end of the day, while we were taking up position on the hospital grounds, many Germans had gathered in a small forest about 2 kilometers away. Their force was a motley group: the remnants of a few combat detachments, plus a few small groups and some individuals who had strayed from their units for a variety of reasons. By the time evening fell, approximately 300 people had gathered there, including several civilians and three women.

Some high-ranking officers took charge of the group. They decided to try and escape by taking the group back through the city by night in order to reach the main road that stretched westward along the bay. They planned to avoid combat and hoped to slip through our lines quietly, counting upon traditional Soviet carelessness and our soldiers' deep sleep.

A slowly moving "Tiger" led the group; a few cars followed it, after which the pedestrians walked in column. At first things went well. They passed our hospital, not even noticing the foxhole where our sentries were sleeping peacefully. Then they passed the location of the regimental headquarters, and had continued on about 300 meters, when the lead tank suddenly fell into a deep bomb crater. The entire column stopped.

Unfortunately for the fleeing group, at that very moment two Soviet artillerymen were making their way to a field gun, which was standing among some shrubs fencing a front yard. They were moving to relieve . . . the sleeping guard. Just as they reached the gun, they saw a car and several German soldiers standing around it some 15 meters away. The two relief sentries quickly woke up the sleeping artillerymen, and the crew of four prepared the gun and fired a shot directly at the car. Panic-stricken Germans broke into a run, and the artillerymen started firing at them with submachine guns. Looking for some cover from the fire, some Germans vaulted fences and ran into yards and houses. Others pressed themselves tightly against a fence, while the majority simply fled. Only a few of the Germans returned fire. The sudden sound of battle woke up many sleeping Soviet soldiers, who joined the artillery crew and opened fire on the disintegrating German column. The Germans retreated back into the forest, leaving behind at least ten corpses in the street.

As we questioned our two prisoners, the sound of shooting faded. Therefore Soin and I decided to send our German "guests" back into the forest, to try and persuade the other Germans to surrender. Once they reached their comrades, they were to spread the word that we were offering a guarantee of everyone's life, if he or she voluntarily surrendered. The "guests" agreed to fulfill this mission but asked us to return their carbines; otherwise they would be treated as deserters. With no questions we disabled their carbines and handed them back to our "truce envoys," who headed off in the direction of the forest. Soin ordered them to return by 6:30 A.M.

In some half hour my battery's field kitchen, along with two additional guns and an ammunition wagon, finally arrived. They brought us our "missing" dinner from the night before, along with the "People's Commissar's 100 grams" of vodka. I received my personal alcohol portion—a flask of the captured Jamaican rum. Along with Nikolay and two other officers, we almost emptied the flask. Some dozed off after filling their bellies with food; others talked with each other while smoking light German cigarettes.

Unexpectedly, a medical orderly of the regimental headquarters entered our room and asked if there was somebody who knew the

152 German language. Four headquarters guards had just carried into
the hospital Lance Corporal Yuriy Kostikov, who had been seriously
wounded when several Germans had tried to break into the headquarters position. In a short skirmish, Yuriy killed four of the attack-
ers on the spot.

Following the medical orderly, I entered a dimly lit casualty ward.
In the light of my flashlight I saw that Yuriy was still breathing, but
his face was inanimate. There was a group of German doctors and
our soldiers beside Kostikov. A doctor, who introduced himself as
the head surgeon, explained that Yuriy's wound was in the abdomen,
which was almost always a mortal wound. I knew that, of course,
but under the influence of the rum, I told the head surgeon, almost
at a shout, that I was making him responsible for Kostikov's life.
Alas, the German surgeons couldn't save the life of the seventeen-
year-old hero.[2]

I returned from the hospital still heated from my contact with the
surgeons. Soin was sitting in a chair half asleep. I roused him a little,
and we both drank up the rest of my rum. Dawn was breaking.
There was no sound of shooting. We both longed to sleep.

Suddenly our sentries came in, both looking frightened. After
their shout "The Germans are coming again!" all of us woke up instantly. In a minute everybody was running toward the regimental
headquarters. By chance I was the last. While running, for no particular reason, I gave a glance at my watch—6:30 A.M. sharp. It seems
as if I wasn't fully intoxicated at that time, because I remembered:
6:30 was the same time that we had ordered our "truce envoys" to
return. An idea flashed through my mind: "Maybe those Germans
were coming in order to surrender to us?" I stopped running and
turned back to look through my field glasses that were always sus-
pended around my neck. I spotted a number of dim human figures,
but I still wasn't sure whether my assumption was true. I hesitated
for a while and then strode forth resolutely to meet the Germans. I
advanced about 100 meters and then looked through the field glasses
again. This time I almost began dancing with joy: I could see a man
with a white bandage on his head in advance of a narrow but long
column. At once my inner nervous tremor calmed down, and in a
minute the whole column, all unarmed, stood before me.

The bandaged "truce envoy" reported to me, and I, being young
and a little tipsy, "raised my peacock tail." I ordered them to form

one rank and to count their numbers aloud. There were 102 prisoners in the group, but not one officer among them.

I took my stand across from the center of the rank and made a speech to the prisoners. (Now I think that my speech was an example of the propaganda of the time, but I remember that I delivered it quite sincerely.) I told them that after they gave themselves up voluntarily their lives would be spared, and later they would have the opportunity to see their families again. I'm not sure that these promises were kept.

The Germans listened to my words carefully. It was obvious that they completely understood my German pronunciation. This fact encouraged me, and I started shouting some slogans. The first was "Nieder mit dem Krieg!" ("Down with the war!"), and in response sounded unanimous "Hoch!" ("Hurrah!"). Even louder was their resounding cheer to my "Hitler kaput!" ("Hitler is finished!"). I enjoyed such a reaction and was eager to continue the meeting. But some disorder on the left flank diverted me from my speech. I saw a few soldiers of our troop who had unexpectedly appeared there. It was easy to guess what was happening—the lads were taking watches off the prisoners. (It was then a custom among Soviet troops to remove any watch from any German. The point was that in the Soviet Union at that time not many people possessed a watch, and it was a sign of prestige to carry one. At the same time, most adults in Germany had an opportunity to get relatively inexpensive watches.) Those soldiers' action prompted me to think of my own self-interest. I told the prisoners: "Now I invite you to give me some good watches as a souvenir for a Soviet officer." In a minute both breast pockets of my officer blouse were full of various watches. Later, I found that most of these watches were the cheapest, die-cast sort.

Then I ordered all our soldiers but one to return to their positions. After restoring order to the rank, I commanded the Germans to follow me. The single designated soldier, armed with a submachine gun, brought up the rear of the column.

We arrived at regimental headquarters. The officer on duty was greatly surprised at the number of prisoners I was leading, and directed us to the next yard. Two soldiers were keeping watch there over a few more prisoners, who were sitting on the lawn. I handed over "my" 102 prisoners to the guards and, utterly proud of myself, returned to the hospital.

154   Soin's field kitchen stood by the front door of the wing. In our room, breakfast had just started. This time, instead of rum, we drank some pure alcohol. After a frugal snack and a short smoke, I lay down on a narrow medical couch and covered myself with my raincoat.

My orderly woke me at noon: "Guard Lieutenant, get up! An order to leave the city has arrived." I could hardly open my eyes. While getting myself in order, I recalled the giddy occurrences of the past night. When I emerged, the battery was ready to march. In regimental column we moved off westward along the Frisch Haff Bay. The main part of the Königsberg garrison had been captured, and we were now pressing the rest of the demoralized enemy toward Pillau.

Only one month was separating us from the victorious end of the war.

Finally—The Great Victory!

By this time the enemy had changed beyond recognition. The Germans couldn't hold fast at any of several lines of resistance on our way westward. By late April we were already within just 15 kilometers of Pillau. Here we celebrated our traditional 1 May holiday in a coniferous forest. Leonid Pryadkin, the division's political department photographer, came to see the regimental artillerymen and took numerous snapshots of us. The next day we entered Pillau without meeting any resistance.

The main part of the Zemland grouping of German forces had been evacuated from Pillau by sea. Its rearguard detachments had retreated to the Danziger Spit (now the Vistula Spit).

After the regiment entered the city, I succeeded in convincing the quartermaster that my battery could be lodged in a small suburb about 1.5 kilometers from the center of Pillau, where all the other detachments were being quartered. My trump card was the wheeled tractor "Lanz Bulldog," along with a large trailer, that our sergeant major had gotten hold of somewhere in the previous week. By means of such property we were able to reach the headquarters in some ten minutes.

We stayed there for two weeks, and it was so wonderful—far from regimental command! The battery's personnel occupied three private houses with no owners (the overwhelming majority of local residents had left the city in March and April).

During the initial days in Pillau we idled about openly. The end of the war was in the air. Only the rare, dull echoes of gunnery, which drifted to us from the Danziger Spit, reminded us that the war was still not over. Then these sounds stopped as well, and rumors came that Germany had surrendered.

In the early morning of 9 May, I received a command: at 10:00 A.M.—a regimental assembly; at 11:00—a solemn division assembly on the occasion of the end of the war. I let the battery's personnel know the long-awaited news and ordered everyone to put himself in order: to sew on a fresh under-collar strip; to brush off the dust from the boots and shoes; and, for those who needed it, to get shaved.

The solemn assembly of our battle-tested division took place on the main square of the city, by the *rathaus* (city hall). By that time the full designation of our division was 87th Guards, Perekopskaya, Order of Suvorov Second Class, Order of the Red Banner, Rifle Division.

The division commander delivered a short speech. The formation accompanied it with resounding hurrahs in unison. Our brass band played marches and the Soviet national anthem. Two photographers shot numerous photographs. When Pryadkin appeared not far from me, I called out to him. Leonid halted, directed his camera's lens at me, and clicked the shutter. In a few days I sent the picture to my beloved Vera.

What were my feelings and thoughts once I learned of the great victory? To tell the truth, there were no wild demonstrations of joy, no loud cheers, no extravagant escapades. There was just an extreme happiness for coming off almost unhurt. There were dozens of strong, friendly embraces and a lot of quick drinks, too. But the main thought that filled my mind at the time was the hope of reuniting soon with Vera, my parents, and my little brother.

My dream was fulfilled on 30 December 1945. I describe the meeting in the final part of the book.

May Their Memory Live Forever

This page of my reminiscences of the war I dedicate to the memory of the soldiers, sergeants, and officers of our battery who fell during the war in 1942–1945. Here are their last names:

Abramov	Sabanin
Avakumov	Savoskin
Gorbunov	Sharafutdinov
Grigoryan	Starykh
Kiselev	Suchkov
Kolbanov	Suleymanov
Loshakov	Tetyukov
Rakhmatullayev	Zhigur

The Kobylyanskiy family in Vinnitsa, 1936. From left to right: the author's father, Grigoriy Isaakovich, at age forty-two; the thirteen-year-old author; the author's five-year-old brother, Tolya; and the author's mother, Evgeniya Abramovna, age forty.

The author at sixteen years of age, Kiev, 1939.

My one and only love, Vera Makovchik, at sixteen years of age, 1939.

The author as a freshman at the Kiev Industrial Institute, 1940.

The author as a Central Asia Industrial Institute sophomore in Tashkent, 1941.

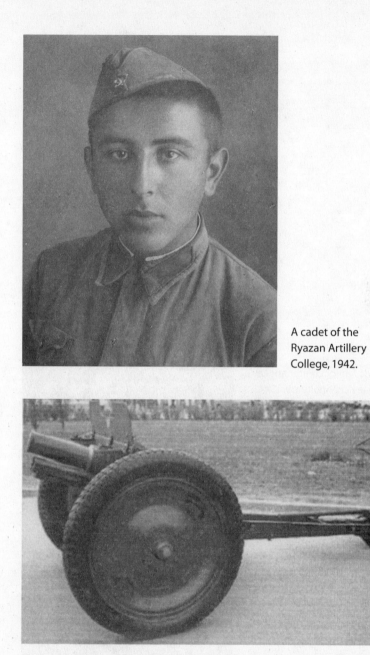

A cadet of the
Ryazan Artillery
College, 1942.

Three-inch regimental field gun (Model 1927/39). (Source: www.battlefield.ru)

Guards Senior Lieutenant Lev
Nikolaevich Vinokurov, 1944.

Guards Lieutenant Ivan
Fedorovich Kamchatnyy, 1944.

Vasiliy Alexeevich Panteleev,
1980.

A gun crew fires near a riverbank, November 1943. (Source: www.battlefield.ru)

After the battle for
Perekop, April 1944.

Lieutenant Boris Glotov (right) and me in Lithuania in August 1944. Six
months later Boris was killed in action in East Prussia.

Guards Sergeant Major
Yakov Stepanovich
Zakernichnyy after his
release from a rear area
hospital, 1945.

East Prussia, 1945. May Day celebration in a forest. From left to right: Brechko,
Kobylyanskiy, and Dmitriev.

East Prussia, 1945. May Day celebration in a forest. A group of rifle regiment artillerymen (from left to right): Karutsyak, Abidov, Voronin, Vasyuk, Lyubchenko, Brechko, Kobylyanskiy, and Brik.

Pillau, East Prussia, May 9, 1945. Victory Day ceremonial formation of the 87th Guards Perekopskaya Rifle Division, awarded with Order of the Red Banner and the Order of Suvorov, Second Class.

Letters to my dearests, 1942–1945.

Pillau, July 1945. Bound for the Motherland. We practice boarding a freight train for our return home. The author is leaning on the short barrel of the 76-mm field gun.

Waiting for my discharge from the army in Kozelsk, November 1945.

We are together at last! Kiev, January 1946.

The author as a junior at the Kiev Polytechnic Institute, February 1947.

There are three of us now! Our firstborn's first birthday, January 1948.

Veterans visiting the Mekenzy Mountains area, May 1969. In the first row (from left to right): Kobylyanskiy, General Tymchik, Berezovskiy, Karpushinskiy, Vinokurov, and Savchenko.

Sevastopol, May 1969. Our division veterans by the monument in honor and memory of the soldiers of the 2nd Guards Army.

Gathering of division veterans in Kiev, May 9, 1970. From left to right: Kobylyanskiy, Korchagina, Vinokurov's wife, Onufreychuk, Livshits-Kanarskaya, Vinokurov, Kochetov, Savchenko, Sapozhnikov, Bamm, and Soin.

Gathering in Kiev, 1971. From left to right: Sapozhnikov, Kamchatnyy, Vera, and me.

Division veterans visiting the memorial on the Mamaev Kurgan, Volgograd, 1977.

During the veterans' gathering in Donetsk, 1980. I am answering questions from the "Red Pathfinders" of Tsyurupinsk.

The author's portrait on
the fortieth anniversary
of the Victory, 1985.

The author's
contemporary portrait,
2006.

The Königsberg Cathedral, still showing battle damage, with the tombstone of the great German philosopher Immanuel Kant in the foreground. Kaliningrad, 1971

Along the Kaliningrad-Baltiysk road, 1971. Memorial marking the common grave of around 2,000 Soviet soldiers and officers fallen in battles on the Zemland (Samland) Peninsula in 1945. By tradition, newlyweds from surrounding towns and villages bring flowers to the memorial.

Along the Kaliningrad-Baltiysk road, 1971. The author near the tombstone of Aleksandr Kosmodemianskiy, Hero of Soviet Union, who died in action there in April 1945.

Kaliningrad, 1971. One of several small fortifications in Königberg's defenses within the city's boundaries. Note the battle damage.

The Bismarckturm on the top of Hill 111.4 (a copy from a prewar German photo).

Part III

Various Reflections on the War

Chapter 14

An Important Factor in Our Victory

In this chapter I do not intend to address the causes of the war or the course of military operations. Nor will I compare the political structures and regimes of the belligerents, or their manpower and military-industrial potentials, or the quantity and quality of their armaments, or, finally, their war strategies. I also do not intend to emphasize the importance of the Allies' contribution to our victory. Certainly, all these factors were extremely important. However, I'm not a military historian, I'm just an ordinary participant in the war and an eyewitness to many historical events. Therefore, I will share with the readers only one of my convictions, which have come from my own experience, that is, from what I've seen myself and what I've obtained from personal contact with my brothers-in-arms.

I'm deeply convinced that a substantial contribution to our victory was the solidarity among the multiethnic ranks of our troops. Today, after the collapse of the USSR, when nationalism is raising its head everywhere, one might believe that factor is a mere fable or, at best, a sincere error made by a person who has been stupefied by the Communist propaganda of that time. Absolutely not! I reach this conclusion based exclusively on the everyday life of the multiethnic personnel in our battery, as well as in other detachments of our rifle regiment.

Here is the approximate ethnic composition of the roughly 100 battery members that I can remember:

Russian—35
Ukrainian—30
Kazakh—14
Tatar—6
Uzbek—6
Bashkir—4
Jew—2
Turkmen—2
Armenian—1
Belorussian—1

When people look death in the eye together, suffer the hardships of war together, help each other through hard times and dangerous situations, and share a crust of bread, they never reflect on their fellow soldier's nationality. I know of no incident of sharp interethnic discord or friction among those who fought alongside me. On the contrary, I remember only many examples of sincere, fraternal friendship between frontline soldiers of different nationalities, and my personal experience confirms this phenomenon. At the same time, however, I do not want to ignore the fact that there were some nationalists, as well as some chauvinists and anti-Semites, among us (although this concerned primarily relationships between different levels of command). From my perspective, these were only rare exceptions.

As far as I remember it, not long before the end of the war, Stalin issued an order to organize a few infantry divisions based upon individual nationalities, particularly Armenian. I remember that at that time the order bewildered me, and I now regard it as a serious mistake, even if it was arranged to please the Diaspora in order to receive some financial support from abroad. In my opinion, anything that divided the Soviet people on the basis of their ethnicity or religion would inevitably harm the Soviet armed forces.

In that regard, I should say a few words about a phenomenon that disappointed me somewhat when I came to learn more about the war veterans movement in the United States. While observing a traditional Veterans Day parade for the first time, I was surprised at the way the colorful procession was divided into separate columns with black veterans, Catholic veterans, Italians veterans, Jewish veterans, and so on, all marching separately. Did not all of you, our companions-in-arms, fight shoulder to shoulder regardless of your ethnicity, skin color, and religion? If so, why then do you march as different associations, first and foremost, and why have I heard nothing here in the United States about the brotherhoods of veterans who fought together or at least served in the same branch of combat arm (as was common in my native country before its collapse)?

What War Taught Me

Naturally, over the course of the war, I gained considerable combat experience. But at the same time, I learned many things that didn't have any direct connection to my artillery profession. I became proficient in using spades and shovels; mastered the riding and care of horses; learned how to roll a *samokrutka* (a hand-rolled cigarette from a piece of newspaper and any sort of tobacco), how to smoke *samosad* (homegrown tobacco) and *makhorka,* and how to make a fire with two pebbles (*kresalo*); developed the ability to drink "moonshine" of any quality; enriched my vocabulary not only with curse words and foul language but also with treasures of folklore—special folk words and wise sayings; and, finally, learned at least two dozen Russian and Ukrainian folk songs.

But the main lessons of life that I received in the war concerned the realm of human character and behavior. At the front, I had occasion to rub shoulders with many dozens of soldiers, officers, and civilians. (In our battery alone, which had a nominal strength of seventy, over three years at least twice that number passed through its ranks. We lost sixteen killed alone, and many were injured or transferred to the rifle companies!) Besides, I had quite a few acquaintances in other detachments of our regiment and division.

There were people of different ages and ethnicities among the men I knew or encountered. The difference between the levels of education was particularly broad: from about 3 percent of the soldiers who were completely illiterate (most of them were natives of the Central Asia republics and hardly understood any spoken Russian) to the less than 2 percent of the officers and soldiers who were highly educated (including those with incomplete institute or university education, like me). But such demographic data are not my concern in this chapter. I want to talk about some aspects of human behavior in the war, which were quite often completely exposed to me. It is fair to say that only under extreme conditions, such as war, do the human soul and mind become revealed in full.

The soldiers, sergeants, and officers around me were, in the majority, respectable people. Some were true examples of courage and
of allegiance to their soldier's duty. Among those, first of all I'd name
Tetyukov, Vinokurov, Zakernichnyy, Panteleev, Kamchatnyy, Ismaylov, Khudoley, Zhigur, Kargabaev, Nemukhin, and Suyunov. (I'd also
like to mention that many people of minority national origin fought
no worse than did the Russians and Ukrainians.)

The behavior of these people fully corresponded to my youthful
ideals of people and of life. But the war opened my eyes to some
negative aspects of human nature as well. It taught me to view
things in a more sober light. I call your attention to the few following stories and facts that did most to enlighten me.

* * *

Twice, in both Ukraine and in Lithuania, I was a witness (and hardly
escaped being a victim) to the nasty behavior of some anonymous
men who served in the division rear units. Both times it happened
when Soviet ground attack Ilyushin-2 (Il-2) airplanes (the Germans
deservedly called them "Black Death") were making their way toward the enemy trenches. As always, the Il-2s were flying at a very
low altitude, and just their thundering roar as they flew closely overhead scared everybody on the ground stiff.

In order to mark the enemy trenches for the approaching airplanes, and to prevent mistaken attack on our own positions, our infantrymen would send up signal flares toward the enemy's location.
On these two occasions, however, some men in our rear service area
(at headquarters, in the political department, in the supply services,
etc.) lost all self-control, became panic-stricken, and, to avoid "friendly
bombardment," started letting off dozens of flares. Those dastardly
cowards misled the pilots into believing our rear area marked the
frontline positions. So on each occasion, our positions came under
an avalanche of fire from our own Il-2s. We deeply despised these
anonymous villains, who put hundreds of comrade-soldiers at mortal risk. But the culprits were never brought to light. These episodes
taught me that in war, one could meet people of that sort as well.

* * *

Here is another story, not so horrible as the previous one but still
very edifying for me. It was late September 1943. The front line lay

2 kilometers from the town of Bolshoy Tokmak, Ukraine. We had been stuck in our trenches before the German Wotan Line for a long time, more than two weeks. That day my turn came for a short pass in the battery rear that was situated in the town. I had thirty-six hours available to wash, change out of my filthy clothing, and rest. The acting commander of the supply platoon, Junior Lieutenant Vasiliy Bondarenko, gave me a cordial welcome. First of all, he ordered his subordinates to warm up a few buckets of water and to fetch a bar of soap and a change of underwear. After I finished all my hygienic procedures, Bondarenko treated me to a plentiful dinner with a good dose of alcohol.

I slept that night like a prince. The next morning, after a large, satisfying breakfast, Vasiliy and I sat outside on a bench and had an unhurried, heart-to-heart talk while smoking hand-rolled cigarettes. At that time, a horse-drawn wagon entered the yard, and the deputy sergeant major proudly reported to Bondarenko, "Ten pairs of repaired boots delivered!" My friend immediately shouted to his subordinates, "Hey, old men! If you need boots, try those on right now!" I became indignant that the supply platoon's men, not the frontline soldiers, got first crack at the boots. And I expressed what I was thinking and feeling to my hospitable host's face. Vasiliy smiled indulgently, then indirectly responded with a rhetorical question: "Can one remain dry after immersion in water?" In such a frank and lucid form, he gave me a lesson on "how to exploit your official standing for selfish ends."

Thanks to this lesson, so to say, "on the lowest level," I stopped wondering about what some commanders of higher rank might be doing. After the meeting with Bondarenko, I had no doubt when a friend told me that our regimental commander more than once ordered and obtained *dozens of meters* of white cotton fabric from our field warehouse for his personal use.

Once, in a recently seized town in East Prussia, I saw a lieutenant and two soldiers, all from our regiment headquarters, entering impressive mansions and removing paintings enclosed by gilded frames. They loaded the loot onto a following wagon. In response to my question, they explained that everything was going back to the regimental command, in spite of the official order that limited *any* of our military men to sending home just one parcel a month weighing up to ten kilograms.

The chief of the regimental personnel department, Captain Ka-zinskiy, exploited his official status in a very barefaced and disgusting manner. He was in charge of only four subordinates, including a female typist. They registered current regimental personnel; counted our battle casualties; mailed death notifications to the families of the KIAs; and processed award recommendations. Can you imagine that by the end of the war, this man, who sat permanently at a desk far behind the front lines, was decorated with five (!) Orders of the Red Star?

The privileged status of many commanders was unlimited. Using the principle of undivided authority as a cover, they behaved arbitrarily without taking anyone else or anything else into consideration. I'm sure that there were many former commanders of that kind among the first postwar "Soviet grandees."

Looking back at my own frontline experience, I discovered that in some degree I was a sinner, too. During a considerable period of time, I made use of my official standing with a view to protect a special person's life (though it wasn't a question of selfish ends, but . . .).

As you may recall, Vera had relatives who lived in the town of Bolshoy Tokmak, and I used the proximity of our position along the front line to this town to pay them a visit. Naturally, I asked them about their life under German occupation. Among other things, I learned that a year before, Vera's cousin had married a village guy of little education, named Shura Chernyy. He was my age. During one of the meetings with the family, Vera's aunt asked me to take Shura into our battery, where I could keep a protective eye on him. The regimental personnel department had no problem enlisting Shura as a wagon driver in our battery. Everything was done legally, and Shura became, informally, my personal ward. I started sinning later, whenever our rifle battalions suffered a shortage of infantrymen.

After heavy casualties in the infantry, the initial way to reinforce the rifle battalions was to sweep other detachments, such as batteries, the field engineer company, and so on, for men to transfer into the battered battalions—supply clerks, drivers, even some artillerymen. We called this action a "total mobilization." Of course, as a wagon driver, my ward Chernyy was an eligible candidate for transfer during these "total mobilizations." But I was always afraid of how Vera's kin would treat me if Shura should perish while fighting as an infantryman. So I often asked the battery commander to transfer someone else. After a year, once I became the battery commander, I taught Chernyy how to operate the field telephone and appointed him as a battery signalman. In this position he was not subject to transfer into a rifle detachment. In such a way, by hook or by crook, I helped him to stay alive.

* * *

The next lessons that the war taught me were about theft and thieves. Unfortunately, during the war I had many occasions to witness thieves in operation.

A young Siberian, Nikolay Starykh, a soldier in my platoon, was an unsurpassed expert and enthusiast in stealing. He couldn't pass by any thing that lay vulnerable or exposed to him—he had a true passion for theft.

Usually, after enemy troops fell back to new lines, our regiment had to make long marches in pursuit. During these marches, trucks of other units would pass us every now and then. Most of the trucks were loaded with a variety of goods, which became Nikolay's plunder. He would leave our column of march, chase down the truck, and climb onto the pile of goods. In the blink of an eye, a wide assortment of items would begin flying off the truck, landing on the side of the road: soldiers' kit bags, loaves of bread, cans of meat, padded jackets, footgear, small shovels, mess tins, or other similar items. Nikolay's expropriation operations lasted only about a minute, whereupon he would fearlessly hop off the moving truck, pick up all his loot, and then return to his position in the column.

Once Nikolay was deeply embarrassed when it became obvious that both his "captured" boots were made for the same foot. He explained his blunder, "I was in too much of a hurry."

I remember how during a night march in Lithuania, Starykh disappeared for at least two hours. After returning, he boasted of his success with an apiary he had encountered in a nearby hamlet. Nikolay emptied a beehive there and treated himself to honey to his heart's content. He brought one honeycomb back to the column and shared some sweet pieces with a few of his friends. Later, the morning light revealed that Starykh's face was swollen and almost unrecognizable: one eye was completely closed by the swelling, the other narrowed to a tiny slit. It looked like the bees had repaid him for his marauding.

On 4 February 1945, Starykh made his last attempt to grab loot before others had a chance. The Germans had just fallen back from a village close to Pillau. Everybody knew that it was common practice for the Germans to bombard mercilessly a village they had just abandoned, within a half hour of their retreat. Therefore, our infantrymen were still waiting outside the village for the barrage to fall. But Nikolay couldn't wait; he went into the village and entered deserted houses one by one to take the most valuable "trophies." As bad luck would have it, he was outdoors when the expected bombardment began. A small fragment of a mortar shell struck Nikolay's chest and killed him instantly.

* * *

Nikolay's iron rule was not to rob from his brothers in arms; moreover, he often shared his spoils with his friends. However, on my military path, I met some thieves of another sort: they "operated" among soldiers and officers who served and fought in the same detachment with them. A few times I became a victim of such "comrades."

The first time I doubted my childish, naive belief that thieves were easily recognizable, and could not exist in a military environment, was as early as 1942. At the time I was still a cadet at the military artillery college. While our platoon was collecting firewood in a nearby forest, a fellow cadet unbuttoned the breast pocket of my soldier's blouse that was hanging among some others and pilfered all the money from it.

The next time when I suffered because of my unwarranted trustfulness was in early March 1945. Unexpectedly I learned that our regimental cashier, a decent and trustworthy person, was going to leave for a week or so to see his relatives who were living in the city of Ufa. That was a special city for me—my sweetheart Vera was living there, too. So I decided at any price to send a gift to her through this man. I hadn't anything suitable, but soon I remembered our young soldier Sharafutdinov, who had recently been boasting of his "trophy"—a beautiful, tiny lady's watch in a gilded case. I found the guy and begged him earnestly to sell the watch to me. Without hesitation, I accepted the price that he quoted. I gave the watch and a note with Vera's address to the cashier. I had no doubts that Vera would be delighted with my gift, and I impatiently waited for her reply letter. Alas, week after week passed, but my "courier" didn't return, and there was no reply from Vera about my gift, which I had praised in advance in my note.

Finally, in early May the cashier came back and explained to me that my watch had been stolen. However, his explanation was strange, and the excuse seemed very dubious. Moreover, thereafter he diligently avoided meeting me. So my attempt to hand a valuable present through "a friend" resulted in receiving one more lesson about the sinful side of human nature.

In the fall of 1945, when the war was already over and we were quartered in the little town of Kozelsk, a brother officer robbed me. I kept my pride and joy—my prized box calf boots—under my bed, in an empty ammunition box. One day, my roommate, who was waiting for a new assignment, received the long-expected call. He snatched a moment when I was on duty, took my boots from the box, and . . . that was the last anybody saw him.

I must admit that, in spite of the lessons I learned in the army, it took me many years to get rid of (to my chagrin, not completely) my youthful naïveté. As the Russian saying goes, "Human simplicity is worse than theft."

* * *

The war acquainted me with one more category of people whose actions entailed or could entail irremediable consequences. The matter concerns only those drinkers who, when full of liquor, become totally unable to control their actions. Fortunately, they were not numerous.

It must be acknowledged that almost all of our troops were "lovers of the bottle." The chief exceptions were our soldiers from the Central Asian republics, whose Islamic faith prohibited them from eating pork or drinking alcohol. They even shunned the "government's 100 grams." All other soldiers never missed a chance to warm themselves up or raise their spirits with vodka or any other strong drink.

There were some drinking binges in our battery as well (naturally, when we were not in action). The most memorable occasions of such sort were in Chulakovka, Ukraine (New Year and Orthodox Christmas 1944), and in Pillau, East Prussia (June 1945). But all our booze-ups went well with no excesses. Usually we finished with loud talk, folk songs, and a little monkey business. But there was among us a man who turned out to be capable of a terrible action when strongly drunk. The matter involved our thirty-year-old deputy sergeant major, Fedor Zhurakhovskiy. Before the war he had served as a militiaman in the city of Kiev. In our battery he became an inseparable friend with a twenty-two-year-old artillery mechanic, a Siberian named Boris Sabanin. Once, when both men were extremely intoxicated, they started quarreling heatedly with each other. Fedor, in a frenzy, shouted brutally, "If you don't shut up, I'm gonna kill you!" Boris provocatively threw open his military greatcoat and dared Fedor: "Go ahead, shoot!" Zhurakovskiy fired a burst that killed Boris on the spot.

Fedor was assigned to the penal battalion after this incident. I think it likely that he survived, because the day of the tragedy was just three months before the war ended.

* * *

I also can't forget our great distress because of the unexpected and inexplicable action of a drunken Senior Lieutenant Tarasov, a rifle company commander. The event happened in early fall 1944, in Lithuania. That day our regiment was in pursuit of retreating German troops. We were moving through a mixed forest along a straight, narrow glade. Our destination was a hamlet located just beyond the forest. When we had approached within 2 kilometers of the hamlet, our column stopped. The forward scouts had already reached the edge of the forest and then returned to report on the enemy. They had discovered that at least thirty Germans were digging in along the outskirts of that hamlet. It looked as if they weren't expecting our appearance so soon, so there was an opportunity to catch the enemy unawares. In a few minutes every company and battery commander received an order: "Deploy into small units. Making no noise, move forward to the edge of the forest. Be ready for a synchronized attack of all units. Start signal—green flare."

Soon, all the infantry companies began deploying both to the right and to the left of the glade. My guns were placed in concealed positions at the edge of the forest. Meanwhile, thanks to my binoculars, I watched the enemy in detail. Some thirty men, most of them with their backs turned toward us, were digging a trench. I couldn't see the tops of their boots, so I estimated the depth of the trench as about a half meter. Nothing seemed to be spooking the Germans, and they looked totally relaxed while they worked. It was impossible to imagine a more advantageous situation! I already anticipated the future success of our surprise attack. At that time, a few orderlies delivered the warning: "Attention to all! About five minutes remain to the flare!" Everybody became tensed for action in absolute silence. But suddenly all our plans and hopes came crashing down as a red-cheeked rider on a white horse rushed out from the forest with a pistol in his hand. It was the blind-drunk Tarasov! Dashingly galloping toward the hamlet while continuing to spur the horse, he gave a shout, "For the motherland, for Stalin!" and began firing wildly. The Germans were startled into action, quickly opened fire at the rider, and took up position in the unfinished trench. At once the horse and rider crashed to the earth, but our "hero" survived the fall. He seemed to sober up instantly and started crawling back to the forest. The enemy's organized fire repulsed our attack, which followed upon Tarasov's "sortie," and we suffered some casualties. When darkness fell, the firing died down, and at daybreak our regiment entered a deserted hamlet. This absurd failure instead of an undoubted victory caused bitter disappointment.

Did the "cavalry attack" entail some consequence to the sot? I don't remember any punishment but know that he continued to serve as a company commander. If I had been Tarasov's commander, he would come out the worse for what he had done!

* * *

This chapter contains mainly negative characters. Does it mean that such people formed a majority at the front? No, and I emphasize, no! I was just talking exclusively about aspects of human character that I had not experienced before the war and did not really anticipate before war revealed them. The prevalent majority of our soldiers and officers were decent people and steadfast warriors. With all my respect, I described or mentioned many of them in other chapters of this memoir.

Letters from Afar

It is well known that every soldier's thoughts during the war were directed toward his family, parents, and sweethearts. The only way to communicate with them was through the military mail system. No envelope and no stamp were necessary if the letter was addressed to or from the front. You just wrote your letter on one side of a sheet of any sort of writing paper (or a page from a copybook); then you folded the sheet so that it formed a triangle, with the blank side out. It remained only to write the address on one side of the triangle. It was absolutely free for both sender and addressee.

It was also very convenient for censorship: the censor just had to unfold the "triangle" and check what was written inside. (All military mail was censored. When the censor found some pieces of inadmissible text, he or she blackened it out. So, once in a letter to my mother I absentmindedly mentioned the name of a city where we had recently fought; the censor blackened it out. The evidence of the censor's scrutiny was a stamp, "Checked by military censor number . . . ," which was usually printed on the blank back side of the "triangle." The serviceman's address was written on the front side of the "triangle." It consisted of the five-digit number of the so-called Field Post Station (that represented the code of the unit), with a one-letter extension (the detachment's code) and the addressee's name. So, my military address was "Field Post Station 19637-E, to Kobylyanskiy."

Everybody at the front was homesick and impatiently waited for letters from home. But the system of mail delivery was so slow! According to my experience, the average time of delivery during stagnant periods of the war was at least three weeks. However, sometimes we went up to two months or even longer without receiving any mail. As a result, you might receive several letters all at once, or, if you were less fortunate, you'd never receive it: sometimes a lot of mail simply disappeared (for example, because of an air bombardment).

* * *

Besides the mail, there was another, more desirable way to contact your dear ones—by going on leave. But, as far as I know, in our division only a few soldiers were ever given leave during the three years of my service. I remember these few occasions. The first leave was an award to gun crew commander Baziroshvili, whose antitank gun destroyed six of Manstein's tanks in December 1942 (see chapter 5).

The second man who was awarded with a leave was a former soldier of our own battery. His first name was Mussa (I forgot his last name), and he was of Turkmen origin. In the summer of 1944, during an ordinary "total mobilization," Mussa had been transferred into one of our rifle battalions. In early fall 1944 he brought in a very important German prisoner for interrogation and received the leave as his reward.

The next lucky man that I knew who succeeded in receiving a leave was my closest frontline friend, Ivan Kamchatnyy. In early January 1945, quite unexpectedly he bumped into our division commander, Colonel Tymchik. Ivan took advantage of his chance: he told our highest commander about his parents' suffering under German occupation and asked for a short leave to help them rebuild the family home. Tymchik didn't refuse; he sympathized with Kamchatnyy because his own wife and two daughters not long before had been suffering under German occupation as well.

In the preceding chapter I mentioned our regimental cashier, who was given leave, too. It turned out that not only frontline soldiers but also rear service clerks were awarded with leave. Why?

* * *

At the front I was one of those who received letters more or less regularly. My main correspondents were my mother and Vera.

Mother's letters were quite short and optimistic. She never complained outright of the difficulties in life that she and my little brother were experiencing as evacuees. But I was able to read between the lines and sensed how they were suffering in their godforsaken village of Inzer, Bashkiriya. I answered mother whenever a pause between battles would permit it. I sent her 600 rubles monthly in order to help them at least a little.

The correspondence with my sweetheart Vera was quite different. The long separation didn't cool my heart; I always remembered Vera and wrote her lots about my feelings. And my greatest joy during wartime was to receive one of Vera's letters. I'm so sorry that I didn't have the opportunity to preserve even one of her letters, though I received many dozens of them.

I experienced a real happiness whenever the regiment mailman brought me a long-anticipated message. I knew in advance that I would find in it not only some news about Vera's life and studies but also many heartfelt lines of love, anxiety over me, anguish over our separation, and hopes for my return. Every letter from Vera was like a holiday for me, and often I shared the joy, which overflowed within me, with my close frontline friends. I read them aloud excerpts from Vera's letters (my friends responded in kind).

One can get a clear idea of Vera's letters and what they meant to me from excerpts of two of my letters to her that I will cite here. The letters were written about one and half years apart, but they are very similar:

> . . . What a happiness came to me today: I received your letter, so wonderful, tender and affectionate! . . . Your letters, my dear Vera, enliven me. There is nothing more joyful and pleasant to me than seeing an answer handwritten by you.

> . . . I know what a happiness it is to hold carefully the letter with the familiar lovely handwriting on it. What a joy it is to take in my beloved's straight even lines at first hastily, and then to read them very attentively, in order to savor them.

I often asked Vera to send me a photo of her, and five times during the war she fulfilled my wishes (the pictures were sent in envelopes). I can't begin to describe my joyous feelings whenever I looked at my sweetheart's wonderful features.

As I mentioned above, all the letters from the front line to the rear and vice versa traveled very slowly, often requiring many weeks before they reached the addressee. One such delay caused Vera to suspect that I no longer loved her. To ease her concerns, I replied with a letter that amounted to a new declaration of love for her, which was the best way to clear up the mess.

To get around some of the censorship restrictions, we often re-sorted to different ruses such as Aesopian language, and so on. For example, to let Vera know that my regiment was going to fight in the Crimea, I wrote, "I hope I'll visit Uncle Misha soon" (my uncle lived in the Crimea before the war). As a result, we found out a lit-tle more about each other's true circumstances. In some letters I described surrounding landscapes and characteristics of the lands where I fought (Lithuania, Latvia, East Prussia).

Once a new topic appeared in Vera's letter: she wanted to join the war. I became uneasy and in my next letter tried to dissuade her from acting too hastily. But soon Vera repeated her wish, and I wrote her the following lines. "I already wrote you about the fate of young frontline women. And you were supposed to heed my words. How-ever, you are still 'ashamed' about not being here. . . . I want only to add that if I should happen ever to lose you, I'll fight only half as hard as I'm fighting now. So you can consider yourself an invisible participant in all that I'm doing here."

Vera neatly kept all my letters. That was a priceless assistance for this memoir in helping me recollect my wartime events and experiences.

* * *

Besides personal letters, there was a special kind of correspondence during the war in our country. Sometimes a regiment would re-ceived unprompted letters with a random, general addressee, such as "To the best machine gunner of the regiment" or "To the bravest scout," and so on. As a rule, girls or young women wrote these let-ters. They wanted not only to inspire the soldier but also to strike up a friendship with him. Usually they received a gratifying answer, and the pen pal acquaintanceship endured.

Schoolgirls made with their own hands a lot of touching and, at the same time, very useful gifts for frontline troops: they knit-ted socks and mittens, sewed nice tobacco pouches or embroidered handkerchiefs. The small parcels were accompanied by warm mes-sages written by a child's hand.

The pen pal relationship didn't bypass our battery either. Two members of the battery, one after another, participated in it. I was the first participant, but the most interesting character in that story was our illiterate soldier Markin.

Mikhail Markin and His Correspondence

I should remind the readers that in May 1943, when our battery received replacements, two young soldiers from a training regiment were among the arrivals (see chapter 6). One of them was twenty-year-old Mikhail Zakharovich Markin, a *kolkhoznik* (a farmhand on a collective farm) from a small, remote village of Ryazan oblast. An unbelievable fact emerged from his assignment interview: Markin was illiterate. Senior Lieutenant Vinokurov's decision to select Mikhail as his orderly also appeared very strange. Vinokurov and Markin were very different sorts of men. Vinokurov was well mannered and highly educated, not at all like the illiterate, rustic Markin.

Believe it or not, but these two opposites coexisted in perfect harmony. And Markin was the main reason for this. His amicability, amenability, and carefulness overcame Vinokurov's inclination to seclusion and occasional irritability. Soon another one of Mikhail's merits came to light. You see, Vinokurov was addicted to strong, hot tea. Thus, Markin's ability to start fires in order to boil water at any time and in any weather was a perfect fit for our battery commander.

Mikhail (nickname Misha) was a born optimist. There was nothing noteworthy in Markin's appearance, but as soon as he met with any brother soldier, his eyes began to shine with joy. His manner of speaking was a folksy one in the Ryazan dialect, and he knew many witty and wise folk sayings.

Markin was particularly cool while under fire, and he always kept his composure in risky combat situations. Many times, when Vinokurov sent him up to our emplacements with a message, Mikhail had to reach us through enemy fire. Nevertheless, as soon as Misha caught his breath after making such a dangerous dash, a pleased smile would spread across his face.

All the soldiers liked Markin and treated him as a soldier who was one of their own through and through. He willingly talked about his past but never explained how it came that he never learned to read and write.

Being completely illiterate, Mikhail still managed an unusual correspondence with his father. He received about one letter every month. Usually, when the regimental mailman delivered a letter to him, Markin just glanced at it to make certain that the handwriting was familiar, then stated: "Thank God, my *batya* [dad] is still alive," and put the "triangle" in his breast pocket. Later, in his spare time, Misha would ask some officer or soldier to read him the letter and to write an answer to his *batya* under his dictation. A few times I was his "clerk." The opening was a standard one, written in an old traditional, rural style: "Good day or evening, dear father Zakhar Ivanovich! In the first lines of my letter, I'm letting you know that I'm still alive and healthy and I wish the same to you." The next two or three sentences were for the "clerk" to write at his own full discretion. Markin approved any topic, any text. The closing of the letter was also traditional and, like the opening, followed Misha's dictation: "After that I remain your beloved son Mikhail. I'm waiting for your answer the same way a nightingale is waiting for summer." (I could never convince him to replace "beloved" with "loving.") As far as I remember, father's letters were only a bit more informative than Mikhail's.

* * *

As I have already mentioned, receiving a letter from relatives or friends was a special event for any soldier or officer at the front. Many shared their fresh news (often bad news) with their buddies in the trenches. The lucky few who received a photo would show it off to their friends. Sometimes I showed the photographs of Vera to my more or less close friends. Once Markin was among them. He was delighted by Vera's beauty and expressed his feelings dreamily: "Eh, my dear! I'd be happy to get a girl who'd send me photos like this."

Soon Misha's dream came close to fulfillment, and I was the initiator of a bit of shady play for this. One day, in the spring of 1943, Georgiy Senchenko, a gun crew commander (and a friend of mine from May 1942), told me about a letter that he just received from his sister, a Chirchik Chemical Technology Institute sophomore. She wrote him about her close friend, a classmate and roommate, Yulya Chernova by name. Yulya, an evacuee from Kharkov, was dreaming of striking up a pen pal relationship with some brave soldier or officer known to Georgiy. Senchenko decided that I would be the best addressee for the girl.

At first I refused categorically—this additional contact was of no use for me; my thoughts of Vera as well as the correspondence with her filled my mind completely. However, my friend was so insistent that finally I yielded to his pressure. I thought it might be a nice bit of amusement or diversion for both Yulya and me. In some three weeks a warm and very patriotic letter from Uzbekistan arrived. There was also a tiny photo of Yulya in it. I responded with a friendly letter, and our correspondence began. I wrote her only two letters.

I shared the news of this pen pal relationship with Vera. Soon it became clear that this "epistolary affair" was seriously distressing to her. To calm my chosen one I decided to find a plausible excuse and put an end to the correspondence with Yulya.

At this time I had a chance but very timely meeting with Markin, in which he repeated his desire to strike up correspondence with some girl. Shortly after, a "clever" plan arose in my mind. I decided to "transfer" the correspondence with Yulya to Markin, just like one member of a relay team passes the baton to the next.

"Guards Junior Lieutenant Kobylyanskiy's heroic death in a recent action" was fabricated as the reason for changing the name of the frontline addressee. Using words that went straight to the soul, I wrote an appropriately sad text on Markin's behalf, and somebody recopied it to make the handwriting unrecognizable.

Soon a sympathizing response came from Yulya to Markin, and Mikhail became a happy correspondent with her. In my turn, I was glad to inform Vera that I was now rid of my pen pal.

Sadly, Markin wasn't fated to receive the long-awaited photo of Yulya. One day in September 1944, when we were fighting in Lithuania, Mikhail was seriously wounded: a shell fragment took off his right foot, just below the ankle. The wound required immediate hospitalization, and we never met with him again. Of course, he was doomed to remain a disabled veteran forever. I know nothing about his further fate. However, I strongly believe that Markin's optimistic personality, his goodhearted nature, and his diligence toward duties helped him to remain standing through the extremely difficult initial postwar years and to find a proper place in life.

Sometimes We Marched in Our Sleep

As everybody knows, at the time of the Great Patriotic War our infantry moved on foot. In spite of serving in a field gun battery, all my subordinates (with the exception of our horsemen and wagon drivers) and I were pedestrians, almost the same as the infantrymen. So, my experience allows me to talk about the marches of our rifle regiment as a whole.

As a rule, when the matter concerns the campaign history of a military unit, a historian discusses the main battles in which the unit took part, names the cities or areas where it fought, and identifies the names of the commanders and particular heroes. However, war isn't just a series of battles or courageous acts. At the same time, war requires exhausting toil and a great deal of patience from the common soldiers. This side of war is not often remembered; therefore, I have decided to describe just one particular aspect of soldiers' toil in wartime—our long marches.

I can't remember a historian, memoirist, or writer who used the total length that a military unit traversed during a war to characterize its war experience. But if the matter concerns some infantry unit, one can vividly imagine how long was the road that a soldier traveled. Once, I plotted on a map the two long legs of the route our division followed during three years of the war:

1. Stalingrad—Stalino—Tsyurupinsk—Perekop—Evpatoriya—Sevastopol—Snegirevka.
2. Yelnya—Belorussian forests—Lithuanian countryside—Königsberg—Zemland Peninsula—Pillau.

It turned out that the combined length of both legs comes to 2,500 kilometers!

These lengthy marches stretched on and on, and in their own way they were difficult, but at the same time this was an inseparable and unforgettable part of the war for our soldiers and me. It wasn't bloodless, either: two times, in April 1943 and in October 1944, our battery suffered losses while marching. In both cases land mines exploded when a gun's wheel ran over them. Nevertheless, decades later, as I recall our marches, I see them first of all as exhausting ordeals, an inevitable labor that wore soldiers down.

Long marches were typical when on some mornings we discovered that the enemy had retreated overnight. During such nighttime retreats, the Germans usually managed to put up to 50 kilometers between them and us (I suppose that they were transported by trucks). And yet we rarely set out at dawn in pursuit of them, as we wanted to avoid German reconnaissance planes. So we usually waited until dark to set out after the retreating enemy, except whenever it was raining, or a thick layer of low clouds blanketed the skies. Sometimes we didn't catch up to the enemy's forces until the second or third night of pursuit, by which time their positions were already fortified.

While marching by night in column formation, we felt relatively safe. Everybody could lose themselves in their own thoughts and dreams, and indulge in quite peaceful mental images or recollections. However, these pleasant reveries or remembrances were usually brief. The accumulated fatigue from the pace of marching and soldiers' efforts to overcome drowsiness quickly ousted any pleasant thoughts. Night marches exhausted everyone, even in good weather, when there was no rain to soak through our military overcoats, making them much heavier, and to turn the dirt roads into muddy morasses that seemed to make every step more difficult and exhausting than the previous one.

Usually we made everything ready for the march by dusk and were off shortly after sunset. Generally, our marches came to an end about a half hour before dawn. As I remember it, we never marched more than 25 kilometers in one night, whereas according to military doctrine, we should have been right on the tail of the retreating enemy. Alas! There were many reasons that excluded this possibility: darkness; bad country roads; a guiding officer's uncertainty at almost every intersection; and, no doubt, our infantrymen's extreme fatigue. Neither threats from higher up nor customary urgings of direct superiors quickened our step.

As a rule, some twenty minutes after our march started, the first brief halt was declared with a typical instruction: "Take a leak!

Rewrap your foot bindings! Horsemen and drivers, check the harness!" Then the pace of the column remained more or less normal till the first long halt. The rest returned our strength, and we continued to pound out the kilometers with renewed energy. But soon our brisk pace would begin to slow down. The sounds of soldiers' footsteps and the rhythmic gait of the horses, muted by the soft ground, the scraps of low conversations, and faint scratch of wheels, all blended into a monotonous, somnolent noise, and gradually drowsiness would overtake the majority of soldiers.

Soldiers would fall asleep while marching, their pace became slower, and the column would stretch in length. Yet some likeness of the column remained because the infantrymen, even while asleep on their feet, continued to walk mechanically with one hand holding on to the back half belt of the overcoat on the man in front of him. It happened quite frequently that the sleeping soldier's hand slid off the half belt, so he continued to walk without his "personal tow." Many times I saw on those nights how a lone soldier gradually veered away from the column. At first he would drift imperceptibly toward the side of the road but soon would move off the road completely and continue his separate journey until he fell into a roadside ditch. The startled wayfarer would rush back to his position in the column, but in just a short while, the same thing could happen again.

Periodically a loud peremptory shout "Close up!" would sound out. It would wake the soldiers up for a while, and they would obediently dress ranks. But soon most of them were gripped by sleep again.

Sometimes an officer seized the opportunity to sleep on the battalion supply wagon for an hour or so. Then a fellow officer would wake him up and take his place in the coveted location.

During halts and some occasional long stops on a dry road, our fatigued soldiers would instantly drop to the ground or into the roadside ditches. They would sleep both in reclining position and while sitting. It was always so difficult to rise to one's feet again when the orders "Fall in! March!" rang out—and the soldiers' legs ached in protest.

One of a few ways to ward off drowsiness during night marches was to have a conversation with a friend, especially if the dialogue consisted only of brief statements. If your friend's reply turned into a long monologue, you could fall asleep to the drone of his voice.

The long march made your feet feel like lead. The constant battle with sleep all night long left you exhausted. It was normally much easier for soldiers in our battery to handle the difficulties of night marches than for our infantry. First, it was possible for any artilleryman to lighten his load by placing his haversack, helmet, and overcoat on the limber or on an ammunition wagon. Second, our gun crew members had an additional opportunity: instead of hanging on to the overcoat belt of the man in front of them, three of them could hold on to the gun (two to the gun shield, one to the barrel). The rest of the crew, usually one to three soldiers, walked along beside the gun. Moreover, if the road wasn't too difficult and all four horses were in the team, one more soldier had the opportunity to sit on the gun carriage for 1 or 2 kilometers. However, it was rather dangerous to make use of that kind of transportation. The sitting person had only to become drowsy for a moment and to lose his balance—and the next second he would fall under the gun's wheels.

Close proximity to the moving gun threatened anyone who marched in his sleep with the same consequence. There were about twenty accidents of this kind in our battery within three years. As I remember it, no fractures or serious traumas followed. I must admit that I also found myself under the wheels of the gun, and what's more—twice! Fortunately, both accidents ended safely.

When we finally halted for the day at an interim destination that had been determined in advance (usually a grove or a small forest glade), everyone had only one dream—to lie down and have a good sleep for as long as possible. However, being a fire platoon commander, I couldn't forget my duties. There was a lot to do before I could lie down: to position and camouflage my guns and limbers; to appoint sentries; to check the condition and care of the horses, and so on. Only after all of that was done could I find a vacant cozy place, spread my overcoat on the ground, and, while using it both as bedding and a blanket, fall asleep in a moment.

Now I'd like to tell you how I gained my experience in choosing a "cozy place" for the day's slumber in one type of weather condition. It took place one day during our extra long march in May 1944. After a few days of overcast sky, bright weather had ensued, but the early mornings were pleasantly cool. One such morning, any place seemed to be cozy: the sun was just starting to rise, and the entire glade was in the shade of surrounding trees and shrubs. But in some two or three hours the shade disappeared, and almost all of us were bathed by sunlight. The bright daylight and the uncomfortable heat awoke almost all members of the battery. Everybody began looking for a new place in the shade. I still can't forget the headache and disgusting feeling of a hangover that I had that morning, as I searched for a new place to sleep. Not many of us were able to fall back asleep. The next morning, many of us were more prudent while choosing a place for sleep. The most reliable choice was to settle down under a wagon, but there were too many others who had the same idea. I preferred (after using my compass in order to anticipate the shifting shade) to lie down beside the proper wheel of a gun with the idea that I would be under its shade until noon. My "scientifically grounded approach" was crowned with success. That day I had an excellent, long sleep.

I remember also a few extra long marches that our division undertook. They happened whenever our division was redeploying to a different sector of the front, and they took place far behind the front lines. In general, the fact and the route of our redeployment were a secret. However, under these circumstances, we even had a slight indulgence: sometimes, in order to hasten our transfer, we were permitted to start the march shortly before dusk or to finish it shortly after dawn.

During these redeployments, *front* headquarters, as usual, set very tight time schedules for us to reach the new positions. It meant that the speed of march must be higher and the marches had to be longer. But human strength isn't unlimited, and by the end of such a march, we could hardly shuffle our feet. Once, in order to quicken such a march if only for a half hour, our division commander used unexpected means. Just before dawn, when the distance to our destination was still about 2 kilometers, we could suddenly hear the sounds of lively march music. Our division's small brass band was playing by the roadside. Perhaps one can hardly believe the stunning effect that this musical encouragement had on us. Our sleep just vanished; soldiers assumed a dignified air; their feet began automatically to step in accordance with the rhythm of the music. The inspiration we received was enough to reach our destination without falling asleep.

The next night the band cheered up our marching troops three times. After the division columns passed it, all seven musicians with their brass instruments were transferred by truck a few kilometers ahead. These short doses of such musical support turned out to be quite useful. Later on, the division command engaged the brass band time and again to raise the spirits of our slowly trudging infantrymen.

While outlining the story on our marches during the war, I had planned to conclude it with the episode about the musical support of the tired marching columns. However, I recently came across an impressive review in the German magazine *Stern*.[1] It was devoted to the published diary of a German soldier, Willy Peter Reese, who fought in 1941–1944 on the Eastern Front. The comprehensive review was full of extracts from this memoir, and one of them in particular caught my eye, as it conformed perfectly to the topic of this chapter. After reading it, I became certain that not only my comrades-in-arms suffered from drowsiness during these seemingly interminable marches. It turned out that even the notorious German cast-iron discipline couldn't withstand the human fatigue and the all-conquering power of sleep. So, I decided to close this chapter with the mentioned extract, which I have translated from the original German:

Last night a troubled order for prompt retreat came in. Actually our march was an escape from a half-locked ring of superior Russian troops. We retreated in some speechless despair, staggering from our tiredness. In spite of the continued march, the sleep was overcoming us: our eyelids were closing up; feet stepped mechanically, but soon we became weak in the knees and we fell. When awakened by the fall and the pain, we raised ourselves with the help of each other and staggered farther with our last bit of strength given by the pain of death.

I think this passage requires no comment.

Chapter 18

Two More Bloodless Aspects of Our Daily Routine

Our Daily Bread

In this chapter, the Russian figurative expression "Our daily bread" should be interpreted, as usual, in the broad sense: "Our food" (sometimes, it could even stand for "Our livelihood"). At the same time, it is well known that bread, as such, has been the staple food in Russia for ages. Even the folk sayings affirm: "Bread is the master of anything" and "Bread and kasha are our food." And, according to the old Slavic tradition, any important or honorable guest should be presented with an offering of bread and salt.

So, let me start with bread, as such.

I remember that each frontline serviceman received a little less than one kilogram (or almost two pounds) of bread a day. When we were in frontline positions, the bread was delivered to us with every arrival of our field kitchen. We received it on the basis of one round, one-kilogram loaf of bread for four servicemen. But, naturally, there was a problem—how to equalize the weight of four portions of the loaf without scales? A bit of folksy inventiveness helped to solve the problem. This honest method of sharing a loaf was known as the "Komu? Komu?" ("To whom? To whom?") procedure. Because this method of distributing the round loaf for a group of four existed everywhere at the front, it deserves to be described in detail.

After receiving the loaf, the group would place it on a towel or on a newspaper and elect one of them to be the cutter and another one to be the guesser. The first elect quartered the loaf with a knife as precisely as possible. The three onlookers either approved the result or asked the cutter to adjust the division. Then the guesser averted his face from the bread, and one of the three remaining soldiers in the group would point his finger at the pieces of bread, one at a time. Each time, while pointing at a piece, he put the same question to the guesser loudly: "To whom?" In response, the guesser called out the name of a soldier, who then received this piece of bread. I had never heard of disputes among participants who used this procedure.

(There is a frontline story that made the rounds on this subject. Perhaps it is a myth. It goes as follows: One night the food, including bread, hadn't been delivered to a rifle company's trenches. About an hour after daybreak, the Soviet riflemen heard a voice from the German trenches: "Hey, Russ! What's happened to you? Why haven't we heard your morning 'Komu? Komu?' yet?"

* * *

Let's get back to the general subject at hand—how we were nourished at the front. By and large, our regimental food and forage supply service managed its duties satisfactorily. In any case, there was no one who starved to death in our regiment, or who had ever been treated for dysentery. It doesn't mean, however, that our soldiers received the authorized amount of each kind of foodstuff according to regulations. I think that every type of food (but bread!) lost an impressive part of its weight or amount on the long way from the central depots to a common serviceman. And the result was natural: as a rule, our regular meal was both low-calorie and tasteless. (Nevertheless, in the last months of the war, we occasionally received a tasty American canned meat, especially the stewed pork. It was a real appreciated sign of the multifaceted American lend-lease program.)

Because of the scarcity of our actual meal ration, all detachments tried to find ways to replenish their food resources or even turned to foraging, which we called the "To be at grass" method of obtaining supplemental food. It wasn't a big problem once we reached Germany: most settlements we encountered were totally abandoned, and we came upon some warehouses as well. Thus there were many opportunities to obtain essential amounts of valuable foodstuffs. I'm sure that readers still remember our "fortunate finds" in East Prussia (see chapter 11). There weren't such opportunities as long as we fought on our own land, except for rare cases. I have decided to describe two of the most memorable of them.

From the day I first joined the 1049th Rifle Regiment until the end of the war, I experienced only one long break in regular food supply. It happened in late January 1943. Our division was headlong in pursuit of the retreating Germans, who didn't even try to slow us with rearguard detachments. So our advance was rapid and out-stripped our supply line.

I don't remember now why our division's rear services lagged far behind the rifle regiments at that time. But, as a result, none of the regiments in our division received bread or other food from the divisional depot for several days running. Fortunately, our regimental suppliers encountered on the barren steppe an unguarded flock of sheep, with at least a hundred head. The sheep were still in good shape. We were rescued from hunger, but there was an opposite side to the coin in this case. Having not had even a crumb of bread, we regularly gorged on the mutton. Soon, the retribution arrived: my body turned out to be unable to endure such a "meat diet." On the fifth day I lost my appetite completely, and even the next evening, when bread had been finally delivered, I still couldn't eat anything. Moreover, my friend Ivan Kamchatnyy discovered that the whites of my eyes had grown yellow. Since I had never before experienced such symptoms, they seriously frightened me. This kind of fear was far beyond the framework of "my classification of fear" (see chapter 6), and I was constantly in a bad mood. The cure came unexpectedly: I found a frozen onion bulb on the snow-covered road, and immediately I had a feeling that it was just what I needed. The feeling was true.

Actually, mutton was a rarity in our meat ration. The main kind of meat was beef. However, from time to time pork appeared in our menu. Many in our battery were glad whenever we had this change, but at the same time a specific problem arose. The point was that roughly a quarter of our seventy soldiers were from the Central Asian republics, and almost half of them were adherents of Islam. They carefully observed the stringent Islamic rules that prohibited eating pork, and so about ten of our soldiers refused this food categorically. By the way, some of them didn't refuse to drink vodka, though that was forbidden too.

The group of such devoted believers found their own foraging substitute for pork in horseflesh, which wasn't prohibited. Sometimes they butchered the carcass of a recently killed young horse, but more often they caught a stray foal. One of our wagon drivers would take care of the young animal and fatten it up. When the foal grew a little stronger and fatter, it was then butchered. I want to note that both believers and nonbelievers from the Central Asian republics liked the taste and aroma of cooked horseflesh. Once our Muslims invited me to taste such meat that they had just cooked over a fire. A small piece of it was enough to put me off horseflesh forever.

* * *

It goes without saying: the "To be at grass" method of obtaining food wasn't a legal one. And many officers, especially at the regimental level, observed the prohibition completely. But on the other hand, the urgent necessity to feed hundreds of hungry subordinate soldiers incited them to take some illegal actions. There were many similar situations during the war, and more than once, circumstances forced the officers to disregard some regulation or an order. Usually, while taking such a decision, the officer had no alternative. And he would mentally suppress any doubts or hesitation by a then popular cliché: "Blame it on the war!" Unfortunately, this cliché was also useful to many dishonest "operators" in the far rear of the country, where they were managing their shady dealings.

Sanitation and Hygiene

It is not a pleasant task—to describe how dirty and unwashed we were for most of the war, especially, to tell the readers how we suffered from lice. But the matter concerns some problems that affected not only a soldier's skin but also his mood and sleep. In other words, to some extent it could, and often did, reduce the soldier's combat effectiveness. Therefore, I decided to talk about this unattractive aspect of our life at the front, too.

As I remember it, each nurse of the regimental medical company had one or two rifle or artillery detachments under her periodic sanitary observation. Naturally, they carried out their inspections only in the daytime and at that only in calm periods. Within my recollection, such an inspection happened only one time (in October of 1942, while we were on the left bank of Volga River). When our inspector appeared at the battery position, the sergeant major ordered everyone to remove his military blouse and to form a rank. He introduced the nurse, Anya Korchagina by name, and ordered us to take off our undershirts and to turn them inside out. Anya thoroughly examined every seam but found nothing suspicious.

This result could have been expected in advance because we had just been at the front for two weeks.

A week after the inspection we underwent another hygienic procedure—the full sanitary processing. We walked almost two hours to reach the army field post for sanitary processing. It was located in a spacious forest clearing. The sanitary field post consisted of two canvas tents. The smaller one was the "lice slaughterhouse," where our uniforms and underwear, including field caps and foot wraps, underwent delousing and chemical disinfection. The larger tent was the field bathhouse.

Between the tents a pile of billets flamed under a large camp kettle full to the brim with water. Several elderly soldiers were working there. They sawed logs, chopped firewood, and threw the logs under the kettle. Two soldiers dealt with the water: they drew the hot water from the kettle and replaced it with cold water for heating.

Our sergeant major placed us at the disposal of a female lieutenant of the medical service, who constantly hurried everybody. First of all we had to strip to the skin.

While entering the "bath tent," everyone received a tiny piece from a laundry soap bar. The officer announced that we had only five minutes to wash ourselves.

In the center of the "bath tent," a large metal cask stood. It was filled with warm water. About a dozen capacious ladles for individual use lay near the cask.

Can you imagine our disappointment when we discovered that the "warm" water was actually only room temperature? So, the bath that we anticipated with pleasure turned into an abbreviated, useless procedure. Moreover, after the sanitary processing, our uniforms and underwear emerged warm, damp, and rumpled. They also emanated an unpleasant smell. On our way back, we discussed the episode and came to the conclusion that the only true goal of the "hygienic action" was to check it off on a report to the commander.

The word "hygiene" is absolutely out of place when one describes the conditions of our life at the front line. Opportunities to rinse your face happened very infrequently, even in summer. Even more rarely would you have the chance to shave.

Changes of underwear took place approximately once a month. Our sergeant major delivered it from the divisional laundry. Usually this underwear was torn and poorly washed; sometimes you could see several odd spots on it.

Naturally, such unsanitary conditions led to the usual result: in our initial winter at the front we, one and all, became lousy. It was a real disaster, especially each cold season. I don't want to let readers in on the disgusting details of our feelings then, or in on the methods of our unsuccessful struggle against these ineradicable insects. Only in late September 1944, as we were fighting in Lithuania, did we manage to get rid of this misfortune completely.

At the front we felt a need for washing our worn underwear and our sweat-soaked foot wraps and uniforms almost constantly. There were only a few short periods, however, when we had the opportunity to do it on our own. In this book, I referred to one such period as "blissful days" (see chapter 6).

Leisure at the Front

Several times during the war our division was withdrawn from the trenches in the front line to the rear for reinforcement and training. As a rule, on these occasions we were in the rear area for no less than a couple of weeks. One way or another, on most evenings of these periods everybody had the rare opportunity to spend time at his personal discretion. Some wrote letters back home, while others reread letters from loved ones far away once more. Some just slept their fill, others, while smoking poor tobacco, conversed with close friends in colloquial language. However, at times many felt a hunger for some kind of group activity, such as an amusement or some sort of "homemade entertainment." Mostly this form of free-time activity arose spontaneously, without formal organization.

Our "Homemade Entertainment"

The most prevailing form of our "homemade entertainment" was to share "soldier's tales" within the group. Only two or three of the men in the battery had the "gift of gab" and were able to hold others spellbound with their tales. Soldiers often asked these natural storytellers to tell them a story just for the entertainment.

A true glib talker was the thirty-year-old reenlisted sergeant major, Yakov Varushchenko. Yakov's stories of his numerous love affairs always attracted younger listeners. In prewar time he had served somewhere in the far east region of the USSR as the manager of a remote garrison officers' club. Yakov was also the dance master at this club. He was a good-looking man and a highly experienced lady-killer. These attributes and his personal contacts as the dance master served him quite well at this remote, godforsaken garrison. Local officers' wives suffered there from idleness and the monotonous lifestyle. According to Yakov, it was no problem to pick up any local lady. In spite of the fact that most details of his numerous affairs normally varied, the happy ending of all his stories became a cliché in our battery: "After that we hit the bottle, ate well, and made wonderful love together."

My good-natured, thirty-year-old friend Senior Sergeant Vasya Panteleev also shared interesting narratives from his bachelor adventures with us. However, most of us preferred to listen to Vasya recite the poetry of Sergey Yesenin. (In prewar years everything written by this prominent Russian poet was semibanned.) Panteleev knew by heart many of Yesenin's touching lyrics and poems. He recited them in a slight drawl, with a sincere feeling. All the listeners were strongly impressed by Yesenin's verse, and absolute silence would reign around Vasiliy during his recitations.

I wasn't a gifted storyteller. Nevertheless, once I became the center of attention among a group of regimental artillery officers for some two weeks. It took place in the early spring of 1945, while we were in the rear area, training for the storming of Königsberg. The reason for my unexpected success was a windfall: somewhere in Lithuania, I had stumbled upon a small Russian book published in Latvia in the late 1920s, entitled *1,200 Funny Stories*. I read the book through the night, and many of its stories became engraved in my memory. So, during those two weeks, I regularly entertained my fellow officers with dozens of funny stories from the book. Below is the only story that I can still remember:

A dignified woman and her adult daughter were riding in a light carriage along the main street of a city. When the phaeton came up to a tobacco store, the daughter ordered the coachman to stop.

"What for?" the mother asked.

"I'd like to buy a gift for my husband—a carton of cigarettes. You know, since he started smoking again, he has begun to perform his matrimonial duties much better."

"Oh, my dear! If so, please buy one more carton. I'd like to give it to your father."

No doubt, the most pleasant and at the same time the most attractive kind of our "homemade entertainment" were, as we called them, the "evenings of Ukrainian and Russian folk songs"—our favorite pastime. The main initiators of these evenings were Lieutenant Grigoriy Brechko and Ivan Maslov, a private. Both knew a lot of

folk songs—Ukrainian and Russian, respectively—and both had nice 209
tenor voices and were good lead singers. The best backup singers
were my close friends Ivan Kamchatnyy and Petr Zhigur, a forty-
five-year-old private, who treated everyone in the battery like a
father and addressed any soldier as "sonny." Both backups could accompany the lead singers emotionally and in fine style.

The four men had only to gather at some appropriate time, and
they would begin singing at once. At first they sang softly as if for
themselves only. But gradually their voices gained strength, and soon
we could hear their singing all over the battery area. Our artillerymen would begin to gather, little by little, around the singing quar-
tet. Soon, one could see as many as fifteen or more men grouped
around the performers. Many would pick up the tune, and the song
would grow in volume. Others just hummed or quietly listened.
The faces of both the singers and their audience would grow lighter.
Some, deeply touched, closed their eyes slightly. It was singing from
the heart and for the good of everyone's soul. The lead singers had
an endless repertoire of songs, so our impromptu concerts lasted up
to two hours, including a short pause for the smokers.

There were two "soloists" in the battery, too. Both sang in their
native languages.

The twenty-year-old Kazakh Ertay Kargabaev, a private, was a
lively and cheerful guy. He had a clear descanting voice (boys' so-
prano) and a wonderful ear for music. Thanks to these talents, Ertay
was able to perform two popular opera arias from the repertoire
of the famous Kazakh opera singer Kulyash Bayseitova, who had
recently been awarded the official honorary title of National Actress
of the USSR. Kargabaev reproduced them with all of Bayseitova's
roulades. I liked his performances very much.

The second "soloist," Rakhmatullaev, a wagon driver, performed
two Tatar folk songs. On the surface, their melodies seemed to be
too simple. Nevertheless, the extraordinary rhythm of these songs
caught the majority's fancy.

Unfortunately, the merciless war acted without exceptions. In 1944
it didn't spare the lives of two of our best singers. In April, Zhigur was
lost on the bank of the Belbek River, and in September Rakhmatullaev
was killed in Lithuania. In April 1945, during the assault on Königsberg, our Kazakh "soloist" Kargabaev was seriously wounded.

Sometimes the division's political department arranged real concerts for regimental or divisional audiences during quiet periods on the front. They were a true joy to us.

There was a small entertainment group in the division that mostly performed on regimental stages. Between the fall of 1942 and Victory Day 1945, they played at least four times in front of our regiment. As I remember it, the group had four musicians, two songstresses, and two satirical singers. (I think they were on the roster of some rifle or medical detachment.) A talented professional musician, Pasechnik by name, managed and directed the group. Pasechnik could also play a variety of musical instruments. He was quite skilled with the piccolo, and I can still remember his wonderful performance of Alyabev's "Nightingale." In contrast, the artistic mastery of Pasechnik's subordinates was only "so-so," and their satirical routines were primitive. Nevertheless, the audience highly enjoyed their performances and rewarded them generously with cheers.

Incomparably better were two concerts given by the army and *front* entertainment ensembles, respectively. Their casts numbered over 100 professional actresses and actors each. Both programs remained in everybody's memory for a long time because of their variety and first-rate mastery.

All of us were especially pleased with the *front* entertainment ensemble's concert. The highlight of its program was the performance of its wonderful chorus that numbered about fifty women and men. On that day, among other numbers, they performed two recently composed songs, "A Swarthy Girl" and "In a Front-Area Forest." Both songs were beautifully melodious, and soon they became very popular across the whole USSR. In addition, I still remember the skillful direction of the young master of ceremonies from the performance that day. His witty remarks and funny comments made the audience roar with laughter again and again.

Chapter 20

Ideological Pressure

Our Sources of Information during the War

No doubt, the majority of our frontline soldiers and officers first of all wanted to know how their families were living in the rear. But the general situation at the Soviet-German front was also the subject of common interest among us.

Since we didn't have any radio receivers in our detachments, the main sources of war information were newspapers. More or less regularly, we received our divisional weekly small newspaper *Za Rodinu* ("For the Motherland"). Its issues always contained a condensed recent Sovinformbyuro report, several brief articles about our bravest soldiers' deeds, and a short poem or the text of a popular song. The full-size central newspapers *Pravda* ("The Truth") and *Krasnaya Zvezda* ("The Red Star") were much more informative and diverse. Unfortunately, they reached us up to two or three weeks late, mainly arriving a few issues at a time.

These newspapers published unabbreviated Sovinformbyuro press releases. As I remember, the full Sovinformbyuro communiqué usually consisted of several paragraphs, each devoted to a particular sector of the Soviet-German front where active operations were in progress, or to successful actions of Soviet partisans and underground groups. Also, obvious examples of Nazi brutality and cruelty to Soviet civilians were often depicted in the communiqué. Some Sovinformbyuro issues contained facts that demonstrated the eminent labor achievements of Soviet civilians, mostly women, working in the deep rear, especially in the production of heavy armament and aircraft.

The central newspapers also printed their special correspondents' articles about specific battles, which often highlighted the individual Soviet soldiers and officers who had excelled in the fighting. Some of these special reporters were talented Soviet writers and poets. The *Krasnaia Zvezda* almost daily published the brief but highly inflammatory articles and political pamphlets of the famous Russian writer Ilya Ehrenburg. He was born in 1891 and from 1908 to 1920 had lived in France. Pablo Picasso, Fernand Léger, and Louis Aragon were among his friends. During the war, Ehrenburg entitled his brief articles with such captions as "Make a stand for Moscow!" "Whip up your hatred against the German invaders!" "Let's take revenge on them!" or just "Kill him!" As a rule, the introductory part of Ehrenburg's articles cited in a very emotional manner some terrible facts of German brutality toward Soviet citizens or POWs and concluded with a slogan that resembled the title. During the war, Ehrenburg's name was on everybody's lips among the Soviet readership.

In December 1942 all the central newspapers reported about an unprecedentedly generous action of an elderly Soviet citizen, Ferapont Golovatyy, a collective farmer and private beekeeper who had purchased a Yak-1 fighter for the Red Army with his life savings of 100,000 rubles (his own apiary numbered twenty-two hives, and one kilogram of honey was worth 500 rubles during the war). Our propaganda described Golovatyy's patriotic action in glowing terms, and soon several of his followers became famous (I remember a shepherd and a cotton grower from some Central Asian republics among them). Later some collective benefactors, such as plants, factories, and the largest state farms, purchased more tanks and airplanes for the Red Army.

Our central press also regularly released the Allies' reports of the main events on the Western Front, including the actions of the French Resistance, as well as occasional communiqués on the battles in the Asian-Pacific theater against Japan. We could also follow some international news in the newspapers.

Starting in 1943, we also often read about successful aerial engagements of Red Army pilots, who often flew American fighters that came to the USSR as a part of the American lend-lease program. The American Bell P-39 Airacobra fighter particularly remained in my memory because our most famous national idol, Three-Time Hero of the Soviet Union Alexander Pokryshkin, piloted this plane during the last two years of the war.

At the same period of time our central press frequently mentioned the French fighter squadron "Normandie—Neman." It comprised a group of French fighter pilots, who had been sent to the USSR by General de Gaulle, the leader of the Free French government. The French pilots flew Soviet Yakovlev fighter planes. They indeed fought heroically.

* * *

From the first part of this book, my readers already know how powerful and intense were the means of ideological pressure on everyone in our country, and how skillfully the Party elite spread its propaganda and dogma among common people. As it was figuratively said later, they "powdered over our brains" or they "hung noodles on our ears." However, over time more and more people grew tired of the long-standing and relentless propaganda. They began to sense that very often, official statements were not quite adequate or fully revealing. Gradually, most people became indifferent or even distrustful of them. Some more experienced readers (as I already was at that time) were able to read "between the lines" of most official publications, particularly the Sovinformbyuro reports. For example, when a report stated that battles of only "local significance" took place on some section of the front, it meant that things looked bad for our side there. (Just recently I found one Russian Web site where one can read all the condensed daily Sovinformbyuro reports. I was curious to read now what had been reported in the last days of July 1943, when our "Ravine of Death" epic was already close to its sad end. Believe it or not, I learned from two reports that on that sector of the front, only intense reconnaissance probes had taken place.)

To sum up what I have discussed, I can state that much of our propaganda was just wasted effort. For example, I had never heard our riflemen shouting, "For the motherland, for Stalin!" when they rushed toward the enemy's trenches; only "Hurrah!" or "Rah!" rang out at the start of an attack.

Another example was the prevalence of a weak interest or even an indifference to the newspapers' substance. Only a handful of members of our battery (of course, including myself) willingly read the central newspapers in a hope of finding something new or interesting. There was, however, another kind of interest in the newspapers among our smokers: they used pieces of the newsprint for rolling their cigarettes. Very soon everybody had learned that the newsprint of the central newspapers was noticeably thinner and so much better for this use than any other one. Unfortunately, we received only one copy of each issue of the central newspapers.

As for Ehrenburg's strident articles, they were really written in a very emotional manner. The author depicted the Nazis' barbarities in strikingly vivid descriptions. But on the other hand, as you read several of these articles one after the other, a feeling of some sameness would appear, and the strength of their impact on the reader would weaken.

I'm not sure that all of our war veterans would agree with my remarks on the insufficient effectiveness of our propaganda. It is quite likely that some of my frontline comrades, especially many young soldiers, who were less experienced than I was in 1944 and 1945, perceived all propaganda statements more trustingly than I did.

A Little about Military Political Workers

Most military political workers in the Red Army were the so-called *politruks* (*politruk* is an abbreviation of the term for "political leader / instructor"), the political deputy commanders at all levels of command down to the company or battery. In my opinion, that institution was just a remnant of the Russian Civil War (1918–1920). At that time, a fairly large number of young Red Army units and soldiers fought under the command of former czarist officers. Because the Bolshevik leaders distrusted most of these officers, the Communist Party established the position of commissar, who was a Party official appointed to keep watch on the military officers. The commissar had the right to countermand any order from his appointed military commander. But what was the reason to keep commissars now, at a time when all future officers had to pass through a rigorous examination of their origins, political convictions, and loyalty to Soviet rule before they were enrolled in a military college? Moreover, many current commanding officers were Party members themselves. Therefore, because I was a staunch supporter of the principle of "unity of command" in the army, I was pleased when an April 1943 decree rescinded the dual command and put an end to the institution of deputy commanders for political affairs at the level of companies and batteries.

As was the case anywhere, there were various sorts of people among the *politruks* and other types of military political workers. Many were decent and honorable men who served their country well.

For example, I keep warm memories and pleasant images of Stepan Sysolyatin. Although a little bit simpleminded, he was a kindhearted and sociable man. All of the soldiers in our battery liked him. He always felt uncomfortable during combat when he observed that everyone was carrying out the commander's orders dutifully on his own, and he sensed that none of the soldiers really needed the motivation or assistance of a *politruk*.

In late May 1943, according to the aforementioned decree, Stepan left our battery as we no longer had the post of deputy commander for political affairs. Sysolyatin remained in our regiment; he filled the vacant post of the 3rd Battalion's deputy commander for political affairs. This was a definite promotion, but a tragic destiny awaited him: at the end of July 1943 he was killed in action during our battle at the "Ravine of Death." The terrible news reached our battery only in the first days of August. All of us mourned over the wonderful man Stepan Sysolyatin.

* * *

For a year or so, our rifle regiment's deputy commander for political affairs was Colonel Grigoriev, a stocky bald man in his midfifties. At that time the rank of our regimental commander was just a major! It was rumored that Grigoriev had been dismissed from some much higher post because he did not "play up" to his commander at that time. Grigoriev was an extremely intelligent, polite, and affable person. Very often he talked individually and sympathetically with the common privates, who complained about the difficult conditions and even poverty that their families were suffering back at home. Grigoriev never hesitated to react. He wrote many official appeals to the local officials for help; in many cases his letters were effective, and the families of our guardsmen received some necessary support.

There were, however, political workers of other sorts. Some wished to emphasize their self-importance. So they constantly meddled in the specific business of the military commanders, openly contradicted many of the commanders' statements, and frequently started arguments and rivalries. Others schemed to get rid of their commander by using such convenient means as daily "political reports" delivered directly and discretely to the division's political department. They used these secret reports as an opportunity to write slanderous information that discredited their respective commanders.

Propaganda Means of Demoralizing the Enemy

Not only *politruks*, our instructors of the divisional political department, and newspapers of all levels were devoted to influencing the Soviet soldiers' morale and ideological perception; our frontline soldiers were also targeted by German propaganda. The most widespread means of enemy propaganda were Russian-language leaflets. The Germans usually dropped these over our lines at night.

The first leaflet, which I found on the ground in the spring of 1943, contained an appeal from the leadership of the "Union for the Liberation of Russia from the Bolsheviks" (the cited name of the union is not quite exact because I don't remember the genuine one). The appeal was addressed to all soldiers and commanders of the Red Army. The leaflet denounced Stalin's antinational regime and let us know that all true patriots of the motherland, all the best representatives of Russian intellectuals, generals, professors, journalists, and doctors, joined in condemning the damned criminal regime. According to the text, many of them had joined the German army, which was bringing freedom to oppressed Russia. (I'm trying to give the main sense of that appeal, since naturally I don't remember its text exactly.) The final part of the leaflet called for everyone who cared about Russia to surrender to the Germans. The leaflet served as a pass for safe entry into the German lines, with the words "Put your bayonet into the ground" as the password (I remember that exactly!). The signature of the secretary of this union or committee, a general with a quite long Russian last name, perhaps Sinelnikov, completed the text.

On the reverse of the leaflet were a few photos. They displayed unfeasible, excellent conditions for the treatment of Soviet prisoners of war. I remember the significant caption of one of the photos: "A loaf of bread for your dinner—for two!" That was twice as much as our quota of bread!

In the summer of 1943 I found another such leaflet. It was a cartoon about the crushing defeat of the Red Army's Southwest *Front*'s attempt to launch a powerful spring offensive.[1] Two ludicrous fleeing figures were depicted: Stalin as an injured bear and Timoshenko (who had led the Southwest *Front*'s badly organized offensive).

In early September 1944, I found a third, rather interesting piece of German propaganda. This time it appeared as a copy of the holiday issue of some Soviet air force unit's newsletter, *Stalin's Falcons* (18 August was the national Day of Aviation). The copy resembled a true Soviet military newsletter, but when I examined it more closely, I found it was mostly devoted to proclaiming the Luftwaffe's superiority over Soviet aviation.

In a month or so I found one more German leaflet (it was my last find). On its right side I saw some ten or fifteen small, cartoonlike portraits of ridiculous, disgusting-looking men, who all appeared different from one another. The only thing they shared in common was an evident Jewish origin. Such a "collection" could provoke only negative feelings about those who were portrayed. Above the group was a heading in large, bold print: RECOGNIZE HIM! Articles in the leaflet described all the purported sins that world Jewry had committed against humanity and, separately, the Jewish domination in the USSR. A cartoon illustrated the latter statement: a smiling Kaganovich (Stalin's closest Jewish apprentice) pulling strings to manipulate Stalin, who was depicted as a cheerless marionette. Can you imagine my feelings while examining that leaflet?

* * *

Now, let me revert to the spring of 1943 to talk about the sole Soviet leaflet I discovered, which was addressed to German troops. When I found it, its sharp, sepia-toned photographs printed on high-quality paper, not newsprint, surprised me. The first part of the text described Hitler's cruel attitude toward thousands of the best representatives of the German people, whom he had imprisoned in concentration camps. Then, the leaflet urged German soldiers to surrender and come over to Red Army side. The "spice" of that leaflet was on its reverse side. On a queen-size bed an attractive, Aryan-looking blonde woman lay with a young, dark-haired man of obviously Mediterranean appearance. The text below the image explained that in Germany numerous *Gäst-arbeiters* (foreign or guest workers) were "substituting" for German husbands and lovers, away at the front to fight against the USSR.

I remember one more method of ideological pressure on enemy troops. In our division was a special propaganda group for demoralizing the enemy. It used a specially equipped truck with a microphone, a powerful amplifier, subsidiary electrical batteries to power the equipment, and a loudspeaker on the roof of the truck. The group was subordinate to the division's political department and numbered about five people. Their mission was to perform periodic propaganda broadcasts in the enemy's direction from a position close behind our front line. This group also dispersed printed leaflets by balloons, which drifted over the enemy's lines.

I read about such groups in the newspapers; I was familiar with our group's chief, Major Vinnik. However, I never saw it operating in our section of the regiment's trenches. I also heard that the Germans used similar means to demoralize our troops, but I never heard one of their broadcasts. I think that the broadcast method to demoralize the enemy's troops wasn't particularly effective.

A Jew at the Front:
A Frank Discussion

As a child, I grew up in a family that didn't observe any religious traditions and holidays. Around the age of eight, my parents taught me
about different sorts of ethnic groups and nationalities, for example,
Russians, Ukrainians, Poles, Jews, and so on. They told me: "Both of
us are Jews, and because of that you are a Jew, too." They explained
this fact in a quiet manner (not as something special), and they never
emphasized it again. Later, when I was a teenager, my school, the
Komsomol, and Soviet mass media all persistently inculcated in me
the spirit of internationalism and the equality of rights of all ethnic
groups. As a result, before the war I very seldom thought about my
Jewish origin. However, within a couple of months after the war
started, I felt almost continuously the sense of belonging to this
"nontypical" people.

The cause of this change in attitude was the outburst of demotic
anti-Semitism that spread quickly and widely in our country at that
time. The old vulgar prejudices against Jews were revived in different levels of society. Here and there you could hear sarcastic accu-
sations, insulting nicknames, degrading anecdotes, and mockeries
concerning Jews. Everything Jewish, mostly mythical or intention-
ally exaggerated, became an object of malicious criticism. Among
many sins ascribed to Jews, one could find their supposed devotion
to the "golden calf," mercantilism, dishonest actions, cowardice, and
a tendency to evade service at the front; finally, even their specific in-
tonations and pronunciation of the letter *r* as a burr were insulted.

Today, I believe that there were then a few grounds for the outburst of that disgusting phenomenon, which had been hidden during the years before the war (or maybe being a teenager, I really
didn't notice it?):

- Among hundreds of thousands of refugees who escaped to the
  eastern provinces of the USSR, Jewish families were a substantial
  part; had they remained under German occupation, they would

have been massacred. So the permanent residents of the eastern regions naturally noted a large percentage of Jews among the newcomers.

- Most of the locals in the eastern regions hadn't even seen a Jew before; some only had heard and believed that Jews had crucified Jesus Christ. And now, the sight of quite healthy Jewish men far from the front repelled many of the natives: "Why are they walking freely here, while our husbands (brothers, sons, fathers) have already been called to the front?" Of course, many of the refugees had not been drafted at their homes because of the rapid speed of the German "blitz": before they could be mobilized, their homes and local draft centers had been overrun. But some of my fellow Jews remained civilians without any valid reason. No doubt, some people of other ethnicities also evaded the front. But everybody knows that what belongs to "others" is always more visible, so the Jewish evaders were noticed most of all.

- The arrival of the large number of evacuees naturally affected the locals' living standards. Food became hard to find; many apartments became overcrowded with new residents. Who could be blamed for all of this? Of course, the evacuees, and first of all the Jews.

- There happened to be rich persons among the Jewish evacuees, and they became the source of certain rumors. Many common locals ascribed to all Jews the myths about countless Jewish wealth, despite the fact that the overwhelming majority of the arrivals actually led almost a beggarly existence there.

- Several unfamiliar customs of the Jewish newcomers, some aspects of their social behavior, and even their way of managing a household were not to some locals' liking.

- Hitler's propaganda persistently represented Jews as the most malicious enemies of all humanity and charged them with all deadly sins. Echoes of that calumny spread across all regions of the USSR.

In my present-day opinion, these were the main reasons for the intensification of hostility toward Jews at that time.

I must add and emphasize that most locals fully and openly sympathized with the evacuated newcomers. They unselfishly helped them to survive and often shared their last crust of bread with them.

The insults accusing Jews of cowardice and of avoiding frontline service deeply hurt my feelings. I can never forget the bitterness I felt while hearing such disgusting, cheap witticisms on that subject. Until I received my military uniform, my only reaction to such "jokes" was to grit my teeth and bear what I heard. How could I, a sturdily built nineteen-year-old guy, explain to every Tom, Dick, and Harry that my status as a college sophomore automatically postponed my military service? So, before 15 May 1942, I swallowed all such dirty insults silently. Because I was forced to listen in silence to such taunts on the subject for nearly a year, my mind became addicted to the topic "Jews at the front line." Thus, even before donning the military uniform, I was focused on understanding how Jews behaved at the front and how they actually fought.

Over the years, I came to the conclusion that there is no direct answer to this and similar questions, if one wants to form a judgment on any particular nationality, ethnicity, or even any large group of individuals. In other words, all groups of people have their own heroes as well as their own cowards. Because of this circumstance, my youthful attempts to generally characterize Jews at the front failed. Therefore, you will find below mostly the facts I encountered at the front and my attitude toward them.

I'd like to start with information on all my close male relatives who were within the limits of the call-up age, from eighteen through forty-five, in 1941. There were four of them, all were my first cousins, and my sole brother was only ten at that time. Here they are with their year of birth and their service records:

Mikhail Ginzburg (1911)—in the army from 1939. Participated in the war first as a military political worker, then as a military engineer, and later as a deputy commander of a motorcar battalion (a special transportation unit, which was at the disposal of an army headquarters).

Naum Ginzburg (1919)—fighter pilot, seriously injured in a dogfight in 1943; a disabled veteran of the war.

Isaak Kobylyanskiy (1922)—my namesake—drafted just after he graduated from high school in 1940. Killed in action in June 1941.

Isaak Vainburg (1922)—in the army from 1940, when he graduated from the Kiev Artillery "*spets*-school." Seriously wounded in

1942; after recovering in a military hospital, continued to fight; a disabled veteran of war.

I didn't include myself in that list, since readers already know about my participation in the war. You can see that even without the fifth person this sort of "family statistic" was entirely positive for Jews.

In the summer of 1942, while I was a cadet of a military college for three months, I took note of the nationality of each instructor and commander I dealt with. There was only one Jew among about twenty of them. I considered this fact as a kind of "positive statistic" again, because if you were of military age and not in a military school, you were fighting at the front.

A more complicated picture appeared before me when I fought in a rifle regiment of a regular infantry division. All frontline regiments numbered on average during the period of war a total of about 500 so-called active bayonets. There were not as many Jews among them as I would have liked. Besides myself, four more Jews were fighting "actively" (as I interpret this word): the antitank rifle company commander Gorlovskiy, the 120-mm mortar platoon commander Plotkin, the 50-mm mortar platoon commander (later, a company commander) Bamm, and the signalman Khandros. (Gorlovskiy and Khandros fell in battle, both in 1943.) All of these men were known as brave warriors, and that made me glad. (Perhaps there were more Jews in our battalions, but I mentioned only those with whom I had personal acquaintanceship).

However, my oversensitive, captious gaze noticed that one could see in the rear detachments, which were fewer in strength, approximately just as many Jews: the head of the regimental SMERSH group Vignanker, the mailman Vin, the security guard of regimental headquarters Shulman, the storehouse stockman Sapozhnikov, and the clerk of the personnel department Yakubman. It was much safer to serve in those detachments, though sometimes they suffered casualties, too. The higher proportion of Jews in the rear detachments, relative to that among the "active bayonets" in the rifle and artillery detachments of our regiment, caused my dissatisfaction.

I'm sure that such relative proportions were more likely to exist in the infantry regiments of the army. At the same time, in the artillery regiments of the rifle divisions, for example, which required more mathematical knowledge from its "active" soldiers, the ratio between the proportion of Jews among the "active" units and the proportion of those among rear detachments would be more even. (At that time, most eighteen-year-old Jews had completed high school education, which was not true of many other ethnic groups in the Soviet Union.) But I just served in a rifle regiment.

No doubt, this relative disproportion in numbers between "actively" and "passively" fighting Jews was obvious to everybody. And it was especially troublesome to me because it could support the rumors about the "Jewish skill" in shirking that you could sometimes hear at the front, too. There were some anti-Semites among our troops, mostly officers, who liked those rumors.

In addition to the outburst of anti-Semitism in the rear territory of our country and the malicious slander of Jews in German leaflets, the "mini-statistic" of our rifle regiment strongly grated on my feelings. I understood that it was absolutely impossible and senseless for one person to struggle with anti-Semitism as a whole, and so I chose my own way: to try, as earnestly as I could, to rebut those anti-Jewish prejudices with my own behavior in battle.

Several of my actions and decisions at the front were motivated precisely by my desire to show those around me that I, a Jew, was at least equal to anyone else. Quite often I acted as a reckless youth, while ignoring danger in a pointed manner. In our battery, I was among the steadfast warriors.

Once, my loyal friend and frontline comrade Ivan Kamchatnyy (a Ukrainian, by the way) wrote about me in a letter to my sweetheart Vera: "He was a good example to others in the battle at the 'Ravine of Death.' I'm proud of him."

Of course, there were other forceful motives in my behavior under fire: patriotism, hatred of the enemy, and adherence to my military oath. Furthermore, there were two specific and personal motives that guided my actions as well. The first motive was the desire to prove to my sweetheart that I deserved her love. The second one, to tell the truth, was my deep aspiration to excel in everything I did. That pervasive sense of perfectionism was still remaining from my school years (in particular, I remember my hidden desire to earn more combat decorations).

Also, in quiet situations, somewhat removed from the front line, I didn't like to yield to my colleagues in the least in other activities, as well. That fact related to some ordinary aspects of life. I remember two appropriate examples: my efforts to improve my ability to drink more liquor without getting demonstrably drunk; and the pains I took to present myself as a neat and polished military man.

I remember two occasions at the front when I consciously took absolutely vital decisions based almost exclusively on the fact that I was a Jew. I describe them below.

In the previous chapter I described the actions of our division propaganda group for demoralizing the enemy. From time to time the chief of this group, Major Vinnik, a Jew, by the way, visited our regiment. Once, in the fall of 1943, Vinnik, probably after getting to know that I could speak German fluently, found me and suggested he could transfer me into his group. "It would be much safer there," he added. My reaction was instant: "Never! We have just a handful of Jews among the 'active bayonets' in our regiment. I can't diminish that number!"

The second case took place in late October 1944. Our division had reached the left bank of the Neman River just across from the city of Tilsit (the historical meeting place of the Russian emperor Alexander I and Napoleon I in 1812). The city lay on the opposite bank, perched on a very steep and imposing height. When I first looked at this daunting panorama, a thought occurred to me: "Lord forbid that we attack the city frontally!" But our headquarters didn't share my opinion, and we were ordered to be ready to cross the river and to storm Tilsit on the night of 31 October. There was an official announcement: the first soldiers who entered the city would receive the most honorable title of Hero of the Soviet Union and would be awarded the Gold Star medal. Despite that enticing promise there were no signs of enthusiasm among our troops. Moreover, almost everyone looked anxious because there seemed few chances of survival. Here are a few lines of the letter to my beloved, which I wrote after receiving these orders: "I am on the verge of a very serious battle, and only the Lord knows what end is waiting for me. This letter might be fated to be the last one." Never before and never after did I write so openly about the forthcoming danger.

During the whole week that remained until the appointed day of the river crossing assault, we kept busy making rafts of logs in the riverside forest and digging trenches close to the river after dusk.

Unexpectedly, on 30 October, an orderly of the regimental personnel group came to deliver an application form for the Military

Engineering Academy to me. Shortly after, a clerk of the group explained to me by phone that the regimental headquarters had received an order to send immediately one qualified serviceman to
the academy, and that I was the only person in the regiment who
had started higher technical education. All the paperwork was to be
completed in just a few hours.

Initially, I rejoiced at the opportunity to avoid the fatal operation and began to fill out the application form. But gradually other
thoughts started coming to my mind: "How can I act in such a way?
It would give the anti-Semites a strong trump card, wouldn't it? And
how can I not share my friends' and subordinates' fates and leave the
battery just on the eve of the appointed dangerous battle?" These
reflections ended with my call to the personnel group—I refused to
seize the "happy opportunity."

The same afternoon the battle order was canceled. That meant I
was in luck once more.

That's all about my experience as "a fighter with anti-Semitism"
during the war.

Did I achieve something essential at that time? Did it do the Jews
some good? I don't think so. Nevertheless, I don't repent any of my
youthful actions. Moreover, I'm sure that at least a few of my fellow
soldiers referred to me while rebutting somebody's sweeping accu-
sations of Jews, their cowardice and other sins at the front. I hope
my comrades' children and grandchildren heard the words of their
objections.

While finishing this rather complex chapter, I see both positive
and negative considerations for the Jews' behavior at the front in it.
I think the reason for such contradictions is the impossibility of giving a sole definition of any whole people, not only of Soviet Jews.

Writing this chapter, I tried to be honest and unprejudiced. And
I still firmly adhere to my youthful belief in the basic equality of all
human beings.

A number of years have passed since the end of the war. Today
everyone can see the official statistics of the Great Patriotic War.
The data demonstrate that the Jews' statistical relative participation
in the war (i.e., the number of participants per 100,000 individuals
of the whole population) was no less than other peoples'. The statistic for war casualties shows a similar ratio.

Women of Our Rifle Regiment

Only men served in our battery. Therefore, my reader, I can't tell you how the women of our regiment specifically fought or served during the war. If you are interested in this matter, there are books, both documentary and fictitious, about the contribution of Soviet women to our ultimate victory, and about some notable female heroes. Nevertheless, I served in a rifle regiment for a relatively long time, and I became familiar with several of our female comrades. Often, during periods when our regiment was in the rear, I had an opportunity to associate with some of them. Sometimes, I had a conversation with a female comrade during our long marches. More than once, my male comrades frankly shared with me their experience concerning women at the front. Finally, several reunions of our division's veterans, both male and female, took place after the war (see the appendix), and I had many conversations with my former female comrades about their lives. As you understand, the main topics of all of our discussions were private matters. In this chapter, I want to share with the readers the bulk of what I have learned from all of these contacts.

In our rifle regiment, and I think in every other infantry unit, the life and fate of most women were very hard. Particularly, our unit was not motorized, so almost all of our "female battle friends" had to march some 30 to 40 kilometers nightly along with the male soldiers. Together with us they got wet or froze; when things went well, they got warm or dried by a campfire beside us. There were a little more than twenty of them in the regiment: telephone operators, a doctor, nurses and medical orderlies, and two typists. (In 1944–1945, a group of two or three female snipers appeared several times in our regiment. Division headquarters assigned them to our regiment for short periods. I know only a little about them and their actions.)

Most of the "female friends" whom I knew came to the regiment after completing short-term schools of practical nursing or signal service schools. Only the senior doctor of the regimental medical company, Vera Mikhaylovna Penkina, graduated from a medical institute before the war; she was mobilized in 1942 as a licensed physician.

Why did many girls choose to go to the front? I think there were a few very different reasons. Some young women were motivated by patriotism; others had become tired of suffering from the deep privations under which the civilian population in the rear areas had long been struggling. There was one more, undoubtedly serious motive: at the front she could find her intended, or at least a "temporary husband"—back home, men had become a rarity.

The least life-threatening places where women served, if one may generally speak about safety at the front, were the regimental headquarters (where they served as typists or telephone operators) and the regimental medical company (where women served in the full range of positions, from senior doctor to medical orderly). In the most serious danger were the girls who served in battalion medical platoons as combat medics. They bandaged the wounded under enemy fire and dragged them away from enemy fire. Most medical orderlies in such platoons were older men, but sometimes a girl served there.

From the first hour of serving in a unit like our regiment, every woman became a subject of undisguised craving. Very few of them remained without a sexual partner; even substantially more rare were those who refused to become a concubine on moral grounds.

Olya

I knew the only girl in our regiment who rejected a lot of "propositions" on principle and who yielded to no solicitations and even ignored some threats. It was the eighteen-year-old blonde Olya Martynova, a former inhabitant of the city of Rostov-on-Don. She was short, chubby, and blue-eyed. So, if she hadn't been wearing a soldier's uniform and boots, one would have taken her for a senior high school student.

Once, in the early fall of 1943, during one of the many overnight foot marches along the dirt roads of Zaporozhe oblast, I found myself beside Olya, and a slow, frank conversation began. I learned that she had come to us that spring after completing a short-term nursing school. Olya had enrolled in the school for patriotic reasons the previous summer, just after graduation from high school. Her parents had remained at home during the half-year-long German occupation of Rostov-on-Don. Just recently Olya had received their first letter full of hopes for her forthcoming return.

Olya told me about the endless importunate (sometimes even compulsory) demands from her for sexual intimacy, which she had experienced from the day when she first joined our regiment. Her words (pronouncing the r's in the nice French manner)—"But I refused all of them. After all, I didn't come here for such affairs"—told me that Olya was different from all the others. She was an absolutely naive, innocent girl, and I appreciated her conscientious attitude.

Olya's refusal to comply cost her very dearly, though. She became the only woman in the regiment who was appointed to a rifle battalion as a combat medic of a medical platoon.

For about half a year, fate saved Olya, but on 1 October 1943, when we started storming the Prishib Hills in the Wotan Line, a shell fragment pierced her chest. Death came instantly.

At that time my platoon was temporarily detached from the rifle companies: with our heavy guns, we were unable to get over the antitank ditch fronting the hills. Finally combat engineers completed a small embankment across the ditch, and we started after the battalions. When we reached the embankment, I saw at the bottom of the ditch two soldiers laying somebody's bloody, motionless body on a stretcher. Looking closely at the tragic scene, I recognized Olya. The medical orderlies told me that she had been killed while rushing to help a wounded soldier.

* * *

The fates of our other women developed quite differently. I don't mean they all survived the war unhurt (to be precise, two women were injured). The point of the matter is about their status: almost all of them became a *PPZh* (the Russian abbreviation for a "campaign wife") of some of our soldiers, mostly officers.

A staff officer, a friend of mine, once told me that the chief of the regimental personnel group, Captain Kazinskiy, was obliged to report to the regiment's commander upon the arrival of any new woman, especially on her appearance and sex appeal. Then, after a short "orientation interview," regimental "higher-ups" decided to which detachment she would be assigned. Often, it actually meant whose *PPZh* she would become. Usually, women didn't refuse such a fate and agreed readily, although the difference in age could reach as much as twenty-five years. Few women were restrained by their future partner's marital status or whether or not he already had children. It was clear in advance that any commander's *PPZh* would have privileges not only in protection but also, within the limits of what was possible at the front, to have a dry warm shelter and a steady supply of food. Making her choice, the girl cherished the hope of getting married; she tried as hard as possible to gain that man's heart. I know only one instance when a *PPZh* reached her goal, but mostly they turned out to be abandoned and, as a rule, remained single to their dying days.

Sometimes, however, females didn't submit to the "higher-ups'" choice. There were rare occasions when an unruly woman, following her own heart, spurned the designated choice, and chose a lower ranking officer, although it might threaten her with serious troubles. Here, for example, is a true story of a "field love triangle" that developed in our regiment and existed for a fairly long time.

Tasya

In the summer of 1943, a female telephone operator, Tasya by name, arrived in the regiment. During the "orientation interview" she caught the fancy of the regimental headquarters chief, Major Bondarchuk. So Tasya's name (I don't remember her last name) entered the roster of the 1st Rifle Battalion, but she herself stayed with Bondarchuk. But one day, because of a business trip to army headquarters, he left our location for a week.

Tasya spent those days in the 1st Rifle Battalion and while there became closely acquainted with the deputy battalion commander, Senior Lieutenant Ivan Savushkin. He was of medium height, chubby-faced, and looked a little simple. Ivan was younger than Bondarchuk by some ten years. Obviously, he was to Tasya's liking, and by the second day they were already inseparable. She never took her loving eyes off the happy senior lieutenant. For them, the "honeyweek" flew by in a moment. When Bondarchuk returned, Savushkin tried to arrange Tasya's "transfer" back to him, as the battalion's official roster stipulated. That attempt just caused a fit of rage and a torrent of threats from the major. From that point on, Tasya had to be with Bondarchuk "in the performance of her duty," but at times she succeeded in having secret meetings with Vanya [Ivan's nickname] "at her heart's summons." The jealous and vengeful major sometimes learned about their previous clandestine meetings but couldn't prevent the next ones. Therefore, he focused his revenge on Savushkin. The difference in their ranks gave him plenty of opportunities for that.

Deputy rifle battalion commander was one of the hardest and most life-threatening positions at the front. Many in the regiment knew Savushkin as a conscientious soldier. I always remember him near Sevastopol, sitting in a narrow crevice of a rock with a receiver clasped to his ear. The battalion CP was located there. The path to the crevice was in the line of sight of enemy machine guns—the corpses of several of our soldiers, who had tried to slip through the danger zone by daylight, gave visual evidence of the extreme hazard of this journey. Savushkin's duties forced him to travel this path to the battalion companies and to the regimental CP time and again daily. Ivan performed all requisite actions fearlessly and diligently throughout the war.

Thirty years later, in 1973, a traditional reunion of our division's veterans took place, and I met Ivan Petrovich Savushkin there. He looked healthy but had grown stout and bald. To my surprise, I saw only one award on his chest—the modest Order of the Red Star. It seemed to be some misunderstanding because most veterans had been decorated generously. I asked him directly whether his grandchildren had lost their grandfather's decorations. Ivan answered with bitterness, "This is damned Bondarchuk's revenge for Tasya's love of me. That beast forbade the personnel department to put me forward for a decoration as well as for advance in rank. So I finished the war as a senior lieutenant, same as I was in 1942."

I don't remember Tasya's subsequent fate. I only know for certain that she never became Savushkin's lawful wife.

Vera Mikhaylovna

An attractive twenty-five-year-old Muscovite woman named Vera Mikhaylovna Penkina conducted herself in a very specific way. Having the quite high rank of captain of the medical service and being

of strong character, Vera demonstrated her independence from the 231
first days of her service in our regiment. She started with firm re-
fusals to a few "hand and heart" offers issued from some regimental "higher-ups." After she saw the lay of the land in our regiment,
Vera chose a "campaign partner" by herself. It was the regimental
120-mm mortar battery commander, thirty-year-old Senior Lieutenant Vsevolod (nickname Seva) Lyubshin. A well-built, brown-eyed,
nice man, he was a descendant of Kuban Cossacks. Before the war
Lyubshin lived in Kazakhstan and worked at a school as a military
science teacher for the ninth and tenth grades. Vera Mikhaylovna
(she required all our officers to use this courteous form of address,
using her patronymic name, while addressing her) wasn't wrong in
her choice. Vsevolod provided almost ideal, by front criteria, conveniences for her. There were six wagons in Lyubshin's battery. Vsevolod transformed one of them to serve as Vera's mobile bedroom
during our long night marches. In the medical company she could
only dream of such comfort. (From time to time her tireless lover
crept in for a short time "to get warm" or "to take a rest." Vera
Mikhaylovna was a very temperamental woman, so soldiers who
marched beside the wagon sometimes could hear some sounds and
guess what was going on under the tarpaulin cover.)

Usually the Vsevolod-Vera couple looked self-confident and cheerful, and it always seemed as if both were destined for each other.

Whenever we stayed relatively far behind the front line, where
the environment was rather calm and safe, Vera Mikhaylovna often
spent days making her rounds in the regimental artillerymen's location. Here she took pleasure from the tasty courses that she ordered
up. Vera liked to drink the "government's 100 grams" (and more) or
some "trophy" liquor, matching our men shot for shot. Becoming
tipsy, she would grow stupid and irritable, and would begin using
foul language.

I still can't forget the shocking action that she committed in January 1945 while intoxicated. At that time, we stayed for a day in some
East Prussian manor. During the several previous months, we had
succeeded in collecting gramophone records with wonderful Russian songs performed by some emigrants from the old Russia, who
were unknown within the USSR. Somehow we had acquired a portable gramophone as well. So, whenever a quiet hour or so came, we

often enjoyed listening to favorite melodies. Both the gramophone and the records were the common property of two batteries (the 76-mm guns and the 120-mm mortars).

On that day, Vera, along with our group of several artillery officers, settled into the spacious mansion. We dined with a lot of liquor, and very soon Vera became intoxicated. She began picking a fight with Vsevolod. To upset him in a most telling and public fashion, she seized our treasure—the cardboard box with our entire record collection—lifted it high in the air, then threw it down with all her might. Everybody froze; only Lyubshin continued extending his begging hands to her and murmuring, "Vera, stop, Vera, stop."

Now I want to tell you the story of a nighttime incident, which took place in March 1945. I believe it shows some morals and manners typical of our front life. The main characters of that event were Vera, Vsevolod, and our new regiment commander, Lieutenant Colonel Kuptsov.

Mikhail Kuptsov, a tall man in his early forties, had accepted that post about a month before, during the heavy combat on the Zemland Peninsula. In March we were withdrawn from the front line to get ready for the coming storming of Königsberg, which was planned for early April. The regiment was encamped in a forest, and we resided in well-built dugouts. At that time, Kuptsov began to familiarize himself with the auxiliary detachments of the regiment. While visiting the medical company, he took note of the graceful Vera. As a senior doctor, she introduced all medical personnel to the esteemed guest.

The next day, shortly before midnight, Kuptsov called up the medical company commander, "Send Captain Penkina to the regimental headquarters' dugout immediately. I have already sent my orderly to escort her." But, naturally, Vera was spending the night with Lyubshin, so the orderly rambled throughout the forest in search of her for a quite long time before finding Vsevolod's dugout. It wasn't easy to rouse Lyubshin from his sleep, and when he was finally completely awake, the orderly had to tell the puzzled battery commander over and over again about who was being summoned and to where. In a few minutes Seva and Vera left the dugout and followed the orderly. When they reached the headquarters dugout that was being guarded by a soldier armed with a submachine gun, the orderly asked them to wait for a bit and went into the dugout. In a minute he emerged, saying, "Only the Guards captain is invited." Vera entered alone.

Meanwhile, Vsevolod lit up a Belomor cigarette and began walking nervously back and forth near the entrance. He had just tossed aside the first stub and was attempting to light the second cigarette when suddenly he heard Vera's desperate scream, "Seva!" In a moment, Lyubshin unbuttoned his holster and drew his pistol, shouldered aside the guard, and burst into the dugout. Aiming his pistol at Kuptsov, Vsevolod seized Vera's hand, and both left the lair of the "higher-up" would-be rapist. (I got all the details of what happened that night from Lyubshin at our veterans' traditional meeting in 1975. He told me also about the consequence of the episode: Kuptsov began taking revenge on Vsevolod just after Victory Day and continued to persecute him until the day of Lyubshin's demobilization from the army.)

The Lyubshin-Penkina "military field romance" came to an end three weeks before the war finished. Concealing her actions from Vsevolod, Vera Mikhaylovna scored a great success: an order for her demobilization arrived at division headquarters. Only when all the papers were ready did she reveal her secret, and then she addressed her chosen one blithely, "Dear Seva, thank you a lot for everything you gave me over these years! Thank you for your love, for your hot caresses! However, darling, you must understand that on Civvy Street you and I cannot be a good match for each other; we are too different. You will find your fortune, and I, mine. Farewell, dear Seva, and be happy!"

Many, including me, were stunned by the sudden and unexpected termination of that romance. At that time, we all considered her as a traitress. But now in retrospect I think she was right.

In 1948, while visiting Moscow, I tried to meet Penkina, but her former neighbors told me that just recently Vera, still unmarried, had left for the Ukraine. That's all I know about Vera Mikhaylovna Penkina.

Vsevolod Semenovich Lyubshin served as an artillery officer a few more years, then retired, returned to his hometown, and got married. I met him several times in the 1970s and 1980s. He is over ninety now.

Anya

A hard fate fell to Anna ("Anya") Kornakova's lot. A medical company nurse, she was assigned to visit our battery regularly, and actually, she came to see our soldiers and officers quite frequently. I was familiar with Anya since 1942, but only in June 1943 did I first hear about her intimate affairs. At that time Anya, a twenty-year-old and well-built girl, fell in love with our new, very handsome chief of regimental artillery, Captain Vasiliy Karpov. Because of Anya's strong sex appeal, I'm not sure whether he was her first lover at the front.

A half year passed, and one day a new secretary-typist, a nice Kievan, Maya by name, arrived in the regiment. After her arrival, Karpov stopped paying attention to Anya. And so she experienced the bitterness of defeat, as well as the deep pain of being dropped by a beloved man, who had abandoned her decidedly and suddenly. But quite soon her negative emotions grew feeble: there were many men who desired to be Anya's lover.

Anya's next "friend" was a rifle company commander (I don't remember his name), but in about a month he was injured and taken to the hospital. Then Anya became intimate with another company commander, Remizov by name. They were together for a long time. He was a typical drillmaster. Remizov's main merits were his stentorian voice and outstanding ability to hold his liquor. But the series of Anya's misfortunes didn't come to an end yet. In the summer of 1944, she fell sick with typhus. It was strange because lice, the main carrier of that disease, were not occurring as often by that time as the year before, especially in her surroundings. Anya returned from the hospital closely cropped. She looked strange, and in those days I couldn't look at her without sympathy. But as soon as her hair grew a little again, something else came to light: Anya was pregnant. In a month she left us and started on her journey home to give birth to Remizov's offspring.

What happened to her at that time was in exact accordance with a popular spicy, indecent wartime joke:

Question: What is the difference between a bomb and a frontline girl?

Answer: The bomb is stuffed in the rear then dispatched to the front. For a frontline girl, it's the other way around.

I learned about Anya's life after her departure from a rather confessional letter from her that I received in 1968. The most painful of Anya's sufferings occurred at the moment she returned to her native village. Shortly after hugging Anya in greeting, her mother handed her a recent letter she had received from Remizov. Informing Anya's mother about the pending return of her daughter, the author of the letter strongly rejected his assumed fatherhood. Remizov wrote, "She had dozens of men like me; and I haven't slept with her for a long time at all." Anya was shocked by her former lover's meanness. Nature, however, continued to run its course, and soon a third person appeared—Anya's son. The next year she already knew that Remizov, after being demobilized, had gotten married and was living with his family in a village about 200 kilometers from hers. Anya sent him several letters, but there were no answers.

At the age of three, the boy began asking Anya who and where his father was. Instead of answering, she began to make everything ready for a journey. With the last of her money they set off to meet Remizov. As one could expect, neither mother nor child was even let in the door.

Anya didn't dare return home and settled in the city of Kalinin (now Tver). She worked as a nurse in local hospitals, then as a medical worker in a kindergarten. In 1950, Anya got married. It seemed that she had at last found her fortune. Alas, her husband died just three years later.

Zhenya D. and Zhenya L.

Only two couples of our regiment turned their frontline love into lawful marriage. The senior secretary of the regimental personnel department, Grigoriy Demchenko, married the most beautiful woman of the medical company, senior nurse Zhenya Domnikova. Since the war they have been living happily together in the city of Kaluga.

The other marriage has a special prehistory. In 1942, a young but well-educated and experienced doctor of the medical company, Nikolay Dudnikov, began courting his assistant nurse Zhenya Lifner. She quickly seemed poised to reciprocate his feelings. But Dudnikov was not the only one who took note of Zhenya. The other was the

Chapter 22

aforementioned Captain Kazinskiy, whose wife had been killed by the German occupiers in 1941. To get rid of his leading rival, Kazinskiy devised a crafty plan. Thanks to his important connections, Kazinskiy managed a promotion for Dudnikov that transferred Nikolay to a more important unit, but one at a "safe" distance from Zhenya—the divisional medical battalion. The promotion raised Dudnikov to the rank of senior doctor, but it also took him out of Zhenya's proximity.

After that, only one problem remained for Kazinskiy—to conquer Zhenya's heart. This task took several months.

In postwar years the Kazinskiys have been living in the city of Chernovtsy, Ukraine.

* * *

After telling the previous stories about our "female combat comrades," I must tell readers something else, too. There were occurrences at the front when women (not through their fault!) brought misfortune.

Let's remember the long night march that preceded the tragic combat near Vishnevy hamlet (see chapter 6). I wrote there: "Our march along country roads was interrupted several times at some intersections because the regiment's advance guard hesitated over which road to take. (They didn't want to disturb the regiment's commanders, who were sleeping in their wagons.)"

Now, I must apologize to my readers—the statement in chapter 6 was true enough but was not the complete story. I should have rewritten the last sentence above (in parentheses) and offered more detail as follows: They didn't dare disturb the regiment's commanders, who were sleeping in their wagons together with their "wenches"—because who knows what might have been happening under the tarpaulin cover at that or any other moment—and so some stoppages lasted up to a half hour. Many soldiers grumbled over the tedious waiting, and most of them understood the reason for the stoppages.

Not far from me at that time, the Number 1 gun crew of my platoon was standing, and I heard them muttering. At the center of the group stood the gun crew commander, the battle-tried senior sergeant, Vladimir Tetyukov. Everybody respected him for his courage, discretion, and kindness. Nevertheless, after several halts

Tetyukov's patience had been exhausted and he spoke out from the heart,—"Remember, boys, my words: Russia won't see victory till the army gets rid of 'wenches.'"

What happened in the morning, you already know from chapter 6. The delays cost us so dearly!

Tetyukov's prophecy didn't come true: despite the presence of "wenches" in the army, Russia did emerge victorious from the war. But Tetyukov didn't see the victory: he was killed just a few hours after uttering his prediction. And the "wenches" *indirectly* caused his death. Indeed, if the highest regimental commanders had not been sleeping with their "wenches," the advance guard would have dared disturb them immediately, we would have entered Vishnevy before dawn, and our riflemen would have had the opportunity to dig in. So our artillerymen would not have been forced to take a mortal risk.

For the sake of justice, I have to note that most of my regiment commanders (there were thirteen of them during the almost three years I spent in the regiment) never forgot the call of duty in favor of love affairs.

* * *

One may ask me, why didn't I mention in my writing many examples of the professional side of women's participation in the war? I already answered this question in detail in the introductory paragraph of this chapter. Nevertheless, I don't want my readers to imagine that most women of our regiment kept busy only with matters of the heart or sexual matters. On the contrary, *almost all of them, particularly the doctors, nurses and medical orderlies, discharged their difficult obligations carefully, sometimes heroically.* Their sense of duty overcame the fear and fatigue. And all of this was done under unique conditions while bearing even more hardships than male soldiers suffered. I would remind the reader that (besides a woman's periodical discomforts) our regimental "female friends" were surrounded by hundreds of male soldiers all day long. With no privacy they even faced the problem of how to urinate or defecate, particularly when we marched or halted for rest in an open country.

Nearly every woman's life at the front, especially in the infantry, was incredibly hard. Therefore, whenever I meet some unfamiliar female veteran of the Great Patriotic War, I always make a mental bow to her, not only for her personal contribution to our victory but also for the hardships that she *certainly* suffered at the front. And I absolutely do not care about any of her amorous adventures that *perhaps* occurred in the remote years of her and my youth.

Author's note: I have changed the last names in this chapter for ethical reasons. Only Martynova's and Tetyukov's last names are genuine.

Chapter 23

The Germans: Recollections of My Feelings and Encounters

During the war I hated the Germans as a whole. To me, the term "as a whole" embraced all the murderous acts that Hitler's troops perpetrated in their own country, in the conquered European countries, and especially on the occupied territories of our motherland. My hatred toward the Germans only strengthened after I became a witness to many terrible atrocities during the war.

One could not but hate the invaders for the "scorched earth" that I saw in the region between the Volga and Don rivers, left behind by the retreating Germans, and for the gallows they set up in a village near Rostov-on-Don, where the bodies of five hanged civilians swung in the winter wind. I hated them for burning the central part of the city of Stalino and for destroying and depopulating Sevastopol, as well as for the hundreds of thousands of youth that they commandeered for slave labor in Germany. However, I also heard of rare instances when some German invaders were not as cruel as most.

I had an opportunity to visit my hometown, the city of Kiev, for one day during the summer of 1944. The city had been liberated only seven months before, and I witnessed its devastation, especially the totally destroyed Kreshchatik, the city's main and most beautiful street. I found only the skeletal remains of the building where our family had lived before the war. The Germans had torched this home of recent construction. I also met a former schoolgirl who had witnessed the tragic sight of the procession of local Jews to their terrible fate at Babi Yar. After seeing and hearing all of this, how could I not feel a fierce hatred toward the Germans?

Yes, there was no way the Germans could repay this debt to me. As I fought on, I tried to take revenge on them for all of their monstrous offenses. No doubt, I rejoiced over each of our local victories. And I also remember how pleased I was when I read published communiqués of German casualties, as well as the reports of the destructive bombing of German cities by the Allies.

However, when it came to dealing with specific, living German individuals (whom I chanced to meet rather infrequently during the war), sometimes my reactions differed from my "general hatred" of the Germans. For example, when I met prisoners I felt a certain triumph of revenge. In other instances, especially, when I encountered feeble old people, women, or children, I felt some sympathy for them.

When in combat, I usually observed German soldiers at a distance of 100 meters or more, so I could see only figures, not faces. The first time I had an opportunity to see them face-to-face was in a village close to the Don River in December 1942. Two Red Army guards were holding a few prisoners in a small yard. A fellow soldier and I went right up to the wicker fence to get a better look at our enemies. Standing in a group, the German soldiers in their dirty and crumpled mouse-gray greatcoats were talking to each other in low voices. They had not shaved for a long time. Some of them scratched themselves here and there continuously, a sure sign that they had lice. None of them paid any attention to us. Only one prisoner, a tall thirty-something-year-old German, stood alone apart from the group. He was bareheaded, and I remember his long hair that was combed back (no Soviet serviceman was permitted to wear such a haircut). However, the main thing that is etched into my mind was the way that he looked at us. There was plenty of hatred and contempt in his gaze! Even in his miserable status as a dirty and lousy prisoner, he had not lost his Aryan haughtiness, a feeling fostered by their "beloved Führer." Although we were eager to shoot that arrogant "Fritz," instead we only used the choicest of Russian swear words.

* * *

In previous chapters you have already read about my face-to-face encounters with German soldiers in close combat in Lithuania, on Hill 111.4 in East Prussia, and during the memorable night in Königsberg.

I also had a few short contacts with fresh "tongues" (Red Army parlance for "prisoners for interrogation") who had just been snatched from the Germans' trenches. The scouts often tried to conduct some sort of preliminary interrogation on their own, that is, without any officers around, and they would ask me to serve as the interpreter. As a rule these encounters had little interest for me because very fresh "tongues" usually were in a state of shock, and the scouts who had seized them were in hurry to deliver their "loot" back to headquarters.

It is worth mentioning here that the German soldiers we captured after February 1945, while they were fighting in their own homeland, looked completely different from the way the previous "conquerors of most of Europe" had looked earlier in the war. The majority of them were tired, unshaven, and sloppily uniformed. Their tarnished look was clear proof that they no longer believed in victory.

I do recall a strange incident, which occurred in late April on the Zemland Peninsula west of Königsberg. Our regiment was advancing westward along the northern bank of the narrow Königsberg Canal. Because there had not been any enemy resistance for quite a long time, we were advancing in column formation. Suddenly somebody gave the alarm—across the canal, at a distance of about a quarter of a mile, we saw a column of armed German soldiers marching in the same direction. Although they outnumbered us by at least two to one and they definitely saw us, they gave no indication of aggressive intent. We soon understood that they were only in a hurry to leave us behind, to reach the crossing over the bay, and to catch up with the main body of German troops. Soon after this strange encounter the canal bent away and our routes diverged. The peaceful enemy disappeared.

In early May 1945, at a time when there was no fighting in this area, a young German soldier approached our battery's position from a nearby forest with his hands up. He unexpectedly halted, took a small harmonica out of his pocket with one hand, and began cheerfully playing the popular tune "Katyusha."

If he thought to disarm our hostility, his ruse worked. The way in which he turned himself in made all of us feel friendly toward him. Smiling ingratiatingly, the tow-haired, blue-eyed, short guy answered all of my questions willingly: Rudi by name, seventeen years old, born in the Sudetenland. He had not taken part in any combat so far. After this short interrogation Rudi performed a long concert for us, first by playing the harmonica and, second, by playing the "trophy" (captured) accordion, on which he performed the famous Russian songs "Black Eyes" and "Stenka Razin." We greeted both songs enthusiastically. Then he performed a few German soldiers' ribald songs and "Katyusha" once again.

I felt no animosity at all toward Rudi. After the concert was over, I ordered that this unusual prisoner be fed and then kept under our own supervision, without anybody else's knowledge. But on the third day a SMERSH group officer discovered our secret. Rudi was taken into custody, and we heard nothing further about his fate.

* * *

Now I'll tell you a bit about the local population. We did not have many encounters with civilians because the overwhelming majority of them had enough time to evacuate the region before we arrived. I do remember a partially discolored poster, which I saw in the vicinity of Königsberg. It urged all citizens, especially women, to evacuate immediately, lest they become victims of Soviet monsters and sexual predators.

We met the first civilians in the small town of Sidlung near Königsberg. It occurred one day in late January 1945 (I described that day in chapter 12). I felt no anger toward the frightened women.

My next meeting with civilians took place on 8 April, during the battle in downtown Königsberg (see also chapter 12). There were several elderly and disabled women in a lobby of a hotel. Seeing those kinds of German civilians, I never gloated over their misfortunes, and perhaps I even sympathized with them a bit.

* * *

I think I ought not to pass over in silence the very troublesome topic concerning the sexual behavior and sexual crimes of our troops in East Prussia. When we first entered the enemy's homeland, we were informed about a strict order concerning the proper treatment of civilians, but I'm sure that many actually violated it. Yet I never heard about any trials regarding these sorts of violations in our division. However, I do know some facts concerning such misbehavior and crimes.

I have already mentioned the whispers about our six scouts' "success" with women they had encountered in a German hamlet, as well as about a Soviet soldier's misbehavior in the lobby of the hotel in Königsberg. However, there were more incidents.

Our division remained in Pillau after the war ended and stayed there until July 1945. There were few civilians in the part of the city where our battery stayed, just women and elderly men, and I didn't

see any children around at all. During the evenings, soon after the
signal "Bedtime to all!" had sounded and all soldiers were already
in their barracks, some reckless and "successful" officers would secretly slip away from their quarters (mostly the "officers' dormitories") to visit their "German girlfriends." As a rule, there was a small
parcel of food and treats in each violator's hands. It wasn't necessary
to know the German language in these sorts of meetings.

You will also read in the next chapter about my former subordinate, Alexey S. by name. There was a temporary but touching romance between him and a German woman.

However, I know an additional, terrible account of Soviet soldiers' sexual assaults. I will describe it below.

Once, in July 1945, when we were at the time located in a rural
hamlet, I met an eighteen-year-old German woman named Annie.
Her figure was definitely attractive, but she looked very unwell. We
had a conversation, and I asked about her health before we parted.
Annie gave a deep sigh of sadness and told me her story, which
touched me deeply.

The hamlet where she was living was about twenty miles from
Pillau. When it became known that Soviet troops were approaching the area in late April, Annie decided to go to Pillau in order to
try and evacuate by sea. So did most of her neighbors. She packed
her few belongings into a shopping bag and set out on her flight to
safety.

It was not a big deal for Annie, who had grown up in the countryside, to get to Pillau. Unfortunately, however, soon after she started
her trek, Annie stumbled and sprained her leg badly. Since she had
to continue her journey while leaning on a stick and hobbling all the
way, the girl could not escape. Russian soldiers intercepted her less
than half a mile from the harbor and ordered her to go back to her
residence.

Instead of a few hours, Annie's journey back lasted a full week.
Time and time again, both day and night, passing Soviet soldiers
stopped her. Nobody ever beat her, they just ordered her to lie
down, and she was afraid to refuse. In some instances she was forced
to have sex with up to three men at a time, one by one. Altogether,
there were more than eighty of these sexual assaults. Annie ultimately made it home, suffering from a high fever when I met her.
Afterward, she was sick for two weeks. "I began growing stronger

just recently, but the nightmares still stay with me," were the last words of Annie's sorrowful story.

I still feel really bitter when recalling these terrible incidents caused by some of our Soviet soldiers. However, at the same time (*but not as an excuse*), I would also like to mention that in 1945, I knew or heard about the aforementioned occurrences only in my own direct environment (of around 300 officers and men). Now I know much more grievous information on this topic, but it is not my personal experience.

I also think that sexual assaults and sexual crimes weren't exclusively Soviet matters, but *characteristic of the entire war. And war is indeed the most awful thing in existence.* (Now all of us know what happened not so many years ago, during the wars in former Yugoslavia.)

* * *

My final encounters with Germans, which returned my thoughts to the war, took place at my Kiev Polytechnical Institute during 1946 and 1947. Dozens of German prisoners of war, under escort by armed guards, worked there to rebuild the institute's half-destroyed buildings. Their job was difficult. The prisoners looked lean and dirty. Their faces were joyless. However, I felt no sympathy for any of them. I mentally addressed them: "It serves you right. You got what you deserved. Why did you come here? Why did you kill our people and destroy our cities and villages? Let the next generations of Germans remember your fate. And don't seek any sympathy from me."

Part IV

The War Ended, but Life Went On

Three Postwar Months in East Prussia

Well, at last the war was over, and I continued to do my duty along-side my fellow soldiers and officers, with whom I'd passed through the ordeal of war together. I'm trying to recall now how we kept busy during the first months of peace.

First of all, we arranged barracks for our three regimental batter-ies in the spacious dining hall of some former factory. We converted one side room of the hall into a bedroom for ten officers. Three other side rooms served as the battery warehouses.

After the artillerymen completed these arrangements, their main work, which became the task of all regimental detachments, was putting the so-called adjacent territory in order. Everyone did it without enthusiasm: all of us knew that the regiment's commander, Rubtsov, would only expand the size of the "adjacent territory" the following day, no matter how much we did. His only goal was to keep all of his subordinate officers and soldiers busy.

For several days running in June all regimental artillerymen worked all day long as farmhands in a field some 20 kilometers from Pillau, harvesting ripe crops. It was hard work, but we didn't mind so much, as it was also productive and a pleasing change of scenery and labor.

Day after day our officers gave lessons in artillery to all the bat-teries—all the artillerymen "studied" over and over again the parts of the gun and how they operated, despite the fact that all of this was already well known to everyone. Moreover, in case of surprise inspection, all the lecturers (including myself) had to prepare writ-ten lesson plans and abstracts of their lectures.

Furthermore, the men in all the detachments listened to hour-long weekly lectures on both domestic and international news.

Two novelties in the field of officers' and soldiers' nourishment appeared in early July. The regimental command established a paid officers' canteen (even though our monthly pay was negligible). Our canteen had its own "specialty"—homemade beer! The regimental secret brewery was in a deserted hamlet not far from Pillau. The brewer was our battery soldier, Alexey S., who was taken from the battery and assigned to this unusual post just by verbal order. Two soldiers from other detachments assisted Alexey, along with a German woman, who was the only inhabitant of the hamlet at that time. She also cooked, cleaned rooms, and did laundry. (From the second night of being hired, this "frau" and Alexey slept together. In a month or so, when we were leaving Pillau to return to the USSR, they hugged and kissed each other, and she shed bitter tears.

Along with brewing beer, the team made a lot of *samogon* for the regimental command, but the best part of the alcohol production, some ten liters weekly, "reached the wrong address": the team secretly delivered it to my battery, and I had it at my disposal. (Alexey never forgot his real assignment.)

At that time the ranks were provided with food in their detachments as usual. However, there was a special novelty in this field as well—three times a day, a medical company representative inspected the freshly cooked meals.

In late May one more memorable event occurred. A headquarters command went out to all regimental detachments: send all your officers and soldiers who have received at least two combat Order decorations to the regimental parade ground.[1]

There were about forty men in our regiment who met this requirement. Four artillerymen were among them: the 120-mm mortar battery commander Senior Lieutenant Vsevolod Lyubchenko and I (both with four Orders); Lyubchenko's subordinate, platoon commander Lieutenant Alexey Brik; and my subordinate, gun crew commander Senior Sergeant Dmitriy Shcherbinin (both with two Orders).

The regimental commander's adjutant formed us in one rank, and Lieutenant Colonel Rubtsov announced that in honor of our Great Victory, a ceremonial parade would be staged in Moscow's Red Square soon, and so he was now going to select candidates for the parade. (This information took my breath away!)

A quite long, freshly hewn stick was in the adjutant's hand. It stood upright with one tip on the ground, and everyone in the rank was ordered to approach the stick in turn. The length of the stick was 170 cm (approximately 5 feet 7 inches), and anyone who was shorter was dropped from the selection. Only a few men qualified for the parade. Shcherbinin and Brik were among them, while Lyub-chenko and I failed this height requirement.

Both lucky artillerymen returned from the parade at the very end of June. They were overflowing with unforgettable impressions and told us about their experiences in detail.

While participating in the ceremony of the historical Victory Parade of 24 June 1945, they saw Generalissimus Joseph Stalin; Marshals of the Soviet Union Georgiy Zhukov and Konstantin Rokossovskiy, who conducted the parade; members of the Politburo; several more marshals of the Soviet Union; and numerous other generals.[2]

Their stories of the preparation for the ceremony were particularly interesting.

First of all, along with several thousand other participants in the parade, they were awarded with one more Order. Shcherbinin and Brik received the Order of the Red Banner. Then every participant received a specially tailored and individually fitted ceremonial uniform, including boots.

While preparing for the triumphal procession, the participants stayed in different settlements near Moscow. They drilled all day long there, especially to master a faultless ceremonial step. The best Soviet musicians, actors, opera singers, ballet dancers, and entertainers entertained them on most evenings (excluding the last week before the parade, when rehearsal marches were held at Red Square after midnight).

* * *

Twice during July our fully equipped regiment marched to the local railroad station to practice boarding and loading on a freight train. The first drill exposed many defects, along with the need to foresee some common things that facilitate towing and loading. The second drill passed successfully.

These useful rehearsals naturally fueled my desire to return home as soon as possible.

* * *

A salary bonus in so-called Occupation Marks (OMs) was an unexpected, nice surprise for us. We received it monthly in cash; the total was equal to our salary in rubles. Unfortunately, at that time there were no Voentorg stores or public markets in or near Pillau where we could spend the OMs. Nevertheless, we were told that everybody would be able to exchange his OMs upon crossing the border of the USSR. The exchange rate was two OMs for one ruble.

In spite of headquarters' every effort to fill up the soldiers' and officers' day with study, practice, or other activities, we had at least three evening hours of spare time each day. In addition to our usual methods of passing free time (see chapter 18), at that time gambling card games with OMs as a stake became very popular among us, largely because we all had plenty of these useless and somewhat dubious OMs. The name of our primitive card game was *Ochko* ("The Spot") or "21."

I ought to confess: I was an amateurish, reckless card player and lost a few thousand OMs. My rival was Sasha Bezuglov, the battery cook. Later it came to light that he was a professional cardsharp. That was a good lesson for me: I never again played cards for money.

With my remaining OMs, some 800 worth, along with a loaf of bread and a small package of cookies, I purchased new gray trousers made for me by a German woman out of trophy ("spoils of war") cloth.

* * *

Our group of ten roommate-officers had another way to dispel, at least temporarily, everybody's postwar homesickness by means of *samogon*. We began our long *posidelki* (sit-together time) about an hour after the signal "Bedtime to all!" had sounded and all our subordinates were already asleep.

We started the *posidelki* with conversation that followed the initial round of drinks. After the next rounds of drinks, our talks became more and more lively. At that time somebody would strike up the first song. All of us liked to sing, and our repertoire was very long. Usually the signal to finish the *posidelki* was given by Lieutenant Dmitriev. As soon as he struck up the "Oy da ty kali-i-nushka . . ." ("Oh, my dear rosebud"), everyone knew: Mitrofan had had more than enough drink. Friends helped him to undress and get to bed. Others cleared the table and aired out the room.

* * *

Lieutenant Talip Abidov, a regimental antitank battery fire platoon commander, shared extraordinary news with me at the end of May.

He was an Uzbek and a good friend of mine. Overnight Abidov had been summoned to regimental headquarters, and there he learned of a secret order for his transfer, placing him at the disposal of the People's Commissariat of Defense (NKO). While reading the order, Talip spotted another Uzbek officer's name. Both had to leave for Moscow immediately. Talip supposed that this matter concerned the formation of an Uzbek military unit, so he would have an opportunity to see his relatives in Uzbekistan. After sharing the news with me confidentially, Talip earnestly asked me to sell him my impressive blackface watch at any price. That watch was the only high-quality trophy that I had obtained from the captured Germans in Königsberg (see chapter 12), and I boasted of it constantly. I refused to take money from a good friend and handed him the watch as a memorable gift.

Only forty-one years later did I have an opportunity to clear up Talip's further fate. It was early April 1986 when I received a letter from him. Abidov wrote that he had just recently gotten in contact with the 87th Guards Rifle Division's Veterans Committee. They were inviting him to take part in the upcoming veterans gathering in the town of Krasnograd on 5 May and gave him my address. I answered him, and we actually met there on 6 May 1986. It was a very touching reunion after being apart for more than forty years. We caught each other up on the main events in our lives, as well as about our families. There were thirty members in Talip's family (counting his wife, Khury-opa, and himself, as well as six children and twenty-two grandchildren) at the time of our meeting. To my surprise, I learned these days that Talip Yuldashevich Abidov, who had been a loyal Communist (and, no doubt, an atheist) during the war, had since become a very religious man. He performed all Islamic devotions regularly and heartily.

The most impressive news that I heard from my friend, however, was the story of Abidov's adventures after his mysterious departure from the regiment. Talip narrated his experience in detail.

At that time, in early summer 1945, the NKO dispatched him to the Central Asia region, and he actually did manage to see all his close relatives. However, our supposition concerning the formation of an Uzbek military unit didn't prove true. Actually, Talip, along with several Red Army officers (all of Uzbek and Kazakh origins), received special official papers that provided them with new Muslim names and some unfamiliar military uniforms. According to the instruction, they were Soviet volunteer advisers, who had decided to support the Uyghur people in its war for independence from the Chinese Kuomintang government.[3] Only a few individuals in our country were informed about this war.

There were not many military actions there, but Abidov, who was the head of an Uyghur unit's artillery, had time to excel. He had organized and conducted an intensive artillery bombardment of the Chiang Kai-shekists' positions. Because of substantial casualties, the enemy had retreated. The local Uyghur military leader invited Talip to a reception in honor of the Soviet adviser for his role in the successful attack. During that reception, the host paid attention to Abidov's notable watch. According to local traditional etiquette, Talip immediately presented it to the hospitable host. In return, Talip received a reciprocal gift, an excellent leather overcoat from the high-ranking host's shoulders.

Talip as well as the other "volunteers" returned home within some ten months. They were all strictly forbidden to share their experience with anybody.

* * *

During our long stay in Pillau, Rubtsov on several occasions found fault with my work, as a rule, undeservedly. Because of my youthful hot temper, I couldn't long restrain myself from expressing my animosity for him. Finally, in late July, after Rubtsov's next groundless criticism, I stated sharply that I didn't want to continue my service under his command and I wanted a transfer to another unit. "Give me your written request!"—was the regiment commander's reaction, and I wrote it immediately. In such a way I found myself in the artillery reserves a week before our redeployment to the USSR.

My Discharge from the Army

In Kozelsk

Before my return to Kiev, our regiment was stationed in Kozelsk, an out-of-the-way, hungry little town, which I remember for its boggy autumn mud and high winter snowdrifts. I spent a little more than four months of service, or rather, of idleness, in the artillery reserves here. Extremely homesick for Vera and for my parents' home, and finding myself in my own country without any pressing duties, I sought with all my spirit to return to Kiev as soon as possible, and I took various steps to bring this about.

Shortly after our arrival in Kozelsk, I had turned in a request to headquarters asking to be discharged on the grounds that I did not have a military education and, separately, asking to take the leave time that I had not been able to use during the war. All my papers were accepted; however, weeks crawled by one after another, but nothing happened. Many of the privates and sergeants from the regiment had already been discharged, but the artillery officers' fates were decided at the headquarters of the divisional artillery in Kaluga. I didn't have any way of pestering the bureaucrats in the personnel department there, so I had to wait patiently. Yet with home and with Vera so close, it became more and more difficult to endure such boredom and idleness!

At the same time, I kept trying to find some way, any way, to get to Kiev, even if only for a short visit. In letters to my parents, I asked them to send me an official telegram about "some serious illness," and I asked them and Vera to look for documents at the institute certifying that I was a sophomore there in 1942. Unfortunately, there wasn't any success in their attempts, either.

The only event that shook the monotony of my time in Kozelsk was my fortuitous, but illegal, brief foray to Moscow. Fortunately, on this occasion I once again came off clean.

As my readers remember, I was a nearsighted cadet in 1942. Unfortunately, I had lost my glasses in Tuimazy, just before our division went to the front. Because of my nearsightedness, lacking eyeglasses, I used field glasses throughout the war to help my distant vision. But now as the war was over, I began to worry about new eyeglasses. In late November, our medical company gave me an authorization for glasses. Thereafter I went to Kaluga, where the divisional medical and sanitary battalion was situated. My request was accepted without questions there, but they told me that I would have to wait for at least two months.

Disappointed, I took dinner at a military canteen and then went to look for our regimental truck to return to Kozelsk. Suddenly an approaching serviceman wearing a short fur coat turned to me, "In an hour I'm going to deliver my colonel's trophy car to Moscow, but it is prohibited to drive alone. Would you like to accompany me?" Without even a moment of pause and reflection, I accepted his suggestion, and soon we started on our journey.

My Last Unauthorized Absence

Two different reasons encouraged me to make this rather rash decision. My seventy-five-year-old grandfather, my beloved Aunt Manya, and her two daughters all lived in Moscow, and I was eager to see them. Moreover, the opportunity to take in the atmosphere of peaceful life in our legendary capital was so enticing! But nevertheless, my decision was thoughtless and risky. I had heard about a lot of military commandant patrols in Moscow, and I didn't have official leave of absence. But I realized this danger long after our departure.

Our journey continued all through the night, and we reached Moscow around daybreak the next morning. Fortunately, I made it to my relatives' apartment without bumping into any patrols. My unexpected appearance was a very joyful surprise for all of my dear relatives. I was very excited and happy, too. First of all, Aunt Manya gave me her husband's dress suit and coat. After a very modest but leisurely breakfast I started on a walk (in my civilian "cover") toward Red Square, the Kremlin, and Lenin's Mausoleum.

Everything that caught my eye in Moscow was novel and amazing, but my growing sense of danger dampened my enjoyment of the walk and the impressive scenery. After bumping into military patrols a few times but not being stopped, I dropped into a brightly lit café. There I ordered a drink of liquor and black coffee for myself, as well as a few chocolate bars for my cousins. That little stop cost me 800 rubles, almost half of my monthly wage. I returned to my relatives' apartment, and late that night my aunt and I went to find a public telephone booth where I could try and call Vera. Unfortunately, there were no phone connections between Moscow and Kiev at that time.

Next afternoon, wearing my uniform, I left my hospitable relatives' apartment and safely reached the Kiev railway station. It is impossible to describe what was going on there in the spacious but extremely stuffy waiting rooms. Thousands of demobilized servicemen and officers filled all the rooms, lobbies, and hallways to overflowing. Everybody was striving to get home as soon as possible. All the exits to the platforms were closed, and the crowd was impatiently waiting for announcements about the next train. I didn't pay much attention to the announcements about destinations, as that didn't matter to me. All the trains from the Kiev station were going to stop at the Sukhinichi station, where I would switch to a local train back to my unit.

Finally I heard something unclear from the loudspeakers, and shortly after that I felt the human torrent begin to carry me to the exit. Once we emerged onto the platform, a race started. The freight train was standing at a distance about a mile from the station building, and the platform was ice covered. Since I was running without any luggage, I managed to pass hundreds of people before I reached the train. However, I barely managed to squeeze myself into a freight car. It was already so crowded that I found room for only one of my legs. I had to pass most of my ten-hour way back, clinging to the freight car in this barely tolerable pose.

Fortunately, no one in Kozelsk had noticed my four-day absence. The adventurous journey came to a safe end.

* * *

In Kozelsk I bunked with another "reserve" lieutenant in a ramshackle little hut, owned by a single, though not old, but astonishingly unattractive woman, who lived there with her sixty-something-year-old mother. We rented a tiny, dark room from her, but we spent no time there except for sleeping. In late November, my roommate unexpectedly left Kozelsk (taking my shiny leather boots with him), and the next day our landlord's mother gave me an ultimatum: either bring a cartload of wood, or sleep with her daughter, or go somewhere else. I chose the least of these three evils—the wood, knowing that the process of my demobilization was already under way.

In the very beginning of December, a captain from the personnel department of the divisional artillery headquarters arrived in Kozelsk to decide upon more discharges. So he was holding my fate in his hands. Following my comrades' advice, I purchased a "quarter" (three liters) of *samogon* before meeting with him. Our conversation took place in my room, and it was very short. Instead of answering his question "So, how are you going to repay someone for your discharge?" I pulled out the large bottle from under my bunk. But he seemed to expect more and began to stare at my new gray trousers that had been made by the German dressmaker out of "trophy" cloth the previous July. In the twinkling of an eye, I changed into my uniform trousers and gave him what he clearly desired. The captain swore that he would take care of everything regarding my discharge in no more than two weeks. He kept his word.

When the long-awaited orders arrived, I received an official leave until 30 January 1946, and the date of my demobilization was 31 January. Thus, I could stay in Kiev a full month while retaining my lieutenant's status.

During my entire journey to Kiev, about forty hours, I couldn't sleep. Daydreams of upcoming meetings with Vera, with my parents and brother, and with friends were flashing before my eyes. It seemed to me that I was approaching my new life, and I hoped so much that happiness was waiting for me.

My Return Home

Before proceeding to the main topic of this chapter, I would like to describe briefly the situations in both my parents' and Vera's families at the time. I had learned about them from my mother and Vera's letters, which I regularly received during my months in Kozelsk.

My father still held his prewar position of chief accountant at the Ukrainian State Association of Livestock Purchase. He was working long hours, as always. My mother ran the household, and my brother, Tolya, was a seventh-grade schoolboy. During the entire year of 1945, their two-room apartment was kind of a passenger way station for at least ten families of close and distant relatives who were on their way back home from their wartime evacuation. Sometimes, there were simultaneously up to ten such temporary "lodgers" in my parents' apartment.

Vera's father had already been working in Kharkov for three months as a supervisor of the South Railroad's train service division. Vasiliy Alexandrovich's job transfer from Kiev was the result of some friction between him and the new minister's protégé. It meant a demotion, but in spite of that, their family's (he, Agrippina Semenovna, sixteen-year-old daughter, Lyuba, and seven-year-old son, Alik) financial and living conditions remained perfect. Their adult daughters, Vera and Nadya, had remained in Kiev. Nadya was now married.

My precious Vera was working at the Artem Works as a rate-setter engineer of the assembly shop. She was living in the same Southwest Railroad apartment building where the family had lived before the war. At her father's request, she was temporarily allowed to occupy one small room of the three-room apartment where their family had recently lived. The family of a senior employee of the railroad occupied the other two rooms.

That was the "disposition" of my future surroundings as I was approaching Kiev.

Happy Meetings

One of the most memorable events in my life was my return home after the war. It started on 30 December 1945 when I, while carrying my luggage (it consisted just of two "trunks" made of empty ammunition boxes), exited the half-destroyed Kiev railroad station building and entered the railroad station square.

It was an overcast morning. Dirty, wet snow covered the small square. The streetcar circular terminal was in its center, and about fifty people were waiting for a streetcar there. I moved to join them. The slush squelched under my feet, and that reminded me about my footwear problem: I was wearing summer boots with soles made of leather and tops made of military cape fabric.

As I headed to the streetcar stop, a man with a wheelbarrow accompanied me. He was persistently offering to deliver my luggage to my house for twenty-five rubles. I decided to wait for the streetcar. (It was not beyond my powers to cross these little more than 2 kilometers that separated me from my parents' house on foot, but at that time I was afraid it would be unfit for a military officer, even for just a lieutenant, to carry large, heavy boxes in the sight of pedestrians. Moreover, with both my arms engaged, I wouldn't be able to salute any approaching officers or respond to any military man's salute.) For a long time, almost one hour, I waited vainly for the streetcar to show up; twice the man with the wheelbarrow came up to me with the same offer, and eventually I relented.

Around 11:00 A.M., I reached the house at 3 Vorovskiy Street and through the back entrance (the front door had been nailed up) I entered a dim kitchen room. There were four doors there—entrances to four families' apartments. This was a definite sign of the so-called communal quarters.

On the second door that led into my father's apartment, I saw with disappointment a huge padlock, but I didn't inspect it closely. I must admit that I wanted to arrive home unexpectedly, therefore I hadn't wired to Kiev the exact day of my arrival. And my parents and Vera only knew approximately about my pending return. Now I was paying for my boyish game—I stood for a half hour or so in front of the locked door.

An unknown neighbor who appeared in the kitchen room for a short time told me, "Grigoriy Isaakovich is working now [it was a

weekday], Evgeniya Abramovna is probably standing in line somewhere to buy something, and Tolya is most likely at school." Later,
another neighbor woman asked me if I had tried to open the door,
since the locked padlock had been just hanging on the latch use-
lessly for a long time. I pulled the door handle slightly and . . . to my
pleasant surprise the door swung open and I found myself standing
in the apartment!

Passing down a long, dark hallway, I opened the door to a room
measuring about 250 square feet (almost everyone in the USSR
would consider it a spacious room). Inside, I saw two wide-awake
teenagers lying on separate beds. One, I instantly recognized as my
brother, Tolya. The other was a beautiful girl with a close resem-
blance to my father's sister, my beloved Aunt Polya. I guessed that
she was my sixteen-year old cousin, Lyalya. Still in their nightwear,
they both jumped out of their beds and dashed to me. After a lot
of hugs and kisses, they began to examine the military awards on
my blouse and the contents of my "trunks," though what was inside them I still can't remember for the life of me. The children got
dressed, made their beds, and then Lyalya moved her homemade
trestle bed out of the center of the room. At that point my mother
entered the room.

My dear Mamochka! How hard it was for you, a tiny woman, to
go through the years of the war! How visibly you have aged! These
years have changed you into a stooped woman with many gray hairs
glistening on your head! But my mother had kept her habits: she
quickly stopped her tears of joy and in a minute begun to fuss over
me, fixing breakfast for her son who had returned safely from the terrible war. Somehow, my father learned about my arrival, and soon
after he came home from the office. Since I had last seen him one and
half years earlier (see chapter 9), his appearance had changed just a
little. He shed a tear, too. And after a small glass of vodka that all
of us drank in honor of my return, he asked my mother, "Can you,
Zhenya, explain why all of this happened so simply, so ordinarily?"

I felt indescribable joy at everything that took place at that time.
However, the thought of another, no less important meeting didn't
leave my head for a single minute: there were just a few hours before
Vera would finish her working day.

After our meal ended, I began to prepare myself for the exciting
reunion with Vera. The very first thing was to attach my military

Order of the Patriotic War, Second Class to my officer's blouse. Vanya Kamchatnyy, while returning to the front lines after his leave, had brought it to my parents last spring. Now, my chest was decorated with all four orders and three medals, namely, the Order of Aleksandr Nevskiy, the First and Second Class Orders of the Patriotic War, and the Order of the Red Star, as well as medals for the defense of Stalingrad, for the capture of Königsberg, and for victory over Germany in the Great Patriotic War. I thought it would be nice to appear before Vera with such an amount of awards.

Next, I neatly sewed on a fresh under-collar strip and polished the tops of my "cape-boots" with black shoe polish. Then I went to the barbershop, where I got a hair wash and hair cut, a shave for my face, and a refreshing massage. I spent almost one hour there, but it was still too early to visit Vera.

At a more leisurely pace, I went from the barbershop to the central Gastronom grocery store to buy a much-deserved present for my sweetheart. It was the first building to be rebuilt on Kreshchatik Street. There I chose the most expensive box of beautiful chocolate mini-figurines (its "commercial" list price was 400 rubles).

While I was standing in a short line at the cashier, an unknown woman offered her ration card: she would buy the box for me, and then I would pay her just 200 rubles instead of its list price. I didn't understand this proposed transaction completely, so I refused her offer. It seemed dubious, and I was afraid it would sully my officer's honor. Upon exiting the Gastronom, I threw a glance at the clock: time seemed to have stopped. To speed it up, I walked at an even slower pace as I headed toward the familiar house at 6 Theater Street, and never before had I moved toward it as slowly as I was moving now. But in spite of my efforts, I arrived at the apartment almost one hour earlier than the time when Vera usually came home. Vera's neighbor, Anna Petrovna, invited me into her living room. I sat there for what seemed an eternity, extremely nervous, while impatiently waiting for Vera.

And finally I hear—my darling is coming in. The neighbor invites her to enter the living room: "Somebody is waiting for you there." I rise. Vera enters. Her eyes shine with joy, but when I try to hug her, Vera suddenly becomes embarrassed and shrinks back a little bit, so my kiss reaches her cheek.

We began our talk in the neighbor's room and continued it in Vera's tiny room, which was crammed with furniture. The conversation was a little incoherent; we jumped from one topic to another, giving each other no time to answer each other's questions. After about an hour of this, we went to my parents. There, during a small tea party, our mutual questioning continued. Late in the evening, I saw Vera home. It seemed to me that she was already getting used to me, and when I hugged her in the lobby of her house just before saying good-bye, Vera didn't shrink from me.

The next morning, after Vera left for work, I visited the town-major's office to register as an officer on leave. The office was conveniently located next to Vera's house, and Vera's kitchen windows faced the office's backyard.

In the town-major's office all my papers were finished very soon. I was authorized to obtain personal supplies from a regiment located at Lukyanovka. Instead of going to its military canteen daily, I chose to take my supplies three times a month as a "dry ration." That somewhat enriched the very moderate ration that my parents' family received, because an officer's ration, both in quantity and assortment of food, was incomparably more bountiful than what my relatives received as their civilian ration.

That day, 31 December 1945, my status of an officer on leave was confirmed until the end of the next month. So I had the right to keep wearing the uniform, to which I had become long accustomed.

On New Year's Eve, all of my local close relatives gathered in my parents' apartment to celebrate my return and to see in the New Year. Vera was by my side the entire time. Guests congratulated me upon my fortunate return from the hell of the war. Many of them were familiar with Vera, and they spoke a lot of warm words to her. I heard these compliments with pride for my chosen one. And only very rarely did I take my eyes off Vera.

The first day of 1946 was a regular workday. I accompanied Vera just to the Artem Works, where she worked, and then strolled down along Vorovskiy Street to the gigantic flea market Evbaz (the "Jewish market") to put an end to my "boots problem." But before I continue this story, let me digress with a description of the general conditions of life in Kiev at that time. I hope it will help my American readers better understand many things in this and forthcoming chapters.

Kiev 1946

Foodstuffs and Consumer Goods

At that time, rationing was still in effect. Every citizen had a ration card. Foodstuffs weren't costly for those who had these ration cards, but the monthly food quotas, especially for fat, meat, and sugar, were extremely small. Moreover, it was often difficult to find a grocery store that had for sale the food item you were seeking. The exact quotas depended on the consumer's category. Workers received the most. In descending sequence after them were office workers, students, children, and finally dependents. The daily quota of bread for a worker amounted to 800 grams, for a student—only 400 grams.

But even with ration cards, it was difficult to buy your daily quota of bread. Outside every bakery door, which was usually closed, you could see a long line of angry people. The door would open periodically to let ten served consumers out and to admit just the next ten waiting in line. During this exchange, a few strong and impudent men would often try to squeeze into the store, and a scramble would ensue, sometimes leading to scuffles. Those who were at the tail end of the line were not likely to be able to buy their bread ration before the store was closed. You could not use the day's bread quota coupon from the monthly ration card on the next day, because it was dated and expired after the marked date. And woe to those who lost their booklet of ration coupons. The booklets were not replaceable, so the owner was doomed to hunger until the next month. You could buy a few food items as well as some consumer goods in different special stores without your ration card, but you would have to pay the so-called commercial prices, which were a few times more expensive than the usual prices. Besides the state "commercial" trade, there were a few public markets and *tolkuchkas* (*tolkuchka* is a crowded area where petty merchants and buyers jostled each other) in the city. Here you could buy everything. Bread, the main food, cost hundreds of times more here than at the state ("ration card") price.

The main *tolkuchka* in Kiev was the Evbaz, but at Hay Market, close to the house where I lived, a brisk secondhand trade in goods went on all the time, too. And the assortment of goods wasn't just secondhand; it was extremely varied. The atmosphere of any postwar *tolkuchka* corresponded to my idea of the early 1920s New Economic Policy (NEP) period that I had gotten from watching movies.[1]

At that time, the huge territory of Evbaz, where today Victory Square is located, resembled an uneasy human sea dotted with dozens of wooden stalls that looked like small islands. Thousands of people moved in every direction, each with his or her own agenda as if displaying the phenomenon of chaotic molecular movement (the so-called Brown's movement).

Upon approaching Evbaz, you could recognize people's figures and then their faces. And you could hear the shouts and haggling of criers and merchants and the begging of numerous paupers.

Different types of people haunted each *tolkuchka*. There you could see small traders, secondhand dealers, petty thieves, swindlers, and so-called dollmakers. These were people who pretended to be buyers. They would arrive at a price for the merchandise with the unsuspecting trader, pull out a wad of money to pay for it, and then quickly disappear with their purchase. But instead of a stack of genuine bills, the "dollmaker" would foist a "doll" on the trader—a stack of newsprint that was cut to the size of a real bill, sandwiched between two real bills. By the time the trader discovered this deception, the "dollmaker" would be long gone.

The overwhelming majority of Kiev inhabitants lived poorly; the rationed food was not enough to feed families. Only a few could afford to buy food at the high public market prices. The outer clothing that people wore was noteworthy. Many, regardless of age and gender, wore military greatcoats (without shoulder straps) or padded jackets; a few wore mouse-gray clothing, which had been fashioned out of German military uniforms. The most prevalent footwear consisted of crude military shoes and boots.

One could see war invalids everywhere. Some of them, especially the legless or armless, were begging for handouts. At that time the government was taking modest care of the war invalids, but many were degraded alcoholics who benefited from their pitiful appearance. They knew how sympathetic most people in our country were and took advantage of it.

The Housing Situation

While retreating from Kiev in November 1943, the German occupiers had definitely kept to their "scorched earth policy." The Nazis had totally destroyed the center of our beautiful city—the main and the most famous Kreshchatik Street and all the adjacent streets. Altogether, hundreds and hundreds of buildings across the city were blown up or burned down during the war. You could see huge piles of rubble on many completely destroyed streets. In some places where formerly a large building had been standing, only a skeletal frame remained. And the empty eye sockets of the window openings in still-standing naked walls looked appalling. Here and there were bottleneck passageways through the ruins. Walking among them, you still caught the indelible scent of burning. Because of the critical shortage of city dwellings, numerous people's fates became gloomy and even hopeless.

At that time thousands and thousands of former Kievans who had returned to their home city from the army or evacuation found themselves homeless, even if their prewar lodgings had survived. In some cases, the municipal government turned over many lodgings that at first were assumed vacant permanently (such as apartments where the victims of the Holocaust had lived) to returning people whose own apartments had been destroyed. In other cases it turned out that neighbors or squatters had occupied many vacant apartments without any authorization. Because of the clash of various vitally important interests, numerous conflicts occurred. There were fierce arguments, sometimes coming to blows. From time to time court proceedings took place. In the simplest cases, those who had violated the law were evicted. But often even the court couldn't arrive at a just decision. Mostly the only way out was to settle one more family in the already inhabited apartment, turning it into a communal apartment and making it overpopulated.

The terms "communal quarters" and "communal apartment" date from the years of the October Revolution in Russia, when in most cities and towns almost all real estate was nationalized. Former owners of dwellings were evicted or deprived of most of the rooms of their lodgings. The vacated rooms were given mostly to common revolutionaries and poor people, who had been living in barracks. In such a way the former apartment turned into a communal apartment or communal quarters. It consisted of a few individual living apartments and some common places for general use (a hallway, kitchen, toilet, bathroom, pantry). There were a lot of inconveniences in this kind of lodging, but the new inhabitants didn't pay attention to them. Despite everything, their living conditions were a significant improvement for them. And gradually most tenants got used to these communal apartments. In later decades, when the government embarked on a modest program of apartment construction, a considerable portion of the new dwellings were projected to be communal quarters for two or three families.

It is appropriate to mention here another powerful source of urban crowding and overpopulation—the country folk. The war not only left terrible destruction in the cities in its wake but also in the countryside. Agriculture and cattle breeding were catastrophically diminished, and most villagers faced starvation. A lot of them tried to find their salvation in the cities. Though Stalin's stringent law prohibited country dwellers from leaving their residence, many, by hook or crook, moved to the cities.

Our still destroyed city wasn't an exception. Because of all the aforementioned reasons, the average space per person in living accommodations had been reduced, I think, to one-quarter or less of its rather small prewar value. I also should remind you that the main municipal services, such as water supply, sewage system, and power supply, were not completely restored in 1946. And it is hard now to imagine the inconveniences that people had to bear at that time.

As an example, I can tell you about the communal quarters where my family lived for fourteen years. Five families, altogether sixteen persons, occupied five rooms, with only one kitchen and one tiny toilet to share among them. For five years there was no gas oven, and tenants never had a water heater or a full bathroom.

The four years of the terrible war and especially the Nazi occupation had greatly depleted the country's economic resources. Because of that, it took a few years to restore the main municipal services and public transportation in most of the devastated cities. However, housing reconstruction, and especially new construction, proceeded very slowly. To a great extent the reason lay in Stalin's priorities—he directed most investments to the heavy and defenses industries. (The world was close to the start of the Cold War era.)

Only in the late 1950s, at Khrushchev's initiative, did mass housing construction begin. The so-called Khrushchev's houses had many inconveniences, but millions of families were happy to have at last their separate single-family apartment. Despite the mass housing construction, the demand for lodging remained strong because of numerous postwar marriages and the subsequent baby boom. The shortage of housing and the endless waiting lists for a dwelling became characteristic features of our society for decades.

I started this long digression just as I was on my way to the Evbaz. Now let us return to this crowded marketplace.

Just as I was about to enter that human sea, two smiling men, a little older than I was, ran up to meet me. The taller one asked, "What are you interested in, Comrade Lieutenant?" Not expecting a dirty trick, I explained truthfully to them my goal. After I told them the required boot size, the shorter one of the two quickly dove into the crowd and disappeared. The "Taller" explained that I could find some footwear only at a certain spot, and he volunteered to guide the "war hero" to that place. The way through the crowd took a few minutes, but the next events developed much more quickly—the "Shorter" was already standing at our destination with a pair of boots in his hands. He announced loudly, "Here they are, and the size is yours. Leather is excellent, and 2,000 rubles is a special price for a frontline officer!" The boots looked immaculate. I tried them on, and after that, pretending to be an expert in leather wares, I knocked on both lustrous soles. "Not bad," I said, "but I can pay no more than 1,750 rubles." The "Shorter" promptly replied, "No problem, no haggle with a war hero. It will be OK." Moreover, when I counted out the seventeenth 100-ruble bill, he stopped me, saying, "It's enough. Wear them in good health!" After taking the money, both dissolved into the crowd.

With pride, I showed the purchase to my father, but he scratched the gleaming surface of the sole with the point of a nail and . . . uttered a low moan: the soles were made of thoroughly waxed and polished dense cardboard. That was my first lesson of my new life. I got rid of the phony boots a year later, when I unexpectedly bumped into the two swindlers at another flea market. They gave me back 800 of my rubles, undoubtedly counting upon another poor victim who might soon come along.

The unhappy purchase damaged my financial status. I came to Kiev having, as it seemed to me, a lot of money—almost 9,000 rubles. By the end of the third day of my new life, as I estimate now, my wealth was less than 7,000. Without a ration card, this amount would buy me no more than 80 one-kilogram loaves of bread.

To compensate for at least part of that loss, I decided to sell a few German watches—the remains of my trophies from my last night in Königsberg (see chapter 12). But in the watch repair shop where the transaction occurred, I was tricked once again. The amount of money I received for the watches was laughably low. That was the second lesson for me.

What Else Happened in January

A day or two after New Year's Day, Vera unexpectedly came home before her usual lunchtime: in order to spend more time together with me on these days, she had announced at the Artem Works that she was going to get married. That way, according to the law of that time, she received three unpaid days off.

Vera and I had no doubts about our future marriage, and neither one of us wanted to postpone it. But we couldn't set the exact date before getting our parents' blessing. My parents knew Vera quite well and had come to love her. We tried to get the assent of Vera's parents in Kharkov by phone. After reaching their number, I began to repeat the solemn vows that I had prepared beforehand. I swore to take care of their daughter, as she was the apple of my eye, and so on. But Vasiliy Alexandrovich cut me off at the very beginning of my speech. He required us to come to Kharkov. "And here we will reach an understanding on that matter," he closed. That turn of events postponed the immediate fulfillment of our dreams. In return we, finally together after a very long separation, acted contrary to the ancient tradition: we stopped waiting for the marriage license and I moved into Vera's room.

In a few days we visited Kharkov. As we expected, we got the OK there. Vera's parents had known me since 1939; they also knew that Vera loved me very much. We all agreed that our wedding would take place in Kiev in early February. Vasiliy Alexandrovich, Agrippina Semenovna, Vera, and I drank lots and lots of strong alcohol to toast the fiancée and fiancé. To tell you the truth, the large shots offered to me by my future father-in-law exceeded my ability to hold them (though I came off fairly well the next day).

During the few days of our stay in Kharkov, I visited the homes of two my frontline friends. Lev Vinokurov was still in the Central

Military Hospital in Moscow. I met his nice elderly parents. They had endured the terrible years of the German occupation. To survive during that lean time, Lev's father, a professor, mastered how to manufacture matches, and his wife sold produce.

The second friend, Samuil Sapozhnikov, hadn't forgotten my "anonymous" remittance to his starving family. As soon as he noticed my "cape-boots," he led me to the shoemaker's shop, where Samuil was the manager. The most skilled workman took my measurements, and in three days a pair of wonderful, shiny new leather boots arrived for me in Kiev. I wore them for many years.

The most serious theme of our discussion in Kiev and Kharkov was my future. Should I look for a job now or continue my education? I had no skills, and I always dreamed of the highest education. That was not only a question of prestige; most people considered it a good route to material well-being. At the same time, I didn't want to be Vera's dependent for the next three and a half years. Vera's opinion was firm—the institute. Our parents both agreed. The final decision was unanimous, and I began to act on it. My action and its result are the topic of the next chapter.

For the two weeks remaining prior to our wedding day, Vera and I were inseparable as soon as she finished her work hours. I closely listened to her every word, admired her, and took pride in her beauty, intelligence, and experience in everyday life.

Every day, just after returning home from work, Vera would start to fix supper. I took pleasure in seeing how skillfully, quickly, and confidently she worked. The aroma of the just prepared meals excited my appetite. Soon we would sit at the table in our tiny room. How tasty was every meal prepared by my chosen one! To my sincere praises, Vera responded smilingly. She promised to feed me with really tasty meals, once the purchase of high-quality ingredients was not a problem. As to her art in cooking, she would say, perhaps, she inherited it from her mother and grandmother.

As I think back on the start of my civilian life in January 1946, I want to recount two funny episodes, which have remained in my memory. Not only are both episodes amusing, but at the same time they illustrate some specific details of daily routine at the beginning of postwar life.

The first one occurred when I was walking along Vladimirskaya Street toward its intersection with Lenin Street. I was about 5 or

6 meters from the corner when an officer turned the corner and walked in my direction. Because I still didn't have my eyeglasses, I screwed up my eyes to try and decipher how many stars were on the officer's shoulder straps, so I could figure out which one of us had to salute the other first. It turned out that the officer held the captain's rank, and my hand started to extend in salute to him. Alas! I had lingered, and the captain's loud voice sounded out sharply, "Lieutenant! Why didn't you salute me? I'm the town-major's aide. Your identity card!" I presented him my apologies, pleading my nearsightedness, but he didn't listen to me, and after showing me his own card, took mine away from me. Then he ordered me to follow him. We reached the town-major's office in five minutes. I was directed into the inner yard, and the officer disappeared. There were about forty officers there, mostly captains, majors, and lieutenant colonels. They were standing in a few random small groups and speaking in low voices.

It was a rule in most garrisons that infractions of military discipline were punishable by ninety minutes of drill. I was strongly disappointed because the drill ground was clearly visible from Vera's kitchen. Our smiling neighbor Anna Petrovna liked to tell us how ridiculous those fat, sweaty officers appeared while doing their drills. Waiting for that kind of shameful procedure, I felt a strong sadness and stood alone by the wall of the building. I didn't want to mix with anyone.

After we waited about a half hour, some captain with a red armband on his sleeve entered the yard. In an instant, a dozen officers ran up to him. They crowded around the captain, and each tried to explain his excuse for not taking part in the drill. They thrust numerous papers toward him, such as hospital certificates, business trip authorizations, train tickets, and so on. But the captain didn't pay attention to any of them. He strongly pushed them aside and walked up to me. The captain asked, "And what is your excuse of not doing the drills, Comrade Lieutenant?" "I have none," I replied. "If so, then I charge you with directing the drill exercises. Take up your duties immediately!"

This unexpected order to lead the drills took a load off my mind. I saluted the captain, and he left the yard. I chose a point not visible to our neighbor and began to give the commands. I wasn't too strict with my subordinates. There were many breaks for smoking before the drill time was up. It was a real "happy ending"!

The second amusing occurrence I will set forth as a dialogue between my brother, Tolya, and me. We were in a streetcar with a few passengers on our long way to Lukyanovka:

> I: Tolya, who were the two demobilized guys who spent the nights in your home last week? I saw them a few times when I visited you late in the morning. They were still sleeping.
>
> T: Well, they were sort of interesting people; they know a lot of jokes and anecdotes. They arrived regularly late at night, and always brought something edible and sweets for all of us. Because of them everybody went to bed after midnight. They never seemed to show any fatigue, but for our parents, staying up so late for several running nights was too tiring. Anyway, they are nice and cheery guys. Unfortunately, they left before they had time to say good-bye to Dad.
>
> I: Were they father's colleagues when he served in the rear?
>
> T: No. As a matter of fact, they showed up unexpectedly in quite a strange way. They introduced themselves as friends of Dad's colleague, but father doesn't remember this colleague.
>
> I: How could that be?
>
> T: I couldn't understand either. They appeared at noon, asked if this was Kobylyanskiy's apartment, and then introduced themselves to Mom. When father returned home from work, mother and I stopped him in the hallway. Mom said, "Grisha, friends of your colleague Mitlyanskiy are waiting for you in the dining room." And Daddy, with not a word, spread his arms wide apart in perplexity. . . . What is the matter with you?!

I fell from my seat, roaring with laughter. Tears blurred my eyes. Finally, I stood up and, still laughing loudly and sobbing at the same time, explained to my brother that Mitlyanskiy was *my battlefront friend, not father's.* As Tolya grasped the mix-up, he burst into laughter and fell down, too. And I was seized by a new surge of laughter as the rest of passengers began to laugh as well.

* * *

Finally, 31 January arrived, and I went to the local *voenkomat.* I handed over the sealed personnel file entitled "The file of Guards Lieutenant Kobylyanskiy" and received some processing papers for my civilian passport. That was the end of my military service.

Farewell, army! Hello, Civvy Street!

Two immediate tasks loomed on my personal agenda: the restoration of my status as a student at the institute and my marriage with Vera. Both of these events determined the ensuing path of my entire life.

Chapter 27

I Rejoin My Alma Mater

It was late January 1946 when I first returned to my institute. Now it had a new name: the Kiev Polytechnic Institute (KPI). This visit added a lot of bitter images to my general picture of the damaged city. The whole left wing of the main building and the former object of everyone's pride—the Large Physics Auditorium that was located in the wing—were unrecognizable; most corridor walls, once light in color, now bore many scorch marks, sure signs of fire. The turret that had formerly crowned the wing was gone. Some window openings were stuffed with bricks, the rest nailed over with sheets of plywood.

The goal of my visit to KPI was to find out how could I regain my sophomore status, which I had lost in the spring of 1942 when I was called up for service after completing my third semester of study. The timing to resume my interrupted studies was appropriate: in some two weeks the fourth semester would begin. Unfortunately, the KII's archive had been burned to the ground in 1941, while the Tashkent archive from its time in Tashkent during the war hadn't been transferred yet, and I couldn't produce any evidence of my former student status. (In July 1943, when my fire platoon had been sent to Soin's battalion's trenches, I asked Kamchatnyy to keep an eye on a small ammunition box where, among my spare underwear, foot bindings, safety razor, toothbrush, and some other personal stuff, I kept my student's record book. Alas, during the memorable *drap-marsh* from the "Ravine of Death," nobody was able to remember and grab that box.)

In the office I was told that in general it was possible to renew my status. It would be enough to produce the dean's attestation that I had completed the third-semester exams. On the schedule of radio-faculty lessons posted on the wall, I found the name of the professor who had been our dean in Tashkent.

I visited him the next day. (I should mention here that my military uniform was the only thing I had to wear at that time.) After I stated my business, the professor responded without hesitation: "I definitely remember you as a student in Tashkent, but I refuse to attest to your status because I have no idea what semester you had completed." I asked him in agitation, "Can it really be true that the officer's word of honor isn't enough for you?" As it became clear that my opponent wasn't going to change his mind, I turned round sharply and walked out of his office, banging the door behind me.

After that disappointing meeting, I visited a few offices of the KPI and ultimately obtained a "conditional" status as sophomore. That meant that I had to pass the next set of examinations in order to restore my full status. Failure would make me liable for expulsion. Meanwhile, I could enjoy most student privileges, including the right to receive a student's ration cards. However, my "conditional" standing did not include the right to receive the student's government education stipend—a loss that I felt deeply. At that time, I had less than 3,000 rubles to my name, and my money continued to dwindle away.

Any advanced student in the Soviet Union was eligible to receive this government education stipend. In 1947, a KPI sophomore's ordinary monthly stipend amounted to 400 rubles; straight-A students received 20 percent more. (In comparison, Vera, an inexperienced engineer, earned 800 rubles a month at that time.) Understandably, the student's stipend was not enough to earn your keep. So only students who received financial support from their parents (some 60 percent of our group) didn't suffer from various shortages. But I had no stipend, and the only income that I managed to earn over the spring of 1946 amounted to just 80 rubles: 30 for tutoring and 50 for ground digging.

The first day of the semester was 11 February 1946. Our permanent "stream" (class) of second-year students of the radio faculty consisted of three groups, about eighty students in all. I could see some fifteen former frontline soldiers and officers among them, including three war invalids and three young women, who were wearing military overcoats. Another dozen students were wearing military overcoats, but they looked so young that it was as clear as day that they hadn't even caught a whiff of actual combat! On the whole, the majority of our class was three or four years younger than me.

The most pleasing discovery of my first day back at the institute was my reunion with five students whom I had known before the war. They had rejoined the KPI prior to the third semester. Both cheerful and lighthearted, Valeriy Andrienko and I had been students of the chemical-faculty in 1940–1941; we both took part in constructing the defensive lines along the Irpen River in early July 1941. Boris Elkun was familiar to me since 1939: we attended the same high school. Abrasha Zaslavskiy, Misha Talalaevskiy, and Nyoma Gorokhovskiy studied in 1940–1941 in the same group as Vera. Gorokhovskiy was hardly recognizable because of his scarred face and fingers: he was a member of a tank crew in the war and had been severely burned when his tank caught fire after a hit from a German antitank shell.

I was as glad to see them again as if I was meeting my own close relatives. I thought that they could share with me their experience of reentering study at the institute after taking several years off. They answered many of my questions but could not help me with the main one: what should be my first step? You can't give a specific answer to this question, because it is impossible to revive just those particular memory cells in one's brain that have been keeping the information that he or she needed.

After a few days of study I realized that a lot of serious difficulties stood before me. In contrast to my knowledge of elementary mathematics, which remained intact, everything that I had studied later, at the institute, was now effaced from my memory. As a result, I was unable to comprehend lectures on different subjects. Instead of my usual self-reliance, I felt myself inferior. This vexed me, and I became irritated.

I remember how tensely I strained my ears to hear the lecture, while trying to follow the long mathematical formulas, their transformations, and the lecturer's train of thought. Alas, I couldn't! My brain had become unaccustomed to such kinds of work. The first pages of my institute notes were filled with gaps and question marks.

Soon I ultimately realized that my ability to understand lectures couldn't be restored by itself. I got the materials for the introductory and advanced courses of mathematics and began studying them afresh. I was working intensively, and in a couple of weeks I noticed that something in my brain was coming alive. It gladdened and encouraged me.

In mid-February I went to the office of the institute's Communist Party Committee (Partkom) in order to register. Seemingly, they paid particular attention to my large number of military awards. Nothing else could explain an unexpected event that occurred in early March. I was invited to the Partkom first secretary's office. Because of the substantial number of war veteran students, most of whom became Party members at the front, the KPI Party organization (about 300 members) was one of largest Party organizations in Kiev. So, its first secretary, Assistant Professor M. L. Kalnibolotskiy, held a high post.

As I entered the office, a tall, unsmiling man in his early fifties stood up from his armchair and greeted me with a handshake. Without further ado, Kalnibolotskiy told me that the Partkom, after reviewing my file, had decided to recommend me to become the president of the institute's trade union committee (Profkom). Recently the Partkom had come to conclusion that Kuznechik, the current Profkom president, was unable to handle his duties. Besides, it was now the right time for him to start the project for his engineering degree. Then Kalnibolotskiy concluded: "We expect that you will justify the confidence of our Party."

I was greatly surprised, or rather overwhelmed, by the offer. Because of my total lack of information about the position, I asked for two days to get to know, at least roughly, what was the actual range of duties to be fulfilled by the president of the Profkom.

My thoughts were in a whirl. On the one hand, the proffered position would guarantee me a good salary. That would be the best remedy against my troublesome sense of being a dependent. Moreover, from Kuznechik's explanation I learned that the Profkom was the distributor of government assistance to hundreds of hungry, unclothed, and shoeless students. There were different forms of assistance: financial aid up to 100 rubles; special coupons that gave an opportunity to buy specified items at the lowest fixed prices; clothes, footwear, fabrics, soap, and even patties stuffed with jam were among the designated items. In addition to all of this, our Profkom also distributed free vouchers toward camping tours, holiday homes, and sanatoriums. Thus, according to the wise saying of the now late Vasiliy Bondarenko—"Can one remain dry after immersion in water?"—a real way out of my present financial difficulties was lying directly in front of me.

However, there were at least two forcible arguments against taking up the offer.

At that period of my life I felt an extreme thirst for knowledge, and my primary purpose was to complete my higher education. Just recently I had begun to believe that I could make up for my lost years of study. Yet now a powerful counterattraction had unexpectedly arisen. (During our conversation, Kalnibolotskiy promised, though: "You shouldn't worry about progress in your studies, we guarantee it.") But receiving falsely exaggerated marks wasn't my goal!

There was another, no less important reason to refuse Kalnibolotskiy's offer. Since wartime I had firmly adhered to the position that in our interethnic situation, a Jew should avoid such types of profitable jobs. I didn't want to be suspected of "warming my hands" in the Profkom.

Eventually, I decided to refuse the alluring offer, and Vera completely approved of my decision.

Two days later, I appeared before Kalnibolotskiy again. This time I started by referring to the fact that I knew nothing about trade union specifics and right away announced that I didn't want to become an example of a Jew who knows how to find and occupy an abundant and profitable place.

Kalnibolotskiy became indignant at my words and accused me of having non-Party views—a serious charge against anyone in our country. But in the end, he accepted my refusal.

Meanwhile, my persistence in studies began gradually to bear fruit. I became more active during lectures and diligently did the homework on my own. The only subject I ignored was the second part of the Sopromat (Strength of Materials) course. I had never studied the first part of that course, and therefore I was planning to take advantage of a war veteran student's privilege to shift the examination in Sopromat to next fall.

By the midsemester I already was familiar with and associated with most students of our class.

In the institute labs we worked in small groups, three or four students in each. I was lucky: my lab partners were nice guys, Vadim Taranenko and Fima Zilberman. (Vadim was of my age, Fima was younger by three years.) We became closer to each other while jointly recording our results after each laboratory assignment. Soon we extended our teamwork method to all labor-intensive homework assignments. My companions clearly demonstrated their responsible attitudes toward our studies. I was pleased with the fact that both Vadim and Fima strove for knowledge and rejected slapdash or careless work, except in those few subjects that were of no importance for future radio engineers. Besides, it turned out that our personalities were compatible with each other, and soon we became friends. Our close friendship lasted for many long years.

At the First Private Communist Party Meeting

The first all-institute private Party meeting that I attended made a special impression on me. This significant event took place at the end of March in the Large Chemical Auditorium that was filled to capacity (the Large Physics Auditorium was still under reconstruction).

I was sitting in one of the upper rows, and I still remember the obvious difference in the color of clothing between the audience sitting in the two front rows and all the others. The former wore dark suits—all represented administration and teaching staff. The rest of the auditorium was almost entirely occupied by an audience of another sort—war veteran students. They were wearing military blouses and tunics adorned with orders and medals. Some of them also wore wound badges (red and yellow strips) on their chests.

I don't remember the topic of that meeting or who delivered the main report, but it is impossible to forget the atmosphere that reigned in the auditorium. Many times heated speeches rang out from the upper rows during the discussion of the report. Young recent officers submitted some proposals or stood up for their viewpoint without restraining their emotions. They addressed the meeting with both enthusiasm and eloquence. Moreover, time and again the seething upper part of the auditorium responded to such fiery speeches with applause.

The most essential thing that I observed at the meeting was the obvious division of the audience into two opposing parties—"Youth" and "Fossils." In the ensuing debate, it was not difficult to identify the members of each faction.

Kalnibolotskiy, who presided over the meeting, commented negatively on each nonmainstream proposal from the young agitators. His unappealing remarks were full of clichés from Party directives, and he delivered them as if they were the highest truths. A few well-skilled public speakers from the front rows rebuffed the impassioned students as well. These representatives of the "Fossils," who had been Party members from before the war, skillfully disproved or even exposed the danger of the students' position. Sometimes you could hear subtle threats in their statements. Naturally, I can't reproduce them now, but their sense could be interpreted as, "Those, who don't support our proposals are standing on a non-Party position." Every expert in Soviet political terminology of that time could understand these words as an indirect threat of expulsion from the Party and even from the institute.

However strange it seemed, in spite of the evident majority of the "Youth" faction, the "Fossils" managed to gain their end. Eventually, all the smooth wordings that they desired were present in the final resolution of the meeting.

In some two years, the rebellious spirit of the young Communists' generation faded away. Verbal and written reprimands; brainwashing at the Partkom; persistent demands to strengthen Party discipline; the Party statute's principle of democratic centralism—all of these against a backdrop of relentless, politically motivated arrests and exiles—fulfilled their evil purpose. The overwhelming majority of Party members turned into a mass of indifferent and passive people. Only a handful of individuals (I wasn't among them) chose another way, which later became known as dissidence.

After two months of my intensive studies passed, I became quite self-reliant. Many students were already convinced of my knowledge. They regularly checked their homework solutions and answers against mine, and some even copied my work. By that time I became able to follow any lecturer's calculations on the blackboard and even to instantly detect some errors in his work.

The second half of that semester passed without any further troubles. Aside from the Sopromat, I approached the coming tests and examinations well prepared.

At the very start of the test period, Vadim and Fima urged me over and over to go ahead and try to take the examination in the ill-fated Sopromat, and not delay it to the fall. Eventually, after several days of hesitation, I yielded to their insistence. My friends designed a special plan of preparation for the examination. The schedule of examinations was favorable to us. First, the date of our group's Sopromat examination was well after the two other groups' scheduled dates. Second, a German-language examination, for which I needed no study, would precede the much more challenging Sopromat exam.

According to my friends' plan, they would collect the contents of all the question cards (three questions and one problem on each) that the professor had handed out to the fifty students in the two other groups during their preceding Sopromat examinations. All we had to do was to pass the German examination ahead of schedule, and then we would have six free days to prepare for the Sopromat exam using the professor's question cards.

It wasn't a problem, especially for me, to pass the German examination (and to score my first A at that). Later, when the due time came, we started to prepare for the Sopromat exam using the copies of the fifty question cards that my friends had obtained in advance. Our work wasn't purely mechanical. Before writing an answer for an exam question, we read the textbook to get to the core of the problem. In such a way we prepared fifty numbered crib notes. My friends assisted me a lot, and a day before the examination I realized that I had mastered the course. My nervousness disappeared. After I had distributed our output between my pockets, the only problem remained: to remember where I hid which particular crib note—in my left pocket or in the right one.

I arrived for the examination shortly before the examiner did. It was the first time we had laid eyes on each other. Once the exam started, the professor invited four students into the classroom by alphabetical order. In some fifteen minutes, when they had begun to prepare their answers, the professor opened the door and asked if there was anyone who wanted to take the examination out of turn, but under one condition: he or she would have no time to ponder the questions before answering them.

I touched my pockets (in order to reassure myself of my knowledge) and accepted the professor's invitation. I chose a question card at random from several that were lying on the examiner's table blank side up. Each card contained a problem and a set of questions. Soon I discovered that the card I had selected was different from any of my fifty thoroughly prepared crib notes. For a long minute, I was in shock. Nevertheless, I forced myself to reread the card carefully and soon understood that *I knew everything the card was asking* and could solve the problem in no time. I answered all the questions with enthusiasm; the examiner just gave a glance at my solution to the problem and without a word put down an A into my record book.

That was the third A which I received in the examination session. I had previously taken an examination in the highest mathematics. V. A. Zmorovich, an assistant professor, was a prominent lecturer of that course. It was rumored among the students that he was stingy with high marks and liked to ask difficult extra questions. I don't remember the details of that examination, except the pleasant sense of satisfaction that my exact answers gave me. I was especially proud of Zmorovich's A, which was a true rarity in our class.

Our last examination was in theoretical mechanics. It brought me one more "A." That was the happy end of my first set of post-war examinations. In this manner, I not only dropped my "conditional" student status and became a full student but, above all else, as a straight-A student I earned the increased stipend of 480 rubles a month, increasing our family budget by more than 50 percent. As a matter of fact, this was my first important achievement on my way along Civvy Street.

Our Young Family

The Marriage

Let's glance back at Vera and me, as we had reached a firm decision to join our fates in matrimony. At that time, in January 1946, Vera was an employed engineer, and I hadn't even a college student's status yet. Vera was renting a room, and I had neither house nor home. My property was miserable; one could put all my possessions in one trunk. In contrast to me, Vera was going to be a bride with a good dowry: her parents had already provided her with a decent wardrobe and a full set of furniture, as well as household goods. She was especially proud of a costly and beautiful dinner set for twelve place settings, which she had purchased the previous spring with the money I had sent to her from the front. Nevertheless, both social and material inequalities were of no concern to us. Our love successfully passed the four-year-long test of our separation, and we looked forward optimistically to our forthcoming marriage.

It is well known that Soviet people didn't have religious freedom, and all religions were oppressed in the USSR for long years. In order to form a family, the groom and the bride had only a simple step to complete—to register their marriage at the ZAGS (civilian registry) office. Moreover, both Vera and I were nonbelievers, so we focused all our thoughts on the forthcoming wedding or, more precisely, on the wedding reception. Our wedding date, 3 February 1946, was set about ten days in advance, and my parents barely had time to complete all the preparations for the ceremony.

At that time, I only had a vague idea of the wedding procedure. I had never even taken part in any wedding as a guest. From the fiction books I had read, I remembered an enchanting large-scale wedding party described in Shishkov's novel *The Ugryum River*, but our upcoming ceremony was absolutely of a different sort. Therefore, I relied on my parents to take care of any problems related to the wedding. My function was simply to do anything and everything they told me to do.

Chapter 28

We prepared for the wedding in a situation of complete disorder regarding consumer services and domestic living standards. Food shortages and high prices, as well as the long lines that stretched out of doors and down the streets at some grocery stores, raised particular problems. The lines arose only in front of stores where rumors had it that scarce foodstuffs would soon arrive.

In order to buy food for the wedding reception, my careful mother set off long before daylight. She was in a hurry so as to not wind up at the tail end of a line. Not many of her attempts were successful, but eventually she managed to buy the most essential items.

Due to the fact that my father was working at a state enterprise that related to the meat and milk industry, he was allowed to buy some meat at the lowest manufacturer's price directly at the meat-packing factory. I purchased the meat, which cost me half of my remaining savings. In spite of my parents' scanty financial situation, their expenses for the wedding were substantial, too.

Because of our very weak financial possibilities, it was no use even to consider a restaurant as a place for the wedding reception. The only choice was my parents' one-bedroom apartment, their part of a communal quarters, despite the lack of conveniences and the inadequate space. Moreover, the house wasn't yet connected to the power grid; therefore, the lighting problem was very serious. To illuminate our apartment during the party, we prepared four carbide lamps that we had fashioned from empty small-caliber shells and two refueled kerosene lamps. Nevertheless, being eager to provide the wedding with electric lighting, I dared to take on a risky and illegal action. Neglecting all safety regulations, I climbed up on the roof and found two insulated ends from the house's wiring. After stripping and bending them into hooks, I connected them to the overhead wires of the street electric lighting. We had electric light! This happy result came just two hours before the appointed time of gathering for the wedding.

The first arrivals were our most important guests from Kharkov: Agrippina Semenovna, Vasiliy Alexandrovich, and their eight-year-old son, Alik. Then other guests arrived. There were about thirty of them altogether: numerous relatives (some were even unfamiliar to me); my former comrades-in-arms Grigoriy Bamm, the mortarist, and Anatoliy Kochetov, the former regimental ammunition service commander; three of my father's colleagues; and our close friend and former classmate Boris Shpilskiy with his wife.

Since my very return to Kiev I had been looking forward to seeing some solemnity, to feeling a special spiritual excitement during the wedding. Alas, there was nothing of that nature. What I remember mainly is the crammed room, as all the guests and participants crowded into the small apartment. The newlyweds had to be satisfied with sharing one chair. Vera's wedding dress was just a beautiful light pink blouse with a brown skirt. I wore my officer's uniform without the shoulder straps. We had plenty of cold and hot dishes spread out for our guests, as well as liquor in the form of diluted pure alcohol on the table. Guests had a fair amount to drink that night.

In order to show how poor most of our guests and we were at that time, I would like to make a few observations about our wedding.

There was no groom's formal suit, no bride's traditional snow-white wedding dress, and there were no wedding rings (I compensated for that deficiency only on our tenth anniversary, when I gave Vera both a golden wedding ring and a gilt wristwatch). We could not even think of a honeymoon, of a journey or cruise. The only moderately costly wedding gift we received was a modest (by modern standards) tea set that the Shpilskiys gave us.

Believe it or not, but we celebrated our wedding . . . before our marriage had been officially registered. I can't remember why we procrastinated on our visit to the ZAGS office. We did it on 4 February, the day after the wedding reception took place. The office was just a plain room with only one clerk. No maid of honor and no best man were required. We just presented our identity cards to the clerk and signed some papers. The whole procedure lasted only fifteen minutes and involved just the three of us. We didn't even have to unbutton our overcoats.

Naturally, our marriage license was dated 4 February 1946. Nevertheless, we celebrated all our anniversaries on 3 February.

Our Newly Created Family

With the wedding celebration over and our family life finally started, we tried to spend every possible free minute together. I recall these days as a period of happy routine.

After an early breakfast we would leave our cramped room, and I would escort Vera to her place of work. Then I would make my way to the KPI. By the end of Vera's workday, I would already be waiting impatiently near the exit of the Works' gatekeeper's office for my beloved wife to appear.

While walking home, we usually discussed various topics and continued to tell each other about different experiences and events that each of us went through during the years of our separation. Vera also told me about many of our prewar classmates' fates.

In contrast to my frontline experience that was no longer of any use to us, Vera's knowledge of daily civilian life was extremely important. Such daily talks became wonderful lessons of everyday wisdom for me, who had donned a military uniform while still just an inexperienced teen.

During these weeks, a few warm gatherings with our prewar friends also took place. We visited some of my relatives in the evenings as well.

It seemed already that our family life had reached a permanent stability. But, as they say, all good things came to an end too quickly. Unfortunately, in mid-March the Southwest Railroad administration ordered Vera to vacate her room because officially she was not a member of the railroad's staff. Both Vera and I were too law-abiding, and we didn't know how to resort to various ruses to keep the room. So we had no choice but to move temporarily into my parents' apartment (actually this "temporary" period lasted for fourteen long years). Of course, our arrival cramped my parents and Tolya noticeably.

A new, not so easy life began in my parents' apartment. It is well known that the coexistence of two families under the same roof often turns into an absolute hell. In our case, however, thanks to Vera's cleverness, benevolence, and tolerance, as well as to my parents' wisdom and patience, it turned into the life of a united family instead. Moreover, the years together left nothing but positive memories of our mutual relations. Over the years of cohabitation, Vera gained the sincere love of my parents, too.

On the day of moving in, my wife reasonably decided not to interrupt my mother's customary way of life. From that point on, Vera managed our young family's household business separately. So a fifth housewife was now sharing the small communal kitchen, and the situation became fraught with potentially bad consequences. In defiance of such expectations, Vera succeeded in establishing good relations with all our neighbors in the overpopulated communal quarters.

Every day after my return to Kiev proved that the sixteen-year-old teenager who had fallen in love with Vera seven years ago had made an absolutely happy choice at that time. The ensuing years just confirmed this conclusion.

After accommodating ourselves to the life in new conditions, Vera and I began to go, more or less regularly, to the cinema to see so-called trophy movies. Most were German and Italian; it seems to me that they were a tiny part of reparations, paid by our recent enemies' governments. Occasionally we went to the Kiev Opera, as well as to both the Russian and Ukrainian dramatic theaters. Later we started to go to our Philharmonic Hall to attend any concert given by prominent visiting performers. We read a lot of fiction, too. One might say we were trying to compensate at least in part for the cultural events that we had missed during the war.

July 1946 was the month of Vera's leave from work and my summer vacation. Vera's parents invited us to spend it with them in Kharkov. Because of Vasiliy Alexandrovich's high rank, their material well-being was quite substantial. They gave us a hospitable welcome. We spent the entire month with them in their comfortable, spacious apartment. Agrippina Semenovna treated us to abundant and tasty breakfasts, lunches, and dinners. We seldom passed a meal without a cup of vodka.

While in Kharkov, I managed to look up both of my former wartime comrades. I at last met Vinokurov, who had been discharged from the Central Army Hospital not long before. His right arm remained disabled forever. The meeting with Lev Nikolaevich was not only warm; it was touching. I managed to visit the Sapozhnikovs as well.

These days in Kharkov, we read some modern novels, and many evenings we went to the movies, dramatic theater, or opera. Both Vera and I had a wonderful July that year.

It wasn't a wonderful time in our devastated country, though. There was so much rebuilding and reconstruction required to repair the extensive war damage—entire towns and cities had to be rebuilt, and our devastated agricultural system and all branches of domestic industry had to be restored. And everything was so far from completion yet!

Chapter 28

Vera and I understood that we would face a lot of difficult problems soon. Nevertheless, we returned home in August in an excellent mood, and we were looking forward to our future together with optimism. With mixed feelings of excitement and hope, we were also expecting to become parents in some six months.

Epilogue

I continued to study at the institute diligently and I achieved noticeable success. In the summer of 1949, I graduated from the KPI,
obtaining the honorable "red diploma" in radio engineering. Upon
graduation I was invited to work as an engineer in the local OKB
(Special Design Bureau) Number 483 of the Ministry of Aircraft Industry. At the end of the same year I became a KPI postgraduate.
In December 1952, after three years of serious scientific and experi-
mental work, I submitted my Ph.D. dissertation in preparation to
defend it before the KPI Academic Council. In January 1953, I was
assigned to the teaching staff of the Taganrog Radiotechnical Institute (TRI).

(I have specified the months when some events took place quite
deliberately. The point is that exactly at that same time, the Stalin
regime's virulent anti-Semitic campaign was reaching its peak.[1] I received the bitter taste of that time in full measure. When I arrived
at the TRI to take up my post, they refused to take me on; instead I
was directed to Moscow and placed at the disposal of the Ministry
of Culture. At first the ministry offered to assign me to the teaching
staff of the Tomsk Polytechnic Institute in East Siberia, but the next
day it canceled the offer and directed me to interview with representatives from four industrial ministries. There was an obvious interest
in hiring me after the interviews, but the next day, after I filled out
the form, which had a question concerning my ethnicity, I was rejected. Fortunately, in March 1953 Stalin died.)

In April 1953 I returned to the OKB Number 483, holding the
post of senior engineer, and at the same time I defended my dissertation, thereby becoming a Ph.D. I always worked in the OKB (in
1960 it was transformed into a research institute) not only diligently
but also with true enthusiasm. I liked my almost forty-five-year-long
creative work in the military branch of both radar technology and
radio electronics. I was promoted many times in the course of these
years (a deputy principal designer, principal designer, a supervisor
of some research projects, etc.) I am the designer or codesigner of

twenty-four inventions and the author or coauthor of more than 100 scientific publications.

In 1967 I became a laureate of the USSR State Prize (in the branch of science and technology). For some substantial achievements in my work, I also received two orders: the Badge of Honor and the Order of the Red Banner of Labor, as well as several medals. I retired in 1993.

My wife, Vera, worked as an engineer, then as an honorable Works' technology bureau chief for more than thirty-five years. She retired in 1980.

Our firstborn child, a son named Alexander, came into the world in 1947, and the second son, named Viktor, was born in 1955. We all lived in my parents' one-bedroom apartment, their part of the communal quarters, until 1960, when our family of four moved into a separate two-room apartment in a house that belonged to the re-search institute where I was working. In 1964 the institute improved our dwelling conditions, and we moved into a three-room apart-ment with approximately 600 square feet of space.

Years passed. Our sons became adults, completed their higher education, and formed their own happy families. Both found jobs to their liking and worked successfully. Three wonderful grandchil-dren became an inexhaustible source of Vera's and my special joy. Reviewing our life, we felt—it was a success!

* * *

In 1992, I suffered an irretrievable and most grievous loss—as a re-sult of incurable illness, my Vera passed away. I lost both my dearest one on earth and my most devoted friend. A year later, I quit my job and in 1994 emigrated to the United States, where our older son had been living since 1990. Here I regularly visit the local cemetery, where my sons and I buried Vera's ashes soon after my arrival.

In the United States, I mostly give myself up to retrospective ex-amination of my past, especially to the wartime years, when I served on the front line in the thick of millions of active defenders of our motherland. I continue to take pride in this part of my life.

At the same time I grew very disappointed with the fact that in America, the great contribution of the Soviet troops and the Soviet people to our common victory over Germany is undeservedly be-littled or passed over in silence. Because of that, I'm trying to spread

in this country as much true information about the Great Patriotic
War as I can. So, in 2003 I translated from Russian into English several fragments of my unpublished recollections of the war. These brief articles were published in the *Journal of Slavic Military Studies*.

This book is devoted to the same goal.

About War Veterans

> Sometime and somewhere,
> While talking of the battles
> And of the sites of fires,
> I'll remember the infantry,
> And my own rifle company . . .
> *From a popular wartime song*

My participation in the Great Patriotic War is a special period of my life, incomparable to any other one. In this book you have already read about the main events that happened to me in the wartime and how I perceived them. But it is necessary to tell you that even after the war, along with my family and my work, the wartime past occupied a noticeable place in my life. Remembering my military service revived my links and common actions with other, similar to me, veterans of the Great Patriotic War. That is the topic of the next few pages.

From the very first months of my civilian life, I realized that I'd never forget my war past, especially the people who fought beside me. Time and again I felt a desire to visit my fallen fellow soldiers' graves and, still more, to meet my living brothers-in-arms.

Readers already know that in the initial postwar years I met Bamm, Kochetov, Vinokurov, and Sapozhnikov. I wanted to meet more of my frontline friends, but I didn't know their addresses. My efforts to find Dmitriy Repin and Vera Perlina through local address bureau services in Moscow and Leningrad failed.

In 1959 our former division commander, retired Major General Tymchik, was appointed as a deputy chairman of the all-Ukrainian DOSAAF (Voluntary Society of Assistance to the Army, Air Force, and Navy).[1] During the war I knew him as a brave and humane commander. At that time I had never had the opportunity to meet him directly. So I decided to visit Tymchik in his office.

First of all I introduced myself to him. Of course, Tymchik didn't remember me, or any of several other names of my former comrades that I mentioned during the meeting. I showed him a few photos of my frontline friends, but the major general recognized no one. However, shortly after I mentioned our four most memorable battles (the Vishnevy hamlet, the Bay of Karkinit, Perekop, and Hill 111.4), he brightened and even told me several interesting details of these events.

Toward the end of the meeting, I told Kirill Yakovlevich about different achievements in my postwar life. I was just about to say good-bye, when he noticed my intentions and asked: "What kind of assistance are you seeking from me?" I convinced Tymchik that the goal of my visit was only to pay my respects to him. As if to justify his query, he explained that most veterans who had come to visit him had asked for some sort of help in finding either a job or housing.

Visiting Memorable Places

In early September 1960, I made my first visit to a place where I had fought in the war. This time I "snatched" a week from my regular leave and went to Tokmak, the former Bolshoy Tokmak. Vera's relatives, especially the Chernyy family, received me with all their hearts. However, the most memorable event of those days was the trip to the Prishib Heights, where fierce combat took place in October 1943. I visited Olya Martynova's grave there and paid my respects.

In the summer of 1971, I gladly seized the opportunity to spend my vacation at a camp on the Zemland Peninsula. My preparation for the trip started beforehand. I studied some guidebooks and maps. Thanks to my home preparation and a visit to the Kaliningrad (the modern name of former Königsberg) Museum of Local Lore and History, I succeeded in finding and photographing some memorable locations of the battles for Königsberg and the Zemland Peninsula. Seeing once again the familiar places of our campaign path from January to April 1945 brought back many memories and strongly stirred my emotions.

Visiting Hill 111.4 was still more exciting. When I reached it, I found that the flat top of the elevation was now a military unit's base. A large group of servicemen, including a few officers, attentively listened to my story of the terrible combat that happened there on the last night of February 1945. With genuine astonishment they looked at the prewar picture of the height with the Bismarckturm tower rising atop it. After I finished the story, soldiers told me that now and then they still bumped into different material evidence of what had happened there over twenty-five years earlier.

I spent another day of my vacation in a stuffy office of the local *voenkomat*. I wanted the clerks to help me locate the common graves where some of my brother soldiers were likely to be reburied. In particular, I intended to pay my last respects to Nikolay Starykh, a Siberian, who perished on 4 February 1945 in the village of Kragau. I looked through about ten very thick volumes of the list of buried warriors. Alas, I never found his name. Why? Was it a consequence of somebody's criminal negligence? Being extremely upset, I went to the nearest common grave and silently paid my last respect to over 2,000 Soviet soldiers. No doubt, some of my fallen comrades were among them.

Veterans' Gatherings

The absolute majority of the Soviet people always considered our victory a nationwide triumph. Therefore, it is not clear why after Stalin's death, during the Khrushchev period, 9 May wasn't proclaimed an official national holiday, and why the mass media (in contrast to fictional works and the cinema) rarely mentioned the Great Patriotic War.

This inexplicable "conspiracy of silence" was broken by the Central State Television a year or two before Khrushchev was "dethroned." There was a series of TV broadcasts about fortunate reunions of some former frontline friends who hadn't seen each other since 1945. I liked to watch these touching stories and even became a little jealous of those veterans' good fortune. Sometimes I even considered whether to search for some frontline friends whose addresses I didn't then know.

These thoughts came to an end in January 1965. Anatoliy Kochetov invited me to a meeting of our division's veterans who lived in Kiev at that time. There were about twenty veterans present at the meeting, but I knew only three of them: Tymchik, Bamm, and Kochetov. Almost all the others veterans had stayed in touch with each other since the war.

Tymchik's proposal to celebrate Victory Day together and to invite nonresident veterans to take part in the gathering was accepted unanimously. We elected an organizational committee (*orgkomitet*) under the chairmanship of Kirill Yakovlevich as well.

During the meeting I learned a little about the veterans there who were unfamiliar to me. All of them were distinctly older than I, and most had served far behind the trenches during the war—at headquarters, in the political department, in the medical battalion, or in various rear services. Naturally, I didn't have much in common with them from my frontline past. Therefore, as soon as I heard mention of the Victory Day reunion proposal, I began eagerly to anticipate the gathering: I hoped to see then some veterans who met my criteria for being considered "*active* participants of the war." (It is necessary to remark that I was still a bit too rigid in clinging to my wartime standards. Later I understood that sometimes the contribution of "nonactive" participants of the war was of no less importance than that of the "active" ones. In addition, during the postwar years I found among the "nonactive" participants many persons who were worthy of respect. Some became friends of mine.)

The second part of our organizational meeting was dedicated to the details of the planned gathering. The Rozhkovs suggested holding the festive meals in their home on Korchevatoe—in the quiet outskirts of Kiev. (The Rozhkovs were married at the front when Fedor managed the division's club and Mariya, whose maiden name was Shevchenko, was a senior surgery nurse in the division medical battalion.) We also discussed the menu for the dinner, the common expenses, and the personal cost for the get-together.

The forthcoming event inspired me. The next day I sent letters to my friends from Kharkov, Moscow, and Tokmak. Besides these I sent four letters to some local offices in hope of finding Kamchatnyy, Karpushinskiy, Abidov, and Kargabaev. Soon I received a nine-page-long, touching reply from Ivan Kamchatnyy. Later Karpushinskiy's response came. Unfortunately, because of different circumstances, both of them were unable to take part in the future celebration. Then Vinokurov and Sapozhnikov told me by phone that it was impossible for them to be in Kiev on the appointed day. And I hadn't received any reply from Abidov and Kargabaev.

On the Victory Day Eve, two dear guests appeared at our home: Vasiliy Panteleev from Moscow and Shura Chernyy from Tokmak. Vera and I received them wholeheartedly. We sat at the table and reminisced about our wartime past until midnight. In the morning Vasiliy, Shura, and I went to the long-awaited gathering.

Some fifty veterans gathered at the event, including a few women who had served in the division medical battalion during the war. The initial part of the celebration was the festive meeting in a modest hall of the neighboring elementary school. General Tymchik opened the meeting with a short congratulatory speech. Then we elected a council for our divisional veterans' organization with Tymchik at the head. Many veterans (myself included) shed tears when a group of schoolchildren from a neighboring school greeted us and performed a touching choral recitation for us.

Veterans continued their celebration in the Rozhkovs' backyard. A long temporary table was set up for about fifty guests. Our festive meal lasted for several hours, since the variety of appetizers and dishes was extensive, and the drinks were plentiful. Toasts were proposed one after another. Every toastmaster emphasized the great contribution of his particular unit or office to the war effort. The toast honored all kinds of military services, including political workers and the rear supply services, but I heard not a single word in honor of the main person in the war—the infantryman. I listened patiently to all the toasts in hope that somebody would mention the infantry, but no one did it. Being tipsy, I couldn't suppress my emotions any longer. I stood up and emphatically proposed a toast in honor of our long-suffering, valiant infantry.

Everybody lingered after the feast was over. We were singing folk songs one after another, as well as popular wartime songs. At the end, everyone drank a final toast before departing, this one that we call the *pososhok* (a small walking stick), which corresponds to the English expression "one for the road."

This successful celebration initiated many ensuing veterans' gatherings, which became a tradition. Three years running the celebration started at the courtyard of the 122nd High School near the Rozhkovs' house. Schoolchildren greeted us and presented tulips to everybody. Then they performed a festive show and finished with a march past the veterans. As they prepared to leave, we warmly thanked the diligent children and their teachers for their greetings and the nice performances. Then veterans went to the Rozhkovs' yard for the festive meals.

In August 1967 a small group of our veterans was invited to the village of Uspenka, which our army had liberated in the summer of 1943 after the successful breakthrough on the Mius front. There was an unusual but warm meeting of several representative groups of different units that took part in the liberation of Uspenka.

The next veterans' gathering deserves a special description.

I'll never forget the solemn and warm days of 6–10 May 1969 when the city of Sevastopol celebrated the twenty-fifth anniversary of its liberation. The civic leaders of the "City of Russian Glory," as Sevastopol is called, had invited a few thousand veterans who either had participated in the heroic 250-day-long defense of Sevastopol in 1941–1942 or had liberated the destroyed city in May 1944. I was among the thirty veterans who represented our division, which had knocked the Germans off the Mekenzie Mountains and broken through into the city.

Along with several Kievan veterans, I arrived in Sevastopol at noon on 7 May. We received a hearty welcome. We saw posters everywhere saying: "Glory to the heroes of the defense and the liberation of Sevastopol!" At the railroad station I met two old friends—Lev Vinokurov and Vasiliy Karpushinskiy. There were long, emotional embraces. Then we were taken with the others to our free accommodations in a junior technical college dormitory. Lev, Vasiliy, and I received a small, tidy room there.

After a short rest, we decided to go downtown. Walking through the lobby, I noticed a sheet of paper on the table. It was a list of registered guests. I read it and discovered that our next-door neighbors were the Rozhkovs, Mariya and Fedor, who had arrived in Sevastopol a day earlier.

Vasiliy, Lev, and I had a terrific afternoon together. The historical city of Sevastopol, which had been completely destroyed by the war, was now totally rebuilt. All of the main streets were decorated for the celebration, the weather was wonderful, and the sea calm. We walked slowly, admiring everything we saw and recalling many events from the war. Every passerby welcomed us warmly. When we grew tired, we went into a small restaurant, had dinner, talked, smoked, drank a bit, and enjoyed ourselves thoroughly until 11:00 P.M.

Still in a good mood, just a little drunk, we were walking back to our dormitory when I told my friends who our next-door neighbors were. After I mentioned Mariya Shevchenko, Vasiliy grew very animated.

"I must see her immediately!" he said. "Mariya operated on me when I was wounded in my side, near Kuibyshevo in the spring of 1943, when I was still serving in the antitank battalion."

Karpushinskiy refused to listen to my advice not to disturb our friends at that late hour. He insisted that I come along because he was not sure they would recognize him. "But, please, don't introduce me at first. Let Mariya try to recognize me by herself," Vasiliy warned me before we reached the Rozhkov's door.

I knocked on the door cautiously; there was no response. After a few seconds, Karpushinskiy impatiently knocked again, and we heard a male voice:

"Who wants to visit us at midnight? We are in bed already."

"It doesn't matter. It's Kobylyanskiy, but I'm not alone, and it's urgent!"

The door opened, and there was the barefoot Fedor dressed in his blue undershirt and black sateen briefs. Mariya lay under a white sheet on a narrow bed. I saw astonishment in her eyes. After a few seconds of silence, Karpushinskiy said, "Hi, Mariya! Do you recognize me?"

"I don't know you!"

"Please, look at me more carefully! You must remember me!"

Mariya turned and addressed me: "Isaak, I have never met and have never even seen this strange man!"

Vasiliy became just a little angry and said: "Now, you'll recognize me for sure!" He approached Mariya's bed, hastily unfastened and pulled down his pants, then turned sideways to Mariya and began to pull his briefs down. Everybody froze.

"Is he crazy?"—the idea flashed through my mind, but I had no time to stop him. Mariya suddenly jumped up from her bed, hugged Vasiliy, and shouted: "Oh, Vasya, my dear boy! My beloved patient, I recognize you now!"

Standing there in her bare feet, wearing only her long white nightgown, she began kissing Vasiliy's face, at first smiling and then beginning to cry. Everybody in the room was similarly struck and moved to tears.

In a couple of minutes, the five of us were sitting there around a table, drinking vodka that had unexpectedly appeared "from nowhere," and talking over what had just happened.

Mariya had identified Vasiliy by the scar left from the operation she had performed on him twenty-six years earlier!

The next day Lev, Vasiliy, and I went to the Belbek River valley in order to find the memorable places where we had fought in early May 1944. Our three-hour search was crowned with success: we found the remnants of my guns' emplacements and the place where Karpushinskiy was seriously wounded. (We were indebted to our taxi driver, an old Sevastopol resident, who rendered an invaluable assistance to our search.)

Over the next three days, we had many interesting meetings and a lot of unforgettable festive events in Sevastopol. The closing event was a grand reception that the Sevastopol Sea Works (the local shipyard) gave for the 2nd Guards Army veterans.

Every year the list of registered veterans of our division's veterans group became longer. Some found out about our council just by accident, others learned our council's address from Moscow, where the 2nd Guards Army Veteran Council was located (our group was one of its several branches). After discovering a familiar name in the registration list, I started to look forward to meeting one more frontline friend. In the fall of 1969 the number of our veterans was approximately 100.

The approaching year, 1970, was a special one: it was the twenty-fifth anniversary of the Great Victory. Our council decided to celebrate this year's Victory Day on a large scale.

I volunteered to set up an exhibition of wartime photos that I had received from many veterans. Some photographs were individual portraits, while others portrayed groups of soldiers and officers. I arranged the photos on six large sheets of thick drafting paper, which we called "stands." Each stand was dedicated to one period of the division's combat history. A professional painter made colorful inscriptions and vignettes on all the stands, so I hoped they would attract every guest's attention. Another one of my initiatives was a success, too: at my request, a designer and three skilled craftsmen of the research institute, where I worked, manufactured 100 beautiful enameled badges for the participants of the celebration. Everything turned out excellently.

On 8 May I made several trips to the railroad station in order to welcome close frontline friends who were arriving from different cities. Eight people stayed at our home: Zhenya Livshits, Anya Korchagina, and three couples—the Vinokurovs, the Panteleevs, and the Chernyys. I was indescribably excited to meet people from my wartime past. At the same time I got a lot of satisfaction from giving them an opportunity to see each other. Vera welcomed and received the guests as if they were relatives or the closest friends. After returning home, all of them sent us letters with many thanks for the hearty welcome and especially for Vera's hospitable reception.

On the Victory Day we arrived at the 122nd High School courtyard long before the appointed beginning of the celebration. The weather was wonderful. I set up all of the exhibition stands along the footpath that led to the center of the courtyard. Groups of veterans gathered there during the day. They looked over and discussed the photos, sharing their memories. I felt true satisfaction.

At that time, the actual fighting banner of our division was an exhibit of the Central Museum of the Soviet Army in Moscow. On Tymchik's demand it had been delivered to Kiev for our gathering. Before the festive meeting started, all the veterans lined up, and the red banner was unfurled. There were a few short speeches at the meeting. Then the schoolchildren put on their program for us. They presented their traditional greeting and then gave us a nice show and a festive parade.

The warm and hearty informal part of our celebration took place in the Rozhkovs' backyard. This time our festive meals lasted long into the evening; the number of toasts was countless. The now gray-haired veterans had a wonderful time. There were long, friendly conversations, and lots of songs and dances.

In general the celebration was an undoubted, big success; the frontline friendship continued; and all our efforts were not wasted.

In later years our veterans celebrated the Victory Day in different cities and towns that marked our division's campaign path in the war: Volzhskiy (the postwar city built on the area where we had started fighting in October 1942), Donetsk (the former Stalino), Kaliningrad (the former Königsberg), Tsyurupinsk, the Cossack village of Razdorskaya, Tokmak, Krasnoperekopsk (in the Crimea), Razdolnoe (in the Crimea). The last veterans' gathering outside of Kiev before my departure from the USSR took place in May 1986. That time we held the meeting in the town of Krasnograd, where in 1941 our then 300th Rifle Division was formed.

At every gathering site, we were given a cordial welcome. There were meetings with local inhabitants, youth, and schoolchildren. Veterans talked about the battles that had taken place in their cities or villages all those years ago.

The "Red Pathfinders" and "Young Students of Local Lore"

In the late 1960s, a new all-USSR schoolchildren and youth movement was launched. Its motto was "Not a single veteran of the Great Patriotic War shall be forgotten! Nothing of the war shall be forgotten!" Thousands of teams of schoolchildren of the Red Pathfinders or Young Students of Local Lore were organized all over the country. As a rule, the most enthusiastic teachers led the teams. They helped the children to discover different details of the liberation of their neighborhood and to ascertain the names of those who had fallen in the battles. During summer vacations, some teachers organized trips that followed the campaign path of our division.

Children who were involved in such activities located veterans among their adult and elderly neighbors or from other regions by correspondence. Children interviewed them, requested photos, corresponded with them, sent holiday greeting cards, and so forth. For example, on each holiday, I received more than thirty greeting cards from children of different towns and villages, which our division had liberated many years ago.

In many schools, small rooms were fitted out as The Room of Combat Glory or, in some roomier schools, The School Museum of Combat and Labor Glory. Everywhere these rooms were decorated with loving care.

Three wonderful and very enthusiastic women achieved the most substantial results: Valentina Nikonova, the supervisor of the Tsyurupinsk District Pioneer House; Olga Fainveits, the teacher of the 151st Mospino High School (Donetsk neighborhood); and Galina Mais, a teacher of the 25th Kaliningrad High School. Without question, the richest and most impressive museum was established in Mospino. It excelled by its professional design, tasteful decoration, and numerous exhibits. I think the local coal mine sponsored the school generously.

Whenever we visited local schools during veterans' gatherings, schoolchildren were the most curious and gratifying audience. They liked to guide us through their museums and displayed open pride in their work. Besides, the children would ask many questions after we shared with them our memories of the war.

* * *

Years slipped by; our children matured; our grandchildren were growing up. And the time came implacably when the veterans' ranks began to thin. One by one, my frontline friends have left this world.

In 1975 our highly respected "soldiers' general," Kirill Yakovlevich Tymchik, passed away. Five years later Lev Nikolaevich Vinokurov departed. In 1985, Vasiliy Alexeevich Panteleev died. Not long ago, in 2003, Ivan Fedorovich Kamchatnyy left this world.

May they be remembered forever!

Notes

Chapter 1

1. Created by a series of imperial decrees issued by Catherine the Great in the late eighteenth century, the Jewish pale of settlement was a western border region of the Russian Empire within which permanent residence of Jews was mandated, extending from the demarcation line to near the border with central Europe. The pale included much of present-day Lithuania, Belarus, Ukraine, Moldova, Poland, and parts of western Russia. Additionally, a number of large cities within the pale were excluded from its regulations and restrictions. A limited number of categories of Jews, such as wealthy merchants, doctors, prominent writers, and composers, were allowed to live outside the pale. After the October Revolution (1917), this residence restriction and other inequalities associated with the pale of settlement were abolished.

2. The first machine-tractor stations (MTSs) were established by the beginning of the 1930s. These MTSs belonged to the government. Each MTS was a production service center that performed contractual plowing and harvesting services for several surrounding collective farms, using the MTSs' tractors, combines, trucks, and so on. (At that time, such agricultural machinery was a rarity in the USSR, which had been left destitute by the years of world war, revolution, and civil war. The government bought it mostly from the United States, interestingly, with money raised by the sale of prominent works of art from the Russian Hermitage and Tretyakov Gallery to Andrew W. Mellon. Mellon later donated his priceless collection to help found the National Gallery of Art.) The Soviet Communist Party had an additional purpose for establishing the MTSs: all of their directors and some key workers were Party members. This established a Party presence at key nodes of control throughout the Soviet countryside.

Chapter 3

1. In fact, the notorious nonaggression pact between Hitler and Stalin, signed by their foreign ministers on 24 August 1939, was a masked collusion over the carving up of Poland and portions of eastern Europe into respective spheres of influence. Hitler was now free to invade and occupy western Poland without fear of sparking a war with the Soviet Union, while Stalin was free to move into the Baltic Republics, eastern Poland, and Bessarabia. All details of this collusion were hidden in a secret Protocol to the Pact. (In the Soviet Union, the existence of these secret protocols was not public knowledge until it was revealed in 1990 at the All-Union Convention of elected representatives from all Soviet Republics.) Thus, prior to 1990, few Soviet citizens had any knowledge of the real basis for the territorial expansion of the Soviet Union at that time.

2. Babi Yar is a grim memorial to the victims of appalling Nazi genocide and anti-Semitism. A ravine lying outside of Kiev, in the autumn of 1941 it became the

communal grave for tens of thousands of Jews from Kiev, including the author's second cousin, a thirty-eight-year-old librarian married to a Russian man, and two of the author's nineteen-year-old female classmates. The Germans spared no one; children, the elderly, and pregnant women were all murdered at Babi Yar. Later, the Germans used the ravine and area surrounding it as the execution and final resting place for tens of thousands more Russians, Ukrainians, Gypsies, prisoners of war, and the mentally handicapped—all people who had no place in Hitler's design for lebensraum (living space).

3. Two days after the war began, the Communist Party Central Committee and the Soviet government created the Soviet Information Bureau. According to the decree, the Soviet Information Bureau's main task was to create and disseminate daily war communiqués, based on information from the Stavka. The Soviet Information Bureau communicated these daily briefs through all central and local newspapers, and all radio broadcasting stations of the Soviet Union.

Chapter 5

1. In late November 1942, Generalfeldmarshal von Manstein, the commander in chief of Army Group Don, was ordered to relieve the Sixth Army trapped in the city of Stalingrad. Von Manstein started his Operation Wintergewitter (Winter Storm) on 12 December. On 24 December the German LVII Panzer Corps was within 50 kilometers of "Fortress Stalingrad," where it ran into Malinovskiy's elite 2nd Guards Army along the Myshkova River. General von Manstein's advance ground to a halt and then went into a long retreat to escape encirclement when the Red Army's Voronezh and Southwest *Fronts* to the north launched Operation Little Saturn into the rear of Army Group Don.

2. NKVD is the abbreviation for the People's Commissariat of Internal Affairs, the organizational predecessor of the KGB (State Security Committee). The regimental Special Departments were counterespionage detachments. In April 1943 all of these departments were removed from the NKVD and placed under the control of the People's Commissariat of Defense (NKO). Their name was switched to SMERSH, which is an abbreviation of the Russian phrase "Death to spies!" As a rule, there was a SMERSH group in every regiment. It consisted of a senior representative, carrying the rank of major or even higher, three or four subordinate officers, and a clerk-typist. The SMERSH group controlled a network of covert informants throughout every regimental detachment. Everybody in the regiment, except the young, inexperienced, or very naive, feared the SMERSH men, and especially their secret informers. The informer could be any ordinary soldier, but in secret he reported on any indiscrete word that could be interpreted as anti-Soviet. The consequences could be extremely tragic.

3. German colonies were established in several rural areas of southern Russia and the Ukraine back in the eighteenth century, at the invitation of Catherine the Great. She offered substantial incentives to the German immigrants. The new colonists built stout, brick homes and buildings in the German style. Their methods of cultivation, ways of housekeeping, and mode of living were much more progressive than in comparable Russian and Ukrainian villages. There was also a big

difference even in the breeds of cattle and poultry. As a precaution, in the first days of the war all residents of German colonies in the USSR had been preventively deported to Kazakhstan.

Chapter 6

1. Tolbukhin's Southern *Front* launched its offensive on 17 July 1943. The author's 87th Guards Rifle Division, in 2nd Guards Army's second echelon, did not cross the Mius River until 21 July. Then on 22 July, it, together with the 49th Guards Rifle Division, the 320th Rifle Division, and strong elements of the 4th Mechanized Corps, launched the last major effort of the Southern *Front* to crack the German defenses around Dmitrievka. For a full discussion of this offensive, and how it fit into the *Stavka*'s plans for the summer of 1943, see George M. Nipe Jr., *Decision in the Ukraine Summer 1943: II. SS and III. Panzerkorps* (Winnipeg: J. J. Fedorowicz Publishing, 1996).

2. The editor has not been able to identify precisely the "Ravine of Death." The author mentions a deep ravine with a shallow stream flowing through it. The terrain west of the Mius River between Dmitrievka and Kuibyshevo is marked by three primary ridges, running from northwest to southeast, divided by two tributaries to the Mius, the Gerassimovka and the Olkhovatchik. Both were major arteries for the movement of troops and tanks during the battle for both sides. Each of these ridges and primary valley slopes is further cut by numerous smaller ravines and gullies. All these locations were the scene of ferocious fighting and horrendous casualties during the July battles.

Chapter 7

1. The so-called Wotan Line was the southernmost extension of Hitler's planned East Wall. It ran from the Sea of Azov in the south northward along the Molochnaya River to a point north of Melitopol. At that point, it left the banks of the Molochnaya and stretched across the land bridge between the Dnieper and Molochnaya rivers, and eventually linked with the rest of the East Wall just north of Zaporozhe. The Molochnaya was the last readily defensible position east of the Dnieper, and most important for Hitler's planning, the Wotan Line shielded the Isthmus of Perekop and the rear of the German Seventeenth Army in the Crimea. It took more than three weeks of hard fighting for the 4th Ukrainian *Front* to overcome the defenses of Colonel General Karl Hollidt's understrength, reconstituted Sixth Army in the Wotan Line.

Chapter 8

1. Penal (disciplinary) battalions and penal companies were formed in the Red Army in accordance with Stalin's famous "Not One Step Back" order, Number 227, on 28 July 1942. Among other things, it directed the creation of penal battalions within each operating *front* and penal companies within each army. As the order stated, all junior and senior commanders and corresponding political workers from all branches of the Red Army deemed guilty of violating discipline by their cowardice or unsteadiness were to be assigned to the penal battalions. Common soldiers

and noncommissioned officers guilty of violating military discipline were sent to the penal companies. Both sorts of penal detachments were placed in the most dangerous sectors of the *front* and army sectors, and assigned to lead any assault, in order "to give the violators the opportunity to redeem themselves with their blood for their crimes against the Motherland." For more information on these penal units and Order Number 227, see David M. Glantz, *Colossus Reborn: The Red Army at War 1941–1943* (Lawrence: University Press of Kansas, 2005), 570–581.

Chapter 10

1. The author's account of this counteroffensive coincides well with the testimony of a German officer from the 5th Panzer Division. Replenished with tanks, artillery, and ammunition from Königsberg's armories and workshops, in the early hours of 19 February, the 5th Panzer Division, together with elements of the veteran 1st Infantry Division, sallied forth from the Königsberg fortifications in order to try and reopen the rail link west to Pillau. After making contact with the 58th Infantry Division outside the Königsberg fortifications and reestablishing the corridor to Pillau, the 5th Panzer Division wheeled to the northeast and joined in a general effort to drive the Soviet 39th and 43rd Armies from the Zemland Peninsula. As the author describes, the German counterattack made progress but failed in its efforts to capture the dominating Hill 111.4. Undoubtedly, it was the tanks of the 5th Panzer Division that the author saw.

For the German account of this action, see Major Baumann's "Armored Group of the 5th Panzer Division in the Defensive Operation," in the transcript of proceedings from the 1986 Art of War Symposium "From the Vistula to the Oder: Soviet Offensive Operations, October 1944–March 1945," Center for Land Warfare, U.S. Army War College, 19–23 May 1986, 407–410.

Chapter 12

1. Colonel Pavel Fedorovich Tolstikov was commander of the 1st Guards Rifle Division of the 11th Guards Army at the time of the storming of Königsberg. The 11th Guards Army was attacking the city from the south, while the 43rd Army, in which the author's division was serving at the time, attacked from the north.

2. Yuriy Nikolaevich Kostikov, born in 1927, was posthumously awarded with the highest national honor, Hero of the Soviet Union. His ashes rest under a marble gravestone by the monument "To 1,200 Guards" in Kaliningrad, not far from the place of his feat of arms. In order to immortalize Kostikov's feat, Yuriy's Moscow high school was named after him in 1950. A few years later a fishing boat of the Baltic flotilla was named the *Yuriy Kostikov.*

Chapter 17

1. Stefan Schmitz, "Eine Kugel pfiff vorbei. Die zweite traf. Das war Erlösung," *Stern,* no. 34 (2003): 118–129. The full memoir has been translated into English and published as Willy Peter Reese, *A Stranger to Myself: The Inhumanity of War, Russia, 1941–1944* (New York: Farrar, Straus and Giroux, 2005).

Chapter 20

1. This advance, southwest of Kharkov, suffered a stunning reversal from Manstein's famous "Backhand Blow"—a flanking counterattack by the XXXXVIII Panzerkorps and II SS Panzerkorps that drove Timoshenko's *Front* back to the east with enormous losses and led to the recapture of Kharkov.

Chapter 24

1. There were two levels of military awards in the Soviet system of decorations: medals, the lower level awards, and orders, awards of the higher level.

2. Generalissimus was the highest rank in both the old Russian and the Soviet military hierarchy. Naturally, in the Soviet Union, only Stalin was entitled to this supreme rank.

3. The Xinjiang Uyghur Autonomous Region is a large area in the northwestern part of present-day China. This region, which bordered the USSR, was formerly known as Eastern Turkmenistan. A few million Uyghurs have inhabited that territory from time immemorial. They are Muslim and have their own Uyghur language. The central government of China has always considered them to be an outcast people. Eastern Turkmenistan became an Uyghur state in 1863, but in 1876 it came under Chinese colonial rule. During World War II, the Kuomintang government headed by Chiang Kai-shek oppressed and discriminated against the Uyghurs more and more pitilessly. The Uyghurs reacted with a national liberation movement (or a religious liberation or a separatist movement—the choice of the movement's name depends upon the political point of view of the person who is defining it). In 1945 the Uyghur resistance changed into an armed uprising. In order to support the Uyghurs in their fight against Chiang Kai-shek, who was an old enemy of the USSR, and sensing an opportunity for further territorial expansion, Stalin secretly sent a group of experienced Soviet officers (all of Central Asian origin) to assist the Uyghur forces as "volunteer" military advisers. The Soviet support, however, didn't last long: after the uprising's religious leader refused Stalin's offer to make the future Uyghur Autonomous Republic a part of the USSR, all of the "Soviet volunteers" were recalled.

Chapter 26

1. The New Economic Policy (NEP) was initiated by Lenin in 1921 to revive the economy after the civil war. The NEP was adopted as a temporary measure allowing a limited revival of free trade inside the country and foreign trade concessions alongside the nationalized and state-controlled sectors of the economy. It was in effect until the end of the 1920s, when the process of forced collectivization of the Soviet peasantry was at its height.

Chapter 29

1. The Doctors' Case (known also as the Doctors' Plot, the Doctors-Saboteurs' Case, and the Doctors-Killers' Case) was the culmination of Stalin's anti-Jewish campaign that began a couple of years after the end of World War II. In 1948, an

308 increasing number of articles in the press accused prominent Jews of "rootless cosmopolitanism," "demolishing national pride," "harboring antipatriotic views," and "fawning over the West." Simultaneously, a deliberate campaign began to liquidate everything related to Jewish culture in the USSR. The Jewish Anti-Fascist Committee was dissolved, its members arrested. Jewish literature was removed from bookshops and libraries, and Jewish theaters, choirs, and drama groups, amateur as well as professional, were dissolved. Hundreds of Jewish authors, artists, actors, and journalists were arrested. During the same period, Jews were systematically dismissed from leading positions in many sectors of society, from the administration, the army, the press, the universities, and the legal system. Twenty-five of the leading Jewish writers, who were arrested in 1948, were secretly executed in 1952. The anti-Jewish campaign culminated in the arrest, announced on 13 January 1953, of a group of "Doctors-Killers," accused of being paid agents of "Jewish-Zionists organizations" who planned to poison Soviet leaders. After Stalin's death on 5 March, the new leadership admitted that the charges had been entirely fabricated by Stalin and his cohorts. The case was dismissed on 31 March 1953.

Appendix

1. DOSAAF was the name of a Soviet paramilitary organization, the Voluntary Society of Assistance to the Army, Air Force, and Navy. The stated mission of the society was the "patriotic upbringing of the population and preparation of it for the defense of the Motherland." To this end, DOSAAF organized and sponsored a network of clubs devoted to paramilitary activities, such as gliding, parachute jumping, boating and sailing, and so on. From the 1960s, DOSAAF also offered facilities for ordinary sports, such as swimming pools, sports halls, and stadiums. DOSAAF financed these clubs, facilities, and activities through membership dues, subscriptions, donations, and a popular quarterly lottery.

Index